Origins of Increasing Returns

Origins of Increasing Returns

THEODORE W. SCHULTZ

BLACKWELL
Oxford UK & Cambridge USA

First published 1993

Blackwell Publishers
238 Main Street,
Cambridge, Massachusetts 02142
USA

108 Cowley Road
Oxford OX4 1JF
UK

Library of Congress Cataloging-in-Publication Data

A CIP catalog record for this book is available from the Library of Congress

ISBN 155786-319–9 (hbk.)

British Library Cataloguing in Publication Data

A CIP catalogue record for this book is available from the British Library.

Typeset in 10 on 12pt Sabon
by Best-set Typesetter Ltd., Hong Kong
Printed in Great Britain by T.J. Press (Padstow) Ltd., Padstow, Cornwall

This book is printed on acid-free paper

Contents

Acknowledgments

As I did for Volume One, in selecting and organizing the collection of papers for this book, I benefited a great deal from the rich editorial experience in economics of Elizabeth Johnson. Margaret Schultz turned to the library to check sources. She also spotted ambiguities and awkward statements. My long time secretary, highly skilled Kathy Glover, stayed abreast of the on-going revisions and saw to it that "permissions to publish" and the introductory parts came in hand.

Theodore W. Schultz

Introduction

The quest by economists to discover the origins of increasing returns has not been in vain. It has led to various advances in knowledge that have contributed to increases in income. What appears to be true is that each advance, as a process, is ultimately subject to diminishing returns. The implication is that there is no known, unique perpetual income increasing process.

The first volume of my collected papers featured Adam Smith's famous theorem that the division of labor depends on the extent of the market.[1] Smith to a considerable degree anticipated the large gains in the productivity of labor which have their origins in ". . . the greater part of the skill, dexterity, and judgment with which it is anywhere directed, or applied (which) are consequences of the division of labour." Various components of human capital are specified by Smith. Clearly, extensions of markets are important but the conditions and the analytics to explain the array of extensions of markets, their origins, and the additional income derived from such extensions were not resolved by Smith.

The first paper in this volume begins with Allyn Young's "Increasing Returns and Economic Progress."[2] I had not discovered Allyn Young's economics during my graduate studies. I came upon it several decades later.

The economics with which I entered Iowa State College in 1930 was fettered by secular diminishing returns with a special vengeance in the case of agriculture which was my field of specialization. My first paper dealt with "Diminishing Returns in View of Progress in Agricultural Production."[3] I had access to forty years of strong data that confuted Marshall's prophecy that the developments in the arts of agriculture would be less rapid than the increasing resistance of the soil.

During the next two decades I was engrossed by economic puzzles pertaining to land, other natural resources, and the price of food. Why had the fraction of personal income of families in most of Europe, England, Canada and the United States devoted to food declined to an ever smaller part of their personal income? According to the concepts that I used in the papers collected in the first of these two volumes, these countries had become "low food drain" entities. From the vantage point of 1990, it was clear that the real price of basic food products had declined substantially. I kept asking myself, "What happened to the economic sting of secular diminishing returns?"

The three papers selected for Part Two of this volume, set the stage for dealing with the fundamental issue of identifying and analyzing various processes that explain increasing returns. Young's concept of increasing returns is compatible with the observed declining economic importance of agricultural land in high income countries.

1 Returns from Research

It became increasingly evident to me during the 1940s that the returns from organized agricultural research in the United States accounted for a large part of the unexplained increases in agricultural production. Expenditures for this purpose had become large. In 1953, I wrote: "If all of the endowments accumulated by Chicago, Columbia, Duke, Harvard, Hopkins, Princeton, Stanford, and Yale were combined and were earning 4 percent, the resulting revenue would have supported only one-fourth of the agricultural research under way at the beginning of the decade of the fifties."[4] My estimate of the lower limit in agricultural inputs saved in 1950 from the adoption of new and better techniques was $1,100 million. The total federal and state expenditures devoted to agricultural research in 1950 was $103 million.[5]

To get at the origins of the increases in agricultural outputs that exceed the increases in inputs one needs to determine the origin of each observable new technique, determine its costs and returns and treat it as an endogenous variable. Using this approach, Zvi Griliches made a classic contribution in his "Hybrid Corn: an Exploration in the Economics of Technological Change."[6] Another approach that has been rewarding is to capture the relevant increases in technical skills and knowledge as components of human capital.

The high rate of increase in agricultural research tells us a great deal about the perceived value of this research. During the period from 1950 to 1988, the world population more than doubled, and so did the world production of food. A clue to the demand for agricultural research is in the more than seven-fold increase in the real expenditures worldwide on agricultural research during the 1950–1988 period.

I continue to ponder the economic meaning of the following evidence. Before the introduction of hybrid seed, the acreage planted to corn in the United States in 1933 was 109.8 million. By 1987 only 76.7 million acres were in corn. On 33 million fewer acres the 1987 production was well over three times that of 1933, 8.25 billion bushels as compared with 2.40 billion. Reckon also the value of the output from cropland released from corn, the decline in the cost of producing corn, and the decline in the costs of feed used in producing animal and poultry products, and not least the large consumer surplus. Such is the essence of the Green Revolution.

Continuing progress in agricultural research is dependent on advances in the sciences. It could be that investments in science research are showing diminishing returns. Big science has become very costly and it entails a great deal of politics. The autonomy of universities is currently being impaired. Academic scientists and economists have become too beholden to government. The harsh truth is we are moving bit by bit closer to centralized control of organized research.

Distortions in economic research have come about in part because of the economic policy biases of some foundations and of most governmental agencies in allocating funds for economic research, and because of the accommodations of some academic economists to these biases in order to obtain research funds. In economics scholarly criticism of economic doctrines and of society's institutions is at a low ebb. Research incentives are beset with distortions.

Within universities, the importance of academic entrepreneurship is in general undervalued. Presidents, deans, department heads, and directors of research find it hard not to be entrepreneurs.

Given our dynamic economy, people cannot escape being entrepreneurs over their life spans. Whether a person is bad or good in performing this function is quite another matter.

Augmentation of income by research is pervasive in achieving economic growth. New knowledge has enhanced the productive capacity of land, and it has led to the development of new forms of physical capital and new human skills. *Fundamental in achieving long term economic growth are the research sectors of the economy.*

Research is a venture into the unknown or into what is only partially known. Whereas funds, organization and competent scientists are necessary, they are not sufficient. An important factor in producing knowledge is the human ability that I have defined as research entrepreneurship. It is an ability that is scarce; it is hard to identify this talent; it is rewarded haphazardly in the not-for-profit research sector; and it is misused and impaired by the over-organization of many research enterprises.

In the quest for research funds, a convenient assumption is that a highly organized research institution firmly controlled by an administrator will perform this important function. But in fact, a large organization that is tightly controlled tends to be the death of creative research regardless of whether it be the National Science Foundation, a government agency, a large private foundation, or a large research oriented university. No national research director in Washington can know the array of research options that the state of scientific knowledge at its frontiers affords. Having served as a member of a research advisory committee to a highly competent experiment station director and having observed the vast array of research talent supported by funds that we had a hand in allocating, I am convinced that most working scientists are research entrepreneurs. But it is exceedingly difficult to devise institutions to utilize this special talent efficiently. Organization is necessary. It too requires entrepreneurs. Agricultural research has benefited from its experiment stations, specialized university laboratories, and from the recently developed international agricultural research centers. But there is the ever-present danger of over-organization, of directing research from the top, of requiring working scientists to devote ever more time to preparing reports to "justify" the work they are doing, and to treat research as if it were a routine activity.

The history of the development and achievements of organized agricultural research and extension activities is a good vaccine for not becoming infected by the gloom and pessimism of doomsday, limits of growth, and the annual crop of new economic crises. No one in Washington or elsewhere in the United States actually knows the environmental specifications that will, over future decades, equate our values with the use we make of our resources. To understand what research entails, a person needs to know the state of relevant knowledge, its frontier and the hypotheses it affords.

Production of knowledge is costly, allocative decisions must be made. Whether or not researchers have a taste for the market, the price signals provided by the market are an essential part of the information that should not be neglected in allocating funds to research and also in allocating one's own time to the research enterprise being pursued.

2 Economic Basis of Traditional Agriculture

The core of my *Transforming Traditional Agriculture*[7] is an analysis of the economic basis of the sources of growth from agriculture in poor countries. I shall summarize the logic and the empirical results with respect to two crucial economic properties.

First, it may come as a surprise to find that farmers in poor countries are in general not inefficient in using (allocating) the agricultural factors of production that they have at their disposal. The reason once understood is simple. These farmers are as a rule subject to particular economic restraints that are typical of traditional agriculture; specifically, they are subject to preferences for acquiring and holding wealth, and to a state of the arts, both of which have remained virtually constant for generations. As a consequence they have long since attained a type of stationary equilibrium. Thus the popular belief that a different (better?) allocation of the existing poor collection of agricultural factors in these communities would substantially increase agricultural production is inconsistent both with economic logic as applied to the behavior of farmers in such an equilibrium and with the available empirical evidence. Strange as it may seem, it is true that on the basis of a strict allocative test, these farmers are more efficient than farmers in most of modern agriculture, because the latter are in a state of disequilibrium, a consequence of their rapid modernization.

Second, when it comes to investment to increase agricultural production, farmers who are bound by traditional agriculture have in general exhausted all profitable opportunities to invest in the agricultural factors at their disposal. This means that the marginal rate of return to investment in agricultural factors of the type which farmers have long been using is low, so low that there is little or no incentive to save and invest. Economic growth from traditional agriculture is too expensive. It means, in practical terms, that adding a few more wells and ditches for irrigation, several more draft animals and implements, and other forms of reproducible capital of the type farmers have been using for generations will increase agricultural production very little, so little in fact that it yields an unattractive rate of return.

These two economic properties are basic in understanding the behavior of farmers in traditional agriculture. The first is the existing *efficient allocation* and the second is the *unrewarding investment opportunity*. What they imply for economic growth from agriculture in many poor countries is that programs aimed solely at improving the economic efficiency of farmers are doomed to fail. Paradoxical as it may seem, farmers in traditional agriculture are generally more efficient by strict economic standards than farmers in the technically advanced countries in using the particular collection of land, labor, and material reproducible capital that they each have at their disposal. Likewise, programs designed solely to induce farmers in traditional agriculture to increase their investment in precisely the same type of agricultural factors they have been using for generations will fail for lack of acceptance, simply because the pay-off is too low.

It may be helpful to distinguish between agricultural inputs that originate from within agriculture and those that are supplied from outside of agriculture. With few exceptions, all the inputs that farmers in poor countries can produce for themselves are low pay-off sources. Virtually all agricultural inputs that hold real promise must come from outside of agriculture. This is obvious for commercial fertilizer, machinery, tractors, insecticides, and the development of genetically superior plants and animals. Though less obvious, it is also true for schooling and other means to improve the skills of farm people.

The high pay-off sources are predominantly *improvements in the quality of agricultural inputs*; these inputs can be acquired by farmers only from nonfarm firms and from agencies engaged in agricultural research, extension work, and schooling. It is therefore necessary to develop ways and means of improving the quality not only of the material reproducible inputs, but also of human agents engaged in farming. Thus far, in our attempts to assist poor countries in modernizing their agriculture, we have been vague and uncertain with regard to these origins of economic growth, and where we have happened to concentrate on the correct objective, we have with few exceptions failed to do things in the right order and in ways that would institutionalize the process.

In closing my Elmhurst Lecture, "Economics, Agriculture and the Political Economy,"[8] I made the following remarks.

> When the dominant social thought proscribes the use of rents, interest and profits and declares that market-oriented competition is blind, the accommodating political economy is severely handicapped in allocating resources for agricultural production. It may use all manner of devices – distributing fertilizer and other inputs by issuing quotas, controlling the migration of farm people from farm to farm and from farms to cities, segmenting the market for agricultural products within the country and allowing no movements between the different areas except as approved by the government, and even preventing farmers from buying and selling to each other.
>
> The heart of the problem then becomes one of knowing what the real economic values are, values to be used in commanding production and consumption. In this context no matter who is making economic decisions, be they planners, managers of collective farms or small private farms, using the information that is thus provided, leads to economic inefficiency. This is not to argue that the supply of valid, usable economic information is costless. It becomes very expensive under the above circumstances for the available supply in many countries has two attributes: the quality of economic information is exceedingly low and very costly. It should also be noted that improvements that are to be had from the work of the agricultural scientists in terms of better plants, animals, fertilizers and

equipment – important as they are when they are used efficiently – in no way solve the problem of ascertaining the real economic value of agricultural products and factors. Nor is the solution to be had by simply using more advanced computer technology.

What are the future cost prospects for agricultural products? In terms of technical possibilities and pure economic opportunities, the prospects for lower costs are good, but in terms of what is being done politically, the prospects are bad. Meanwhile, international food conferences produce a lot of weak reports, and social thought produces strong ideologies. But reports and ideologies do not produce food. Fortunately, plants and animals do not read reports nor do they discriminate against the ideology of any government. One thing is certain – what farm people will be able to do holds the key to our story.

The last paper in Part Four pertains to the economics of the family. We have learned a great deal from our economic approach to family behavior.

In this paper I took the hypothesis that the fivefold increase in real wages per hour of work in the United States since 1900 had swamped the within-family and the intergenerational personal distributions of income. What matter most are the increases in the value of human time over time.

While we have learned a great deal from our economic approaches to family behavior, it is my contention that our analytical work should be extended to relate the economic changes in the rest of the economy to those in the family exemplified by the "life span revolution" and by large shifts in relative prices in commodities, durables, and services. There is the hard-to-explain neglect of the highly competent family income studies based on the permanent and transitory income concepts. Then, too, the entrepreneurial behavior of families as economic conditions change is being neglected in our analytical work.

3   Rediscovery of Allyn Young's Economics

Young's "Increasing Returns and Economic Progress," 1928, was until very recently neglected. Economic events during the 1930s and 1940s were not auspicious to the idea of economic progress. The Great Depression, the massive unemployment and the drastic declines in incomes dominated the agenda of economists. Then too, the premature and sudden death of Young may have discouraged discussions of the merits of Young's thesis.

Important new evidence on the roots of Young's approach is now at hand in *The Life and Political Economy of Lauchlin Currie* by Roger J.

Sandilands, Duke University Press, 1990. I am deeply indebted to Sandilands for guiding me to the origins of the analysis of Young's 1928 paper and in helping me to obtain access to useful published documents. Nicholas Kaldor's *Notes* on Allyn Young's LSE Lectures, 1927–29, edited by Roger J. Sandilands, appeared in the *Journal of Economic Studies*, 17, No. 3/4, 1990, and are exceedingly useful in finding the origins of Young's ideas.

Young's approach to the origins of increasing returns entailed a proliferation of Smith's division of labor. Young stressed the *togetherness* of the various increasing returns activities. What he wanted to ascertain was the *sum* of the interacting effects of all of the various increasing returns activities.

There is much to be said in favor of examining the proliferation of increasing returns that high income countries have attained as an integral part of their modernization. There are increasing returns that are due to:

Division of Labor
Specialization
Advances in Technology
Augmentation of Human Capital
   Schooling, Education
   Learning by doing
   Acquisition of Knowledge
   Spillover of Knowledge
Ideas and Knowledge as Economic Entities
Institutions as Economic Entities
Economic Organization
Restoring Economic Equilibrium

Allyn Young did not appeal to data to support his idea of increasing returns. Had his life been spared, given his impressive statistical abilities, the required empirical analysis may well have been in hand.

We now have vast bodies of data that reveal large unexplained residuals in productivity increases which are a measure of our ignorance of economic growth.[9] Concealed in these unexplained components of growth are various elements of increasing returns.

"Tensions Between Economics and Politics" is the last paper included in this volume. It is mainly a critical review of the interactions and the limitations of the integration of economics and politics.

We have Young's assessments that the most fruitful and illuminating generalization in all of economics is that "the division of labor depends on the extent of the market." Does collective choice require a political market? Are the properties of a political market comparable to those of the economic market when it comes to division of labor, specialization, advances in technology, human capital and the other origins of increasing returns? At issue is the extent to which people belonging to a particular nation would be served better by substituting part of the activities of one of these markets for the other. Meanwhile, there is no lack of tension.

> Tensions between economics and politics, like those in marriages, are part of the human condition. Appeals to the idea of the political market have not reduced these tensions, nor has development economics. The dominating effect of development economics has been to overburden the political sector with economic functions that governments are not capable of performing efficiently. As a policy legacy it is a liability.

Gerald M. Meier closes his essay, "The Formative Period," with an excellent summary of this new branch of economics: "Some may summarize the mainstream development economics of the 1950s as being structural, shaped by trade pessimism, emphasizing planned investment in new physical capital, utilizing reserves of surplus labor, adopting import-substituting industrialization policies, embracing central planning of change, and relying on foreign aid."[10] Would that we had a critique on why this variety of development economics had such a bad start.

Theory and evidence are critical in assessing knowledge, whether of economics or of politics.[11] Whatever the reasons, agriculture has been the victim of more than its share of bad economics. Parity prices for farm produces based on 1910–14 relative prices is a vulgar economic concept. Supply management, production control by means of acreage allotments, and the dumping of farm products abroad to the tune of Food for Peace are also bad economics.

A major mistake of much of the new development economics has been the presumption that standard economic theory is inadequate for analyzing the economic behavior of people in low-income countries. Models developed for this purpose were widely acclaimed, until it became evident that they were at best intellectual curiosities. Increasing numbers of economists have come to realize that standard economic theory is as applicable to the scarcity problems that confront low-income countries as to the corresponding problems of high-income countries.

Another mistake has been the neglect of economic history. Classical economics was developed when most people in Western Europe were barely scratching out subsistence from the soils they tilled and they were condemned to a short life span. As a result, early economists dealt with conditions similar to those prevailing in low-income countries today. In

Ricardo's day, about half of the family income of laborers in England went for food. So it is today in many low-income countries.

Not all of the useful parts of economics were at hand when economists began to study the economic behavior of people in low-income countries. We now have a comprehensive concept of capital that does not exclude human capital; an economic concept of knowledge, the economic value of which can be identified and measured; a concept of the economic disequilibria that occur during modernization; a concept of human agents with ability to deal with disequilibria; and a concept of the nature and significance of the distortions of economic incentives.

Economic Growth with no economic disequilibria is not possible.

Economic Theory that omits the role that entrepreneurs play in economic modernization is on a par with omitting the Prince of Denmark in presenting Hamlet.

Specialization, human capital and economic modernization go hand in hand. Truly, the most distinctive feature of our economic system is the growth in human capital. Without it there would be only hard manual work and poverty except for those who have income from property.

4   Summary

Allyn Young's concept of increasing returns is a basic extension of Adam Smith's increase in income from the division of labor limited by the extent of the market. The declining economic importance of agricultural land and of most other natural resources in high income countries was in large measure a consequence of the increases in income from substitutes for land and for other natural resources. The origins of these substitutes come mainly from organized research activities.

The success of agricultural research is not in doubt. But there are reasons to be concerned. Scientists and economists have become too beholden to government. Economic policy biases are harmful. In economics scholarly criticism of economic doctrines and of society's institutions is at a low ebb. Incentives are beset with distortions. Academic entrepreneurship is in general undervalued. Production of Knowledge is costly, allocative decision must be made. Price signals should be reckoned in allocating funds for research.

Advances in agricultural research have made the green revolution possible. Most developing countries have pursued economic policies that have reduced incentives favoring the modernization of agriculture.

The farm family, especially so in agriculture, is a flexible and robust economic entity except under communism.

The rediscovery of Allyn Young's economics brings an advance in theory into the search for the widely observed increases of returns in many countries throughout the world.

Meanwhile tensions between economics and politics appears to be a part of the human condition. Yet despite many economic policy mistakes many people throughout the world have achieved a real increase in income.

Notes and References

1 Theodore W. Schultz, *The Economics of Being Poor* (Blackwell, Oxford, 1993): see Part II, No. 8, "Adam Smith and Human Capital."

2 Allyn Young, "Increasing Returns and Economic Progress," *Economic Journal* (Dec. 1928), 329–42.

3 Theodore W. Schultz, "Diminishing Returns in View of Progress in Agricultural Production," *Journal of Farm Economics*, 14, No. 4 (Oct. 1932), 640–49.

4 Theodore W. Schultz, *The Economic Organization of Agriculture* (McGraw-Hill Book Co., New York, 1953), pp. 114–15. The total endowment of these Universities in the late 1940s was about $600 million.

5 Ibid., p. 115, table 7.7.

6 Zvi Griliches, "Hybrid Corn: An Exploration in Economics of Technological Change," *Econometrica*, 25 (Oct. 1957), 501–22.

7 Theodore W. Schultz, *Transforming Traditional Agriculture* (Yale University Press, New Haven, Conn., 1964).

8 See below, Part IV, No. 2.

9 Moses Abramovitz, "Resource and Output Trends in the United States since 1970," Occasional Paper 52, National Bureau of Economic Research (New York, 1956), p. 11.

10 Gerald M. Meier, *Pioneers in Development*, 2nd series (World Bank, Oxford University Press, 1987), 17–38.

11 In this and following paragraphs I have borrowed freely from my Elmhurst Lecture (Part IV, No. 2 below).

Part I

Searching for Increasing Returns

Part I

Searching for Increasing Returns

1

On Investing in Specialized Human Capital to Attain Increasing Returns*

Allyn Young began his classic paper, "Increasing Returns and Economic Progress"[1] with these words, "My subject may appear alarmingly formidable, but I did not intend it to be so." My subject may seem no less formidable. To attain and then to gain from increasing returns by allocating resources for this purpose suggests that it is a pursuit beyond the capacity of proper economics.

The idea of increasing returns has not fared well in current growth economics, although it played a considerable role during earlier periods in the thinking of economists. Presently the analytical core of economics belongs to diminishing returns embedded in equilibrium. Surely no economist wants "to go back to a state of innocence before diminishing returns . . ."[2] But it seems as if we have become locked into diminishing returns in existing states of equilibrium. Thus, we forgo having a growth theory to analyze classes of changes that give rise to increasing returns. Allyn Young's paper should have sprung this lock, and it could have opened economics so that economists could pursue increasing returns.

* First published in Gustav Ranis and T. Paul Schultz (eds), *The State of Development Economics* (Basil Blackwell, 1988), pp. 339–52. I am indebted for the criticism and suggestions I received from Zvi Griliches on what I left out on the Residual Issue; from James Heckman for his critical assessment of parts of the evidence I had used; from Robert Lucas, noting his results hold even under constant returns; and from Sherwin Rosen, a memo. of suggestion which is a gem. George Tolley alerted me to studies of the externalities in cities; and, Jacob Frenkel on international trade studies. T. Paul Schultz called attention to Schumpeter on disequilibria and to my having omitted the limitations of specialization. Richard Barichello provided several helpful suggestions. I am indebted to George Stigler for his comments and for restraint in using his economic razor. John Letiche with good grace helped me in clarifying various issues and alerted me to the extensive growing literature on related issues in international economics (see footnote 37).

It should have made room for economic growth events that result in increases in output that exceed the increases in inputs, including the gains derived from "Adam Smith's famous theorem that the division of labor depends on the extent of the market."[3] One wonders why economists have not pursued Young's approach. It could be that he turned economists off by asserting, "I suspect, indeed, that the apparatus which economists have built . . . may stand in the way of a clear view of the more general or elementary aspects of the phenomena of increasing returns . . ."[4]

It may be elementary but it is often overlooked that increasing return activities do not exist in the axiomatic core of general equilibrium theory, whereas each and every increasing returns event implies that there is a disequilibrium. When such a disequilibrium occurs, there is an opportunity to gain from a reallocation of resources. The human agent who sees such an opportunity and who acts to take advantage of it is an entrepreneur.

Two serious flaws of growth economics are the result of the omission of the properties of the disequilibria that occur during the growth process and the omission of the economic value of the contributions that entrepreneurs make as they deal with these disequilibria. To explain the occurrence of observable economic disequilibria during the growth process is a much neglected part of economics. Schumpeter's approach to economic development is a notable exception.[5] His theory is based on changes in economic conditions that originate from within the economic system. These changes occur as a consequence of what a special set of entrepreneurs do when acting within that system. Schumpeter's entrepreneurs are innovators who create particular economic changes.

I begin with particular pertinent ideas of economists before economic growth models were invented. Some of the early ideas about economic progress have a comprehensiveness that has been lost in the highly specialized parts of today's economics. I then turn to the economic measurements that have all but eliminated the *residual* but in doing so have concealed most of the evidence pertaining to the economics of increasing returns. Lastly, I consider more fully particular aspects of increasing returns with special reference to specialization and human capital.

1   Ideas before Growth Theory

Above all there is the magnificent idea pertaining to the division of labor, its origin and its income-producing capacity. The economic importance of the division of labor is presently underrated. It holds the key to specialization, to investment in specialized human capital, and to classes of increasing returns.

The early idea about the substance and scope of diminishing returns was far from clear. It was all too much land-specific, whereas it is applicable to all factors of production. The rational producer cannot and does not try to avoid diminishing returns; he does not try to grow (Abba Lerner's phrase) ". . . the world's food in a flower pot."[6] Ricardo's concept, based on "the original and indestructable powers of the soil," is a burden in comprehending the increases in the productivity of agricultural land over time.

The early economists observed that agriculture is not only land-specific but that land is location-specific and that nature is niggardly. Their assessment of the then state of knowledge pertaining to agricultural production was, in large measure, correct. They could not have anticipated the development of various substitutes for farm land that have become available since then.

The limits of land productivity, which did in fact seriously limit the economic possibilities of increasing the production of food in England at that period of history, became an essential part of Malthus's theory of population. Thus, it may be said that this particular dated version of temporal "diminishing returns" placed an indelible mark on the history of economic thought.

Lest we forget, distinguished early economists were also bent on land reform. Smith, Ricardo, and Hume viewed agriculture as an unprogressive sector. Hume accused farm people of having a predisposition to indolence. His defamation of them is terse: "A habit of indolence naturally prevails. The greater part of the land lies uncultivated. What is cultivated, yields not its utmost for want of skill and assiduity in the farmers."[7] Smith and Ricardo saw manufacturing and commerce as progressive, whereas agriculture was the sinecure of an unprogressive landed aristocracy. Notwithstanding the notable increases in agricultural production during the period from the first edition of Marshall's *Principles* (1890) to the eighth edition (1920), the preface to the eighth edition indicates that Marshall had not freed himself from Ricardo's static situation assumption and logic with its unique scarcity of land as a factor of production despite changes in economic conditions.[8] There is then a backward jump to a *growth model* with no land in Harrod's Dynamic Economics.[9]

The belief that there is a specific *law of diminishing returns* that holds everywhere over time in agriculture is still held by the followers of the Club of Rome. No less an economist than Colin Clark in 1941 came to the conclusion that the world was in for a dramatic rise in the prices of primary products; namely, by 1960 ". . . the terms of trade of primary produce will improve by as much as 90 percent from the average of 1925–34."[10] (To speak of such a violent relative increase in these prices as an "improvement" is a neat twist.) His projection went off in the wrong direction. What went wrong? It was not his population variable that did it. The upsurge in population that occurred was larger than he had assumed. So, too, was the rate of increase in industrialization. Clark simply assumed no relaxation of diminishing returns from land, which turned out to be wrong. Could it be that the less agricultural land the better? – to wit Hong Kong and Singapore! Mark Twain would have enjoyed this approach to economics.

Neither Clark's Ricardian land, nor Harrod's no-land economic growth model is acceptable. Instead, there are compelling reasons and strong empirical evidence that support the idea of "The Declining Economic Importance of Agricultural Land."[11]

The basic point is that agriculture is not immune to changes in economic conditions that give rise to increasing returns. Consider the Green Revolution in wheat in India: it began in 1966 – production that year was 11 million tons; by 1984, India's wheat production had increased to 46 million tons. While we await a theory of economic growth to rationalize this extraordinary production event, common sense suffices to alert one to look for increasing returns in agriculture, especially in view of what happened in the Punjab, where the rates of return to land, fertilizer, equipment, labor, and to the enterpreneurship of farmers all increased.

What the early English economists observed were the increases in production by various manufacturing industries in England. They attributed a part of the additional production to increasing returns. The favorable changes in economic conditions in their day came to be known as the Industrial Revolution. As an economic process it had much in common with what is now referred to as the Green Revolution in agriculture.

Critics of the early versions of increasing returns argued that the simplistic notion of "improvements" did not suffice to explain such returns. Later, the critics used theory to show the monopoly effects of increasing returns. It became more telling. It implied that increasing returns are incompatible with competition. Therefore, monopoly would prevail. Since monopoly was in fact not pervasive, increasing returns were not pervasive.

Marshall's view of the tendencies to increasing returns with which he concludes Book IV are: (a) Increasing returns from scale effects are either *external* or *internal*; (b) ". . . the part nature plays in production shows a tendency to diminishing returns, the part which man plays shows a tendency to increasing returns." Man's part in agriculture conforms to the law of increasing returns (Book VI, chapter X, section 8); and (c) "The *law of increasing return* may be worded thus: an increase of labour and capital leads generally to improved organization, which increases the efficiency of the work of labour and capital." In essence, "Increasing Return is a relation between a quantity of effort and sacrifice on the one hand, and a quantity of product on the other."

Marshall's stress on the economic importance of the health, vigor, and the acquired abilities of people foreshadows what we now treat as human capital and so does his assessment of knowledge: "Knowledge is our most powerful engine of production. . . . The distinction between public and private property in knowledge . . . is of great and growing importance: in some respects of more importance than that between public and private property in material things."[12]

From Irving Fisher, a great economist, we have an all-inclusive concept of capital which includes human capital and which in turn includes specialized human capital, an important source of increasing returns.[13]

2   Enter Economic Measurement

Early economists were not inundated with statistics. They were spared the burden of statistical proof. They relied on history and on personal observations. Now we place our trust in hard data provided they are sanctioned by theory.

A long list of competent studies sponsored by the National Bureau of Economic Research devoted to measurement – brought to a head by Abramovitz[14] drawing on the work of Stigler, Kuznets, Kendrick, Fabricant,[15] Moore, Rees, Long, and still others – reported large gains over time from total factor productivity which became known as The Residual and as The Measure of Our Ignorance. To dispel this state of ignorance some economists were sure that the basic facts were in error. Others relabeled ". . . these changes as Technical Progress or Advance in Knowledge . . ." and thus, left the problem of explaining growth in total output unsolved.[16]

It is instructive to recall the search for explanations and the ideas that were advanced for the increases in measured output that exceeded the increases in measured inputs. Among the many solutions for this puzzle of the Residual, one looks in vain for references to increasing returns. No Smith, no Marshall, no Allyn Young. The idea of increasing returns was no longer kosher.

Studies by Denison and those by Jorgenson-Griliches loomed large in this search. In the process they clarified and improved the basic data.

Denison's approach is decidedly different from that of Jorgenson-Griliches. They disagreed head-on in a series of polemic publications which dealt with their differences on measurements and on explanations. As economic literature, these papers are major contributions.[17] According to Denison, a substantial part of the postwar growth in national output was due to an increase in productivity; according to Jorgenson-Griliches, almost all of the increase was due to an increase in factor inputs.[18]

In my early efforts to make room in economics for human capital I took advantage of Fisher's all-inclusive concept of capital. In principle, my approach in making my first estimates of "Capital Formation by Education,"[19] was akin to that of Jorgenson-Griliches. In retrospect it was simplistic of me to have published estimates of stocks of reproducible tangible capital, of educational capital in the labor force, including on-the-job training capital, for 1929 and 1957, in the United States.[20] It took a lot of on-the-job experience for me to learn that the simplifying assumption that capital is homogeneous is a disaster for capital theory,[21] and the assumption that the heterogeneity of various forms of measured capital as economic conditions change can be transformed for any given date into a homogeneous stock of capital, is subject to serious doubts.

Capital is two-faced, and what these two faces tell us about economic growth, which is a dynamic process, are, as a rule, inconsistent stories. It must be so, because the cost story is a tale about sunk investments, and the other story pertains to the discounted value of the stream of services that such capital renders, which changes with the shifting sands of growth. But worse still is the capital homogeneity assumption underlying the aggregation of capital in growth models. The dynamics of economic growth is afloat on capital inequalities because of the differences in the rates of return when disequilibria prevail, whether the capital aggregation is in terms of factor costs or in terms of the discounted value of the lifetime services of its many parts. Nor would a catalog of all existing growth models prove that these inequalities are equalities. But why try to square the circle? If we were unable to observe these inequalities, we would have to invent them – because they are the mainspring of economic growth, because they are the incentives to invest in growth. Thus, one of the essential parts of economic growth is concealed by such aggregation.[22]

The measurements of Jorgenson-Griliches are an important achievement; nevertheless, their estimates do not reckon the differences in marginal productivities and in rates of return as these change over time. Thus the differences in the incentives during each of the dated years to invest in the formation of capital are blunted, if not concealed, in the aggregation process. One must look elsewhere for evidence pertaining to increases in productivity associated with increasing returns events.

As I ponder Denison's 1985 update, *Trends in American Economic Growth*, 1929–82,[23] I find his changes in the labor component quite similar to that of Jorgenson-Griliches in terms of reasons that account for the magnitude of the changes over time. It is difficult to compare the two approaches on capital. Denison reports no change in land as an input, which is not land as I know it.

Denison's "output per unit of input results" seems plausible in view of his accounting of the factor inputs. Among his 12 explanations for the changes in the measured output per unit of input, there are several that open the analytical door a good bit to get at the origins of the rates of return associated with increasing returns. He states that his scale effects gave rise to opportunities for greater specialization. On this issue I am attracted to Denison's approach, but no supporting evidence is reported.

The difficult measurement problems stressed in the preceding section, including estimates of the effects of scale, education, and disequilibria, are identified and dealt with by Griliches in his agricultural productivity studies. Three of his key papers on these issues are cited below. Most of his results appear in "Research Expenditures, Education, and the Aggregate Agricultural Production Function."[24] Griliches notes that had he "assumed equilibrium and constant returns to scale, it would have begged some of the most important questions we are interested in."[25] For the purpose at hand, in explaining "cross-sectional differences in output per man, of the two variables, wage rates and education, the latter is the 'stronger' one and 'survives' the introduction of other variables whereas wage rates do not."[26] He found substantial economies of scale in agriculture. His results confirm the existences of disequilibria, and the observed behavior reflects the producers' actions to reduce them. In the case of fertilizer, the value of the marginal product exceeded the fertilizer price by a ratio between 3 and 5. Faced with this large disequilibrium, farmers increased their application of fertilizer at a rate of over 7.4 percent per year. This equilibrium gap (VMP/factor price) declined from about 5 in 1949 to 2.7 in 1959.[27] There was still a substantial disequilibrium at the end of this period.

3   Increasing Returns, Specialization and Human Capital

The idea of increasing returns has become a spoiler at this high table of theory. It conjures up the ideological issues of the value and distribution of *the surplus* and of the *unearned profits* in a capitalist economy. It is also bent on spoiling a part of the usefulness of the axiomatic core of economic equilibrium. But for all that actual, observable, increasing returns appear to improve the economic lot of man.

It is helpful to think of each increasing returns occurrence as an economic event. Most increasing returns are small, micro events, as in the case of a farmer's increase in corn yields made possible by hybrid seed. Such micro events can, as a rule, be identified and measured, and their economic effects are in general ascertainable. But when increasing returns are attributed to large macro events, for example, to the Industrial Revolution, the measurement of the inputs and outputs and their precise effects on productivity is exceedingly difficult to do.

Increasing returns are transitory events. They have a lifespan that is clearly observable where these events are small and occur under open-market competition. When an increasing returns event occurs, there is information that it is worthwhile to reallocate resources. Human agents, acting as entrepreneurs, respond to the expected profits to be had, and their actions account for the transitory nature of these events.

It is hard to think of nature as a substantial source of increasing returns. They are, for all practical and analytical purposes, consequences of the activities of man. They may have their origin either within or outside of the economic system. Those that originate from within would be included in Schumpeter's Theory of Economic Development.

How frequently do increasing returns events occur? Do particular events of this type spawn a series of related events? Does the economy have a built-in capacity to create them? In large measure these questions reach beyond the scope of this essay.

The linkages of increasing returns to specialized human capital via specialization will be considered following a few comments on specialization.

We have a myopic view of specialization. We do not reckon the vast extent of the specialization that has occurred over time. For industry, we know about the pin factory. For agriculture, we blithely assume that there is nothing comparable to a pin factory. In international trade, however, specialization has long been a part of trade theory and its applications.

Agriculture is not immune to specialization and to returns from specialized human capital. Today's modern farmer is no Crusoe. The Corn Belt farm family no longer produces eggs, milk, vegetables, and fruit for home consumption. Such food items are purchased. So is the electricity, gas for fuel, telephone service, water not infrequently piped in from off farm sources and paid for. Corn farmers no longer produce their own seed corn. They buy hybrid seed appropriate to their area. Production expenses consist mainly of inputs produced by industry. The production of pigs has become specialized into: (1) producing breeding stock, (2) farrowing and through weaning, (3) producing feeder pigs, and lastly (4) finishing their growth into hogs to suit the market. Yet the myth persists that there is virtually no specialized human capital within agriculture.

It behoves us to keep in mind Marshall's dictum that "Knowledge is the most powerful engine of production." Is it true? In agriculture it is true – the costs and returns from agricultural research tell us so. Studies of the economic value of agricultural research began to flourish following Zvi Griliches's classic PhD dissertation on hybrid corn, its research costs, and social returns. We now know that the rates of return to expenditures on organized agricultural research in general, since about 1930, have been much higher than the going normal rates of returns on physical capital investments.

What is noteworthy is that agricultural scientists, by virtue of their acquired professional skills, are specialized in human capital. Furthermore, specialization abounds in modern agriculture. Scale effects on returns are well known. The contributions of human capital to increases in farm and farm household productivity are receiving increasing attention. An important factor in the economic success of agricultural research is the specialized human capital of agricultural scientists.

Finis Welch has shown that the value of farmers' education in production is high as agricultural modernization occurs.[28] Welch succeeded in separating the *work* effect from the *allocative* effect of education. The favorable returns to the schooling and higher education of farmers are, in large measure, the result of the allocative effects of education. This acquired allocative ability functions as a specialized form of human capital.

Specialization abounds in our cities and factories, in commerce, manufacturing and in light and heavy industries. But what about the professions? Since economists are not averse to being thought of as one of the knowledge-producing professions, I turn to the production and distribution of knowledge in the United States based on the authority of Fritz Machlup. His 1962 book is a rich vein of information on the vast extent of the specialization that prevails.[29] The last book from Machlup's fertile mind is on the economics of information and human capital within the core of economics.[30] The extent and complexity of the knowledge producing professions bespeak human capital specialization and it accounts in good measure for much of their productivity.

Specialization, however, has its limits. It, too, is subject to diminishing returns. When it is carried too far, there will be losses from the consequences of overspecialization. Not to be concealed is the fact that economists are also vulnerable to overspecialization in what they do. An economist who specializes on what farmers do, fails to comprehend the economics of agriculture as an integral part of the economy. Hayek could say with good grace, "Nobody can be a great economist who is only an economist," and he added, "An economist who is only an economist is likely to be a nuisance if not a positive danger."

I now turn to a brief search for economic thinking and for additional evidence to assess the hypothesis which implies that specialized human capital is an important source of increasing return events. I shall not belabor the vast amount of evidence bearing on the performance of entrepreneurs that reveals the rate at which the gains from increasing returns events are realized.

The trade effects of human capital on the composition of the goods that are traded could account for the so-called Leontief paradox, which asserts that contrary to trade theory, capital-rich countries export labor-intensive goods. We now know that the labor services entering into such goods are human-capital-intensive. A capital-rich country exports the services of specialized human capital.

In his *Treatise on the Family*, Becker extends his analysis of the division of labor within the household to that which occurs in international trade. Members of the household specialize their investments and time; "moreover, with constant or increasing returns to scale, *all* members of efficient households must be completely specialized."[31] So, too, the fundamental source of much of the gain from trade is from the advantage of specialized investment and the division of labor. Viner and other trade economists featured and understood the economic reasons why similar countries gained from trade, namely, the gains are a consequence of investments specializing in particular types of human and physical capital and products that utilize such capital intensively.

In a recent paper, Becker returns to his argument that increasing returns from specialized human capital are a strong force creating a division of labor in the allocation of time and investments in human capital between married men and married women.[32]

The economics of two-way trade in similar products between similar countries has been further explored by Daniel Gros.[33] He also argues that increasing returns to scale made possible by specific human capital specialization explains this class of trade. The evidence in support of his argument is as yet sparse.

Rosen came to the issues at hand in his "Substitutions and Division of Labor,"[34] then came his "Specialization and Human Capital," with the following telling argument.

Incentives for specialization, trade, and the production of comparative advantage through investment are shown to arise from increasing returns to utilization of human capital. Indivisibilities imply fixed-cost elements of investment that are independent of subsequent utilization. Hence, the rate of return is increasing in utilization and is maximized by utilizing specialized skills as intensively as possible. Identically endowed individuals have incentives to specialize their investments in skills and trade with each other for this reason, even if production technology exhibits constant returns to scale. The enormous productivity and complexity of modern economies are in good measure attributable to specialization.[35]

Lucas in his Marshall Lectures, "On The Mechanics of Economic Development,"[36] focuses on the interaction of physical and human capital accumulation and on systems that admit specialized human capital. I shall cite a few clues to his approach. " 'Human knowledge' is just human, not Japanese, or Chinese or Korean . . . differences in 'technology' across countries . . . are not . . . about 'knowledge' in general but about the knowledge of particular people." Knowledge is a form of human capital and human capital is an engine of growth.

Lucas assigns a central role to his concept of the *external effects* of human capital. These effects spill over from one person to another, people at each skill level are more productive in high human capital environments, and human capital enhances the productivity of both labor and physical capital. Where Lucas refers to "human capital accumulation as a *social* activity, involving *groups* of people, in a way that has no counterpart in the accumulation of physical capital," it should be restricted to that part of human capital which gives rise to the external effects. In this context, the capacity of human capital as an engine of growth is determined by the returns attributed to the external effects of human capital.

A country's human capital at any given date is an important economic fact in analyzing the production possibilities of the country. The productivity value of this human capital "endowment" depends in large part on its composition in relation to the market opportunities for the services of each part of the composition. What matters in this context is the heterogeneity of human capital. In labor economics, the distinction between general human capital and firm-specific human capital of workers is useful analytically. The concept of specialized human capital encompasses a large number of forms of human capital that pertain to increasing returns events.

Is it possible to anticipate particular forms of specialized human capital that have a high probability of generating increasing return opportunities which would warrant investment in them? It is my contention that it can be done and that it is being done.

In large measure, expenditures on research and development (R&D) qualify. Broadly defined, R&D are major sources of technical advances that originate out of basic and applied research which entail specialized human capital. Thus R&D scientists create new and better techniques for production, the applications of which give rise to increasing return events. Consider organized agricultural research throughout the world. It has become a sizeable subsector of the economy, with annual expenditures equivalent to about 8 billion 1985 US dollars. Then take a close micro look at the acquired scientific ability of a top flight geneticist who devotes his research to increasing the productivity of plants (crops). He is an important cog in the organized agricultural research wheel that has increased greatly the food-producing capacity of agriculture. The prospects are that this important source of gains in agricultural productivity is still far from having been exhausted. Thus, continuing and also increasing investment in this class of specialized human capital is warranted.

Another class of investment in specialized human capital that results in increasing returns over the life span of human beings is exemplified by investment in primary schooling. What is at stake is the acquired ability to have mastered a language sufficiently to *read* efficiently and to *write* with competence. Here, too, marked advances have been achieved in many low-income countries since World War II, measured by the increases in primary schooling. There is a large body of evidence which shows that in countries where agriculture is being modernized, the rate of returns to primary schooling of farmers is high. There continues to be a vast underinvestment in such schools, viewed here as specialized human capital. The high rate of returns to it is a clue that it is a source of increasing returns at this juncture of economic growth.

I have argued that specialized human capital is an important source of increasing returns, and growth theory that excludes the formation of such human capital is far from adequate. Growth theory also excludes the contributions of entrepreneurs to growth. Appreciating the interdependence of these two phenomena is crucial, both for the advance of growth theory and for the explanation of growth experience. On various important issues pertaining to economic progress, early economists had comprehensive insights that growth theory has omitted. Smith's division of labor made possible by specialization constrained by the extent of the market, is a fundamental insight. So are Marshall's tendencies to increasing returns. What is hard to explain is the long silence on the part of economists following Young's classic paper. During the era of the puzzle of the Residual, economic measurement research was unencumbered by Smith, or Marshall, or Young. The search was not for evidence on increasing returns.

There are now indications that specialization, human capital and growth are on the research agenda of a number of economists.[37] Our myopic view of specialization is being corrected by appropriate lenses. Investigations are now at hand and under way that show that specialization, specialized human capital, increasing returns, and growth go hand in hand.

Notes and References

1 Allyn J. Young, "Increasing Returns and Economic Progress," *Economic Journal* (Dec. 1928), 527–42.
2 This phrase is from John Hicks, *Capital and Growth* (Oxford University Press, Oxford, 1965), p. 134.
3 Young, "Increasing Returns," p. 529.
4 Ibid., p. 527.
5 Joseph A. Schumpeter, *The Theory of Economic Development* (Harvard University Press, Cambridge, Mass., 1949). See also his *Capitalism, Socialism, and Democracy* (Harper and Brothers, New York, 1942), chapter 12.
6 Abba Lerner, *The Economics of Control* (Macmillan and Co., New York, 1941), p. 161.
7 David Hume, *Writing on Economics*, ed. Eugene Rotwein (University of Wisconsin Press, Madison, 1955), p. 10. I am indebted to Nathan Rosenberg on this point.
8 Alfred Marshall, *Principles of Economics* (Macmillan and Co., London, 1930). In the preface of the 8th edition, dated October 1920, the following paragraph appears:

> There have been stages in social history in which the special features of the income yielded by the ownership of land have dominated human relations: and perhaps they may again assert a pre-eminence. But in the present age, the opening out of new countries, aided by low transport charges on land and sea, has almost suspended the tendency to Diminishing Return, in that sense in which the term was used by Malthus and Ricardo, when the English labourers' wages were often less than the price of half a bushel of good wheat. And yet, if the growth of population should continue for very long even at a quarter of its present rate, the aggregate rental values of land for all its uses (assumed to be as free as now from restraint by public authority) may again exceed the aggregate of incomes derived from all other forms of material property; even though that may then embody twenty times as much labour as now.

9 R.F. Harrod, *Towards a Dynamic Economics* (Macmillan and Co., London, 1948), p. 20.
10 Colin Clark, *The Economics of 1960* (Macmillan and Co., London, 1953), p. 52. The "introduction" is dated May 15, 1941.

11 See below, Part II, No. 1, "The Declining Economic Importance of Agricultural Land."

12 Marshall, *Principles of Economics*, book IV, "The Agents of Production," chapter 1, pp. 138 and 139.

13 Irving Fisher, *The Nature of Capital and Income* (Macmillan and Co., New York and London, 1906).

14 Moses Abramovitz, "Resonance and Output Trends in the United States since 1890," *Occasional Paper 52* (National Bureau of Economic Research, New York, 1956), 23pp.

15 Solomon Fabricant, "Basic Facts on Productivity Change," Occasional Paper 63 (National Bureau of Economic Research, New York, 1959), 49pp.

16 D.W. Jorgenson and Zvi Griliches, "The Explanation of Productivity Change," *Review of Economic Studies* (July 1967), 249–83.

17 Five of the principal publications on these issues appear in "The Measurement of Productivity," *Survey of Current Business* (US Department of Commerce, 1972), part 2, 52(5), 1–111 It is also available as Reprint 244 of the Brookings Institution, Washington DC.

18 Ibid., p. 1.

19 Theodore W. Schultz, "Capital Formation by Education," *Journal of Political Economy*, 68 (Dec. 1960), 571–83; reproduced in Schultz, *The Economics of Being Poor* (Blackwell, 1993), Part II, No. 2.

20 Theodore W. Schultz, "Reflections on Investment in Man," *Journal of Political Economy*, Supplement, 70 (Oct. 1962), 1–8.

21 Hicks, *Capital and Growth*, p. 35.

22 Theodore W. Schultz, "Human Capital: Policy Issues and Research Opportunities," in *Human Resources* (National Bureau of Economic Research, New York, 1972), 1–84.

23 Edward F. Denison, *Trends in American Economic Growth 1929–82* (Brookings Institution, Washington DC), table 8-1, p. 111.

24 Zvi Griliches, "Research Expenditures, Education, and the Aggregate Agricultural Production Function," *American Economic Review* (Dec. 1964), 961–74.

25 Zvi Griliches, "Specification and Estimation of Agricultural Production Function," *Journal of Farm Economics* (May 1963), p. 421.

26 Ibid., p. 425: see also "The Sources of Measured Productivity Growth: United States Agriculture, 1940–60," *Journal of Political Economy* (Aug. 1963), 331–46.

27 Griliches, "Research Expenditures," p. 968.

28 Finis Welch, "Education in Production," *Journal of Political Economy*, 78 (1970), 35–59.

29 Fritz Machlup, *The Production and Distribution of Knowledge in the United States* (Princeton University Press, Princeton, NJ, 1962), pp. xix and 416; *Knowledge and Knowledge Production* (Princeton University Press, 1980), pp. xxix and 272; and *The Branches of Learning* (Princeton University Press, 1982), pp. xii and 205.

30 Fritz Machlup, *The Economics of Information and Human Capital* (Princeton University Press, Princeton, NJ, 1984), pp. xvi and 644, foreword, and introduction.

31 Gary S. Becker, *A Treatise on the Family* (Harvard University Press, Cambridge, Mass. and London, 1981), 20–21.

32 Gary S. Becker, "Human Capital, Effort, and the Sexual Division of Labor," *Journal of Labor Economics*, 3(1) (1985), 533–58.

33 Daniel Gros, "Increasing Returns and Human Capital in International Trade," PhD dissertation (University of Chicago, 1984).

34 Sherwin Rosen, "Substitutions and Division of Labor," *Economica*, 45(1) (1976), 861–68.

35 Sherwin Rosen, "Specialization and Human Capital," *Journal of Labor Economics*, 1 (1983), 43–9.

36 Robert E. Lucas Jr, "On the Mechanics of Economic Development," *Marshall Lecture* (Cambridge University, May 1985). I am dependent on a draft dated March 1985.

37 Paul Romer, "Dynamic Competitive Equilibria With Externalities, Increasing Returns and Unbounded Growth," PhD dissertation (University of Chicago, 1983). For the extensive, growing literature on these issues in international economics, see the references cited in Elhanan Helpman and Paul R. Krugman, *Market Structure and Foreign Trade: Increasing Returns, Imperfect Competition, and the International Economy* (MIT Press, Mass., 1985); Avinash Dixit, "Strategic Aspects of Trade Policy," paper delivered at the Fifth World Congress of the Econometric Society, Sept. 1985; and R.W. Jones and P.B. Kenen (eds), *Handbook of International Economics* (North-Holland Publishing Co., Amsterdam, 1984).

2

On Economic History in Extending Economics *

Economics consists of a body of knowledge that has become large and complex, as every graduate student will testify. Economists, however, seldom assess the extent to which it is useful. We know full well that our ability to make accurate predictions is very limited, which does not imply, however, that what we know is not in some respects useful. But it is fair to say that the record of those economists who indulge in making projections is no better than that of demographers who keep on making population projections. We tend to feature the theoretical foundation of economics but appear to be unaware of the weaknesses of many of its implications. It is my contention that, despite the vast quantity of current statistics, the empirical foundations of economics remain weak. Moreover, to discover the possibilities of extending and improving the usefulness of theory, we must strengthen its historical base.

If recent past economic events were sufficient to determine which of our many speculations and theories are valid empirically, there would be no role for economic history in strengthening the foundations of economics. If long-past recorded economic behavior were devoid of new and better information than that available from current sources, there would be no point in turning to economic history for such information. There are, however, strong reasons why current events are not sufficient and why particular long-past historical events are a source of some much-needed information in our endeavor to verify and extend the knowledge base of economics.

The scientific prestige of physics rests in large part on knowledge that has been verified by means of controlled experiments. Astronomers,

* First published in *Economic Development and Cultural Change*, 25, Supplement (1977), 245–50. © 1977 by the University of Chicago. All rights reserved. I am indebted to Gary Becker, Robert Fogel, Arcadius Kahan, and Donald McCloskey for their helpful comments.

however, have accumulated an impressive body of knowledge not by running experiments but mainly by analyzing the differences in the history of various celestial bodies.[1] Although economists may hanker to do what the physicists do, it is a will-o'-the-wisp. One of our analytical opportunities in advancing knowledge about economic behavior is akin to those of astronomers. *Herein lie the importance and necessity of economic history.*

I shall begin with a few remarks on the dependency of economics on historical observations, and then comment briefly on some of the strong and weak attributes of economic history, and last, I shall consider several specific research opportunities.

Although economic history consists of many fragments, there is much more of it tucked away in our minds and in our literature than we realize. McCloskey's brief survey of the accumulated literature is very useful.[2] What we believe we know about history that gets embedded implicitly in our assumptions and approaches to economic problems is a mixture of valid and invalid historical insights. We are both richer and poorer in this respect than we really know.

Since all observable economic events are historical, I find it convenient to distinguish between the short- and long-retrospect approach in analyzing economic events. I shall classify any study that examines the economic behavior of people long past as economic history. So that a couple of my studies will qualify as economic history, I shall arbitrarily declare events that occurred 50 or more years ago as economic history![3]

Most economists are born with a strong urge to sell their wares to policymakers; economic historians have an extra gene, which accounts for their desire to reform the historians. Leaving policy aside, I see historical economists as pursuing two general objectives: (1) to reinterpret history and (2) to extend economic knowledge. My view taken here favors the second objective. Professional taste and highly gifted economists aside, I am not convinced that it is an efficient use of an economist's time to try to persuade historians that some aspect of received history is invalid. It leads to protracted controversy that can be very time consuming. No doubt the lag on the part of historians in accepting our precious findings is reduced somewhat by such controversies, but this is of little consequence. I know that this is a debatable proposition.

The endeavor of adding to the stock of economic knowledge is beset by unsettled issues. Standard theory tends to confine economists to what is essentially a closed analytical system, whereas societies are open-ended both now and in times past. What this statement implies is that useful contributions to economics are not necessarily confined to testing the implications of received theory against historical evidence. To develop useful extensions of theory may appropriately be the ultimate goal, but it frequently is not the objective that motivates creative thinking.

There are numerous historical insights with respect to development that are not a part of the core of theory. What is known about the changes over time in the heterogeneity of capital as new forms are added to the stock of capital and about the various income elasticities of the demand is not derived from theory. For instance, one of the more useful, measurable concepts in studying economic development is the income elasticity of demand for consumer items. We know from observation, not from theory, that the income elasticity of the demand for food is not only less than one but that it is between .5 and .7 in India and less than .3 in the United States, and we know which food items become inferior goods as the level of income rises. Again, Kuznets was not testing a hypothesis derived from theory when he found that the share of personal income accruing to the owners of property assets in the high-income countries declined historically from about 45 to 25 percent.

In this connection, there are two points to keep in mind: (1) we perceive many of the effects of the principles of utility and of scarcity that are not parts of theory, and (2) we often overlook the fact that the observable properties of most economic entities contain various attributes which are a consequence of what has happened to those entities in the past. Accordingly, when they are observed they are not free of their history. On the first point, let me paraphrase and apply to economics what Bridgeman the physicist said about physics. Economic behavior is more complex than our thoughts about it. Our thoughts, however, are more comprehensive than our economic language, our language is more comprehensive than standard theory, and standard theory is more comprehensive than mathematical economics. One can walk to many locations that one cannot get to by airplane. Each of these modes of approaching economic behavior, however, from thought to mathematics, has its advantages. But, even so, what is known from the combined contributions of all of them is subject to doubts.

On the second point, there are very few basic economic concepts that are not affected by history when it comes to measurement. They are in general not "history-less."[4] To clarify this idea, a new terminology is required to denote the presence or absence of the effects of history on observable economic entities. Jorge Luis Borges, in one of his fascinating short stories, develops "a character named Funes who cannot forget any detail of what he sees, hears, feels or experiences." It is, for him, a terrible situation. Taking the name of this character, we shall call an economic entity *funes* that, so to speak, "remembers" the past and *afuneus* for one that "remembers" nothing. In applying this story to physics, Victor F. Weisskopf notes that "electrons are very afuneus objects." The arrangements of crystals, however, differ widely depending on what they experienced in the past. In economics, the indifference system and the concept of a general economic equilibrium are afuneus. Observable land, labor, and capital are very funes entities. No matter where we observe them, they contain properties that have been determined by their history. I shall return to these as factors in production presently. Consumer items are also funes. Consider food: in India, food consists largely of farm-produced components; in the United States, only about one-third of the cost components embodied in the food that we use in our homes originates in farm production. Clearly, what food is, in fact, depends very much on the history of the economic circumstances where it is being observed.

The implications of the above two points are that the frontier of economic history takes us beyond hypotheses that can be derived from received theory and from analyses of current economic data, and are marked by their history, as anyone knows who thinks about what is not taken into account in cross-sectional, empirical studies of economic events.

1 Some Strong and Weak Attributes of Economic History

Problem-oriented economists are bedeviled by a flood of theories not knowing how to distinguish between useful and useless theories; they are also troubled by unclean facts, not knowing what these facts conceal and omit when it comes to using them in empirical work. Despite the recent impressive advances in quantitative techniques, very few university economists are engaged in "making data" that will stand up under strong empirical analysis. They appear not to have the time, patience, or resources to produce the data that are really needed.

Economic historians have several advantages in this connection. They produce their own data and in doing so they may be less vulnerable to omissions and errors that are concealed in the now available current economic data. Although large sums have been spent on "controlled economic experiments," they tend to be barren because it is not possible to *control* all of the ever-changing economic circumstances influencing the people within the experiment, and because the people concerned outmaneuver the controllers. History, however, is replete with marked changes in economic circumstances, and the economic responses of people to them are on record. They are sources of real observable events that occurred under conditions that approximate what might be called "economic experiments" that took place under conditions that were not contrived. Unlike the physicists, we cannot accomplish much by organizing controlled experiments, but we can, in effect, do what astronomers do as they acquire observations of various celestial bodies older than the earth.

On another point, I am impressed by the apparent advantage that the instruction in economic history has in getting graduate students involved in real research, as I see the term papers that emerge which contribute much to students' experience in learning how to use their analytical tools in research.

Economic historians are, however, also burdened by several disadvantages. Theoretical economists who dominate economics do not read the contributions that emerge from the work in economic history. Who is to blame? In part, it is a consequence of the propensity of economic historians to reinterpret history, so they publish in journals read by historians. It is my belief that the journals that specialize in economic history are not efficient in reaching economists. The fraction of the pages in our leading economic journals devoted to economic history is very small.[5] Why? It could be that their editors are strongly biased toward theory and its applications to current economic situations. Alternatively, it could be that economic historians have had little to contribute to economic knowledge or that they have not learned how to present their findings so that they would challenge the rank and file of economists. An argument can be made for the latter of these views. In support of this view, a decade and a half ago I would not have predicted that our leading economic journals would be devoting a large number of pages to human capital studies. It would appear that these studies are in demand by readers of these journals.

Another disadvantage is the apparent lack of enough academic entrepreneurs in economic history in developing markets for their PhDs, in acquiring research funds, and in developing viable research workshops as an integral part of graduate work. A few notable exceptions, for example, Kuznets, Fogel, and North, convince me on this point. I trust it will not be in bad grace for me to note the aggressiveness of the entrepreneurship of agricultural economists who acquire both public and private funds in large amounts for research, who account for nearly a fourth of the PhD output in the United States, and who won the singular acclaim from Leontief for their use of theory in combination with observable facts.[6] I am sure that the strong and weak attributes of economic history that I have featured are not the last word on this topic.

2   On Research Opportunities

I have argued for research, the purpose of which is to increase our under-standing of economic behavior. I have also argued that it is not sufficient to rely wholly on hypotheses derived from standard theory. Nor do I believe that we know enough about economic behavior presently to develop useful economic theories that are capable of explaining (1) population growth, (2) the interactions between private rights in physical and human capital, (3) the development of economic institutions, and (4) investments in new forms of capital that embody new techniques.

Although each of these four issues is exceedingly important and although each has been on my agenda repeatedly, the more I have become involved in searching for solutions, the more I have come to realize the heterogeneity that bedevils each of these issues. For instance, fluctuations in birth rates in high-income countries are beset with many puzzles, and so are the demographic transitions in low-income countries. Private rights in capital are not confined to property. There is a lack in historical perspective inasmuch as the question is not being investigated of why the economic contribution of private property has declined so markedly over time relative to that of human capital. Human capital also entails rights, although enmeshed in human rights. An economic theory to deal comprehensively with the changing interactions over time between the rights of private property and human capital rights is not as yet on the horizon. Some progress is being made by treating particular economic institutions as endogenous entities that are created and altered in response to the requirements of economic development. But even so, we are unable to explain the simple historical fact that agricultural experiment stations were among the first to be organized and publicly supported as useful scientific research enterprises, and it is also true more recently in the organization of international research centers. I have long been critical of the way economists treat technology. While it makes sense to analyze the cost and returns from a particular new and superior input — for example, hybrid corn – it is a disaster to lump the vast array of all manner of new techniques by evoking the assumption that these techniques are homogeneous capital entities. The all too convenient term "technology" that is entered into many models is truly a Pandora's box. In fact, each technique is a specific form of capital, and until we are prepared to deal appropriately with the heterogeneity of capital, the prospects of developing a generalized approach to explain changes in technology are dim.

Population, private rights, institutions, and the changing state of the productive arts are on my private list of research opportunities in economic history. But it is the better part of wisdom for me not to incur the additional risk of going beyond what I have said. As I turn to some of the lesser unsettled issues on my list, I am reminded of a scene from *The Mikado*: "I've got a little list when victims must be found" of economic offenders "who might well be underground." The rest of my remarks will be restricted to several of the lesser research opportunities on my list.

1   Recent developments in economics in analyzing the economic behavior of households have led to all manner of new ideas about the family. One of these ideas raises the following question: Is there an economic explanation for the pronounced historical shift from the extended to the nuclear family in Western countries? William J. Goode provides a useful analysis of this shift from the point of view of a competent sociologist.[7] He sees it as having occurred as a consequence of economic modernization. But what precisely is it about modernization that accounts for the obsolescence of the extended family? Four different explanations come to mind: (1) as production activities are modernized, the market is extended which enhances the comparative advantage of the nuclear relative to the extended family; (2) as the incomes of families rise over time, the shift toward the nuclear family is a pure income effect; (3) there is less need for intrafamily insurance as markets develop; and (4) there is less demand for many children, as the price of the time of mothers increases. Looking at current evidence, I see no way of deciding which of these explanations is valid, or whether all are required, except that the post-World War II undoubling of families is largely an income effect, as Dorothy Brady has shown. The essays in Peter Laslett's *Household and Family in Past Times*[8] contain several bodies of information that appear relevant in answering the question at hand.

2   In the controversy over the effects of the cultural difference among families on their investment in the human capital of their children, there are two key questions: (1) What can be done to distinguish between the income and price effects on one hand and the cultural effects on the other? (2) Are the observable cultural differences among families the consequence of identifiable historical economic circumstances under which subsets of families have long lived? Settling these questions will require a good deal of analytical work and historical evidence. There is much to be said for concentrating on the historical experiences of special sets of families within various populations. For instance, Occidental Jews have historically made much larger investments of this type relative to those made by Oriental Jews. Why? Chinese who have long lived in enclaves throughout South Asia have invested much more in their children than have the indigenous families. So have the Mormons relative to

the rest of our population. why? Our knowledge about intergenerational investments in human capital would be advanced by an appeal to such historical records.

3   There have been many city-states. I have in mind the Hansa towns of the North Sea and the Baltic and the city-states of the Low Countries. Add to these the city-states that once flourished in and about the Mediterranean – Pisa, Genoa, Venice, and many others. I see them as natural economic laboratories, the records of which might contribute substantially to the extension of economic knowledge. These city-states appear to have attained a higher level of personal income than that of adjacent sovereign countries despite the fact that there were few natural resources within these city-states.[9] Whereas our own economy has become too large and too complex to isolate the evidence for determining the effects of the size of the market on its productivity, city-states, so it seems to me, have been unique "experiments" for getting at the effects of the extent of the market. Furthermore, it is highly plausible that the people in these city-states invested much more in their human capital than did the people in the adjacent countries. Would the records support this proposition? This view of city-states rests partly on the findings of Theodore and Frances Geiger in their study of Hong Kong and Singapore,[10] two currently viable city-states within the very low income heart of Asia, with virtually no cropland or minerals, with only human resources, and in which personal incomes are far above Asian standards. We can and we should pin down factually the economic effects of the extent of the market by turning to the historical records of long-past city-states.

4   One of the important factors influencing the incentive to invest in human capital is the life expectancy of any population. Presumably, as life expectancy increases it creates an incentive to acquire additional human capital. There is a study which says that between 1950 and 1974 the life expectancy of low-income countries increased about 40 percent.[11] Although the implications of this development are complex, the direction of the prospective investment in human capital is clear. But we have no verified explanation of the factors that account for this remarkable rise in life expectancy in low-income countries. The data on this issue are bad, and it will be very difficult to discover the real explanations. There is, however, another way of taking our bearing on this issue: Why did the increases in life expectancy occur at a very low rate historically in Western Europe and during the early period in North America? We might also find out a good deal about the rate at which the demographic transition occurred. How much of the long-term economics of the decline in fertility is a consequence of the rise in life expectancy?

5   There is embedded in the history of land rents and the income of landlords a major economic puzzle. Presumably farmland is a critical limiting factor in increasing the supply of food. In fact, only about one-tenth of the land surface of the earth is suitable for growing crops. Yet since David Ricardo's day, the supply of farm-produced food has increased manyfold. Even western Europe, with its large, dense population and despite its original poor soils, has become an exporter of wheat. What is the economic explanation for the remarkable decline in land rents and the fading away of landlords as an economic class in Western countries since Ricardo gave us his classical diminishing returns on land? The historical implications of the theory and what in fact has happened since then are two very different stories. As yet, economic theory has no satisfactory explanation. The more intensive application of capital and labor to land, which is an integral part of Ricardo's approach, cannot explain this part of economic history. No one has been as cogent as Jan Pen in analyzing the historical decline in farm land rents as a share of income.[12] I am convinced that the key to this puzzle is in the development of man-made substitutes for land. For want of theory and empirical analysis, we do not have the necessary economic knowledge. Would that economic historians could solve this puzzle.

In summary, the purpose of my approach to the role of economic history is not to rewrite history. It is to identify particular long-past economic circumstances for the purpose of extending our knowledge of economic behavior. With respect to theory, it is frequently necessary to go beyond received theory that implies that some useful extensions of theory are required. It also implies an ability to perceive sets of historical events that are for the purpose at hand: "natural" economic experiments from which economic historians can glean observations of the type suggested by the five research opportunities I have belabored.

Notes and References

1   See Carl Sagan, *The Cosmic Connection: An Extraterrestrial Perspective* (Anchor Books, Doubleday & Co., New York, 1973).

2   Donald M. McCloskey, "Does the Past Have Useful Economics?," *Journal of Economic Literature*, 14 (June 1976), 434–61.

3   McCloskey uses 20 years as the dividing line: my 50 and his 20 reveal the effect of age.

4   The first part of this paragraph draws on Victor F. Weisskopf, "The Frontiers and Limits of Science," *Bulletin of the American Academy of Arts and Sciences*, 28 (Mar. 1975), 15–26.

5   McCloskey, "Does the Past Have Useful Economics?"
6   Wassily Leontief, "Theoretical Assumptions and Nonobserved Facts," *American Economic Review*, 69 (1971), 1–7.
7   William J. Goode, *World Resolutions and Family Patterns* (Free Press, New York, 1963).
8   Peter Laslett (ed.), assisted by Richard Wall, *Household and Family in Past Times* (Cambridge University Press, Cambridge, 1972). Laslett's own definition leads him to declare that the families appearing in his data are nuclear families. Many of them, however, are not nuclear families by my concept of families.
9   See John Hicks, *A Theory of Economic History* (Oxford University Press, Oxford, 1969), and William H. McNeill, *Venice: The Hinge of Europe* (University of Chicago Press, Chicago, Ill., 1974).
10 Theodore Geiger and Frances M. Geiger, *Tales of Two City-States: The Development Progress of Hong Kong and Singapore* (National Planning Association, Washington DC, 1973).
11 Bernard Berelson and staff, "World Population: Status Report 1974," in *Reports on Population and Family Planning* (Population Council, New York, 1974), p. 7.
12 Jan Pen, *Income Distribution: Facts, Theories, Policies*, trans. Trevor S. Preston (Praeger Publishers, New York, 1971).

3

The Value of the Ability to Deal with Disequilibria*

No matter what part of a modern economy is being investigated, we observe that many people are consciously reallocating their resources in response to changes in economic conditions. How efficient they are in their responses is in no small part determined by their "allocative ability." The ability to reallocate is not restricted to entrepreneurs who are engaged in business. People who supply labor services for hire or who are self-employed are reallocating their services in response to changes in the value of the work they do. So are housewives in devoting their time in combination with purchased goods and services in household production. Students likewise are reallocating their own time along with the educational services they purchase as they respond to changes in expected earnings along with changes in the value of the personal satisfactions they expect to derive from their education. Consumption opportunities are also changing, and inasmuch as pure consumption entails time, here too people are reallocating their own time in response to changing opportunities.

The main purpose of this study is to explore how education and experience influence the efficiency of human beings to perceive, to interpret correctly, and to undertake action that will appropriately reallocate their resources. The central questions to keep in mind are: To what extent are these allocative abilities acquired? Are education and experience measurable sources of these abilities? What factors determine the economic value of the stocks of such abilities that various individuals

* First published in *Journal of Economic Literature*, 13, No. 3 (Sept. 1975), 827–46. Reprinted by permission of the American Economic Association. I am indebted to C. Arnold Anderson, Gary S. Becker, Mary Jean Bowman, Issac Ehrlich, Richard B. Freeman, Wallace Huffman, D. Gale Johnson, Lawrence W. Kenny, Donald N. McCloskey, Jacob Mincer, Marc Nerlove, Lawrence S. Olson, George Psacharopoulous, and Margaret Reid for their comments on an earlier draft. I am grateful to the Ford Foundation and NIE for their grants supporting my studies of the increasing value of human time, of which this is a part.

possess? The starting point is the concept that the behavior of human beings is governed by the criterion of optimization under constraints that are specific to the circumstances confronting each person. I assume that there is a competitive factor market that encompasses the aggregate of individual decisions and that the terms of trade are being adjusted to bring these decisions of individuals into a mutually consistent relationship, in the sense that supply tends to equal demand. With respect to the particular abilities under consideration, I assume that the demand for them is determined by the events that give rise to the observed disequilibria and that the supply is one of the components of human capital.

My plan is to investigate the following topics: (1) the concepts of human abilities, (2) the equilibrating activities of individuals to regain equilibrium, (3) the idea of the stationary state, (4) two economic states compared, (5) extending the role of entrepreneurship, (6) the elements of a theory, and (7) an interpretation of a substantial amount of evidence.

1   Concepts of Human Abilities

Our knowledge of a person's abilities consists of inferences drawn from his performance. An ability is thus perceived as the competence and efficiency with which particular acts are performed. What a person does we shall treat as a service, and we shall consider only those services that are deemed to be both useful and scarce, which implies that they have some economic value. The service attributed to any ability has a time dimension; that is, a certain amount is accomplished *per* hour or day, in a year, or over a life time.

There are various classes of abilities; they include the ability: (1) to learn, (2) to do useful work, (3) to play, (4) to create something, and (5) specifically for the purpose at hand, to deal with economic disequilibria. Since what is done can be observed, it is convenient to assume that the observed performance is related to a specific ability. Although these various classes undoubtedly overlap and interact, it is useful to proceed with qualifications as if each class has a special set of attributes. There comes a point, however, at which this reductionist approach is misleading for it postulates the separability of abilities; whereas normal human beings possess hierarchies of integration among abilities.[1]

Much attention is given in our schools to the testing of aptitudes and intelligence: I.Q. tests, for example, are designed to predict school performance. There are tests to ascertain verbal and quantitative abilities, presumably to predict performance in education. Partly to limit the supply and partly to assure standards of performance, professional associations promote tests to determine who is "qualified" to practice law or medicine. The limitations and misuses of these various tests aside, their usefulness in determining, economic performance is very limited.[2] Obviously, these tests are not designed for that purpose. Economists are still hard pressed in explaining the wide variance in the earnings profile of people over their life time. The role of differences in abilities is yet in large part unknown. Virtually no attention has been given to the role of abilities with respect to the time spent and the satisfactions obtained from engaging in play, in creative activity, and in pure consumption, in spite of the fact that time is valuable and its economic value has been rising secularly and markedly in high income countries. Although changing economic conditions are pervasive in a modern economy, the efficiency with which people adjust to these changes has not yet become a part of standard economics. One of the reasons why this is so arises out of the analytical neglect of the equilibrating activities of human agents.

2 Equilibrating Activities to Regain Equilibrium

Determining precisely what people do who are not in equilibrium is not one of the notable achievements of economics. What people do is, in general, concealed in the assumption that their optimizing behavior is such that they regain equilibrium instantaneously. However, it is unlikely that they would be able to do this in fact; but more important, even if they were able, it would not normally be economic for them to make all of the required reallocations of their resources instantaneously. Thus, regaining equilibrium takes time, and how people proceed over time depends on their efficiency in responding to any given disequilibrium and on the costs and returns of the sequence of adjustments available to them. The analytical core of general equilibrium theory is not designed to analyze the specific actions and performances of people who are engaged in these equilibrating activities.

Our closely reasoned general economic equilibrium[3] rests on two basic concepts: (1) the human being is an optimizing agent whose behavior is governed by constraints that are in part peculiar to him, and (2) the market provides the auction at which all individual offers are acknowledged and the terms of trade are established for equalizing supply and demand. General equilibrium theory yields many meaningful implications[4] that are useful in organizing economic knowledge, and more important, in guiding economic analyses. Although it is used predominantly to explain market-oriented activities, it can be extended to encompass various non-market activities, as it has been in analyzing household production, investment in education and in other types of human capital, as well as in examining the sorting and mating behavior leading to marriage and fertility, and the time and purchased services that parents invest in their children. In all of these applications, theory is an essential analytical device, a method, or an approach, in studying aspects of economic behavior. It is, however, a serious mistake not to distinguish between the analytical properties of the theory and the fact that human beings are not always in equilibrium and the further fact that they do not regain equilibrium instantaneously.

Instead of extending parts of general equilibrium theory to analysis of the optimizing equilibrating behavior of individuals, it is all too convenient to treat the observable state of an economy, whatever its apparent disarray, as if it were nevertheless in a state of equilibrium. Using this approach, the economy is deemed to be in equilibrium each and every day regardless of changing economic conditions. To make it so, all that is required is to assume that the costs of information and of transactions are such as to provide the conditions that are required for an economic equilibrium. The usefulness of the concepts of search for information and of transaction costs is not in doubt, but when they are applied as indicated, they merely conceal the disequilibrium that persists into the next day and for more days to come.

What we want to analyze are the various equilibrating processes that are observable activities of people, especially of people living in an economy characterized by high incomes and by continuing modernization. It is true that some of the adjustments to secular changes in relative prices of factors and products have been on the agenda of economists. The role of lags in economic adjustments has, in fact, received much attention. Many sophisticated econometric studies using lags have been published. The achievements of these studies are cogently evaluated by Marc Nerlove.[5] They concentrate primarily on the problems of statistical inference, although there are some extensions of economic theory to explain the equilibrating activities that are revealed by such lags.

The approach of this paper is to extend the concept of entrepreneurship. I shall postulate a supply function of entrepreneurs that takes into account their abilities to deal with disequilibria. Before turning to this approach, I shall comment on the perceived realities of the stationary state, on two very different economic states, and on the inadequacy of the received treatment of entrepreneurship.

3   The Idea of a Stationary State

A stationary state implies zero growth, and it also implies that the economic value of allocative abilities would be zero. If the supply of resources and the demand for their services were to remain constant long enough, the economy would arrive at a stationary state with no economic disequilibria. Currently, long-standing unsettled social issues are being raised once again in evaluating the economic growth of our modernizing economy. Doubts about the ultimate value of economic growth are persuasive and are multiplying. Zero economic growth, coupled with zero population growth, is viewed by many as a condition of an ideal society. It could be that birth and death rates are tending toward a population equilibrium.[6] However, with reference to zero economic growth, the rank and file of people *act* as if they prefer the increasing range of choices and opportunities that they obtain from positive economic growth. I am not implying that they are unconcerned about some of the more obvious social losses entailed in modern growth.

The economist is far from successful in reconciling the views of the articulate intellectuals with the revealed preferences of people generally. The economist wants to be accepted as an intellectual, but he knows that the preferences of people are fundamental to his analytical work. Even if he had the courage, it would be cynical and less than candid for him to assert that intellectuals typically are biased by living in a sheltered, affluent enclave. But regardless of the facts on this point, an economy is supposed to serve the preferences of people, not the particular preferences of economists.

The idea of economic progress predates the theoretical work of the early English economists, who were not, however, of one mind about the value of what was then called the "progressive state." For Adam Smith, "the progressive state is in reality the cheerful and hearty state . . ." while "the stationary state is dull." Ricardo concurred.[7] John Stuart Mill, in contemplating the progressive changes in the economy, was "not satisfied with merely tracing the laws of movement." Akin to some of the current protest, he too was troubled by the ultimate purpose of these "progressive" movements. He maintained that rich and prosperous countries could derive real advantages from the stationary state. (See Mill as edited by Ashley.)[8] For these countries to forego such advantages meant paying too high a price for further improvements in the productive arts and for the additional accumulations of capital.[9] Marshall, in turn, disagreed sharply with his eminent predecessor by saying, "But indeed a perfect adjustment is inconceivable. Perhaps even it is undesirable. For after all man is the end of production; and perfectly stable business would be likely to produce men who were little better than machines."[10]

Judging from the economic behavior of "ordinary" people before and since the time of Mill, they prefer an economy with "progressive changes." Moreover, since Mill's time modern economics has developed specialized sectors, the purpose of which is to improve the productive arts. The accumulation of capital has gone on apace. We have created an economy that is organized to produce this type of "progress." Such is the economic reality we shall investigate and try to explain.

4   Two Economic States Compared

Once an economy arrives at an equilibrium and if henceforth the supply of resources and the demand for their services remain constant, custom could fix rents, wages, and the interest rate, and the economy would continue to be efficient.[11] They could be efficient prices in the sense that no appreciable stresses and strains would arise as long as economic conditions remained unchanged.

It may be helpful to compare the realized over-all efficiency under two very different sets of conditions. A simple comparison between traditional and modern agricultural conditions highlights the difference. Let me state the inference that emerges before elaborating on the underlying circumstances or on the implications they have for applications of theory. The basic inference is that farm people under traditional conditions are closer to an economic optimum, given the resources that are available to them than are "modern" farm people in view of the new and better possibilities that are constantly crowding in on the latter. I use the term "farm people" advisedly because in this context it is not only farm production that matters, but also household production and the investment in human capital by farm people. Farm people in India, say before the green revolution, were closer to an optimum use of the resources at their disposal than the farm people, say, of Iowa, have been since the early thirties in view of the many complex changes in resources and associated opportunities with which they have been dealing.

The reasoning underlying this inference can be stated simply. Farm people who have lived for generations with essentially the same resources tend to approximate the economic equilibrium of the stationary state. When the productive arts remain virtually constant over many years, farm people know from long experience what their own effort can get out of the land and equipment. In allocating the resources at their disposal, in choosing a combination of crops, in deciding on how and when to cultivate, plant, water, and harvest, and what combination of tools to use with draft animals and simple field equipment – these choices and decisions all embody a fine regard for marginal costs and returns. These farm people also know from experience the value of their household production possibilities; in allocating their own time along with material goods within the domain of the household, they too are finely attuned to marginal costs and returns. Furthermore, children acquire the skills that are worth-while from their parents as children have for generations under circumstances where formal schooling has little economic value. This simplified economic picture of traditional farm life, which includes knowing how to live with variations in weather, strongly implies a high level of general economic efficiency.[12] It also implies that there is, for all practical purposes, no premium for the human ability to deal with secular economic changes.

For contrast, I now look at farm people who live in a modernizing economy. Here they deal with a sequence of changes in economic conditions, which are in general not of their own making because they originate mainly out of the activities of people other than farm people. For this reason Schumpeter's theory of economic development is far from sufficient to explain most of these changes. The changes are nevertheless endogenous for the reason that I stressed at the outset. They have their origin predominantly in the useful contributions that flow from organized agricultural research and from improvements in the inputs that farm people purchase and use in agricultural and household production. Accordingly, the *demand* for the ability to deal with the new and better production possibilities is in large part determined by organized agricultural research and by the nonfarm firms that produce the inputs that farm people purchase. Furthermore, it takes time to reallocate resources in arriving at a new equilibrium. Moreover, additional changes occur even before the reallocation called for by the preceding change has been completed. Hence, the implication is that "full efficiency" is kept beyond the reach of farm people.

5   Extending the Role of Entrepreneurship

Whether or not economic growth is deemed to be "progress," it is a process beset with various classes of disequilibria. In response, individuals in many different walks of life engage in optimizing behavior, which entails reallocating resources to regain equilibrium. All of them are in this respect entrepreneurs.

The concept of the entrepreneur rarely appears in the theoretical core of economics. When it does, it is confined to businessmen, thus it excludes laborers who are reallocating their labor services, and it excludes housewives, students, and consumers who are also in the act of reallocating their resources (consisting, to be sure, largely of their own time). In standard theory, it is hard to find a treatment of the supply of entrepreneurship. An exception is Gary S. Becker's "supply curve of entrepreneurial capacity".[13] When entrepreneurs appear in economic analysis, the role attributed to them as businessmen is confined to dealing with risk and uncertainty. The rewards, however, for performing this role are not allowed in general equilibrium theory, for it implies a "zero profit" for this role. In fact, it is obvious that every equilibrating activity entails elements of risk and uncertainty, and it is also obvious that individuals improve their economic position, and in this sense rewards accrue to them as a consequence of their regaining equilibrium.

Although the entrepreneur is a stranger in general equilibrium theory, he has been around for a long time in parts of our economic literature. The entrepreneur appears early in the writings of French economists,[14] but they are only descriptively at home in the work of the early English economists, and it is their work that has become the core of received theory. In Schumpeter's theory of economic development, the role of the entrepreneur is confined to those who engage in activities motivated by profits in the market sector.[15] What they do is, however, only a part of the story because households and individuals both within and outside of the market sector are also present. The entrepreneur as seen by Schumpeter *creates* developmental disequilibria; but his function is not extended to deal successfully with all manner of other disequilibria as they occur within the economic system. In his approach, the mainspring of development consists of the "creative and innovative responses" of the entrepreneur. Edwin F. Gay, Arthur H. Cole, and Leland H. Jenks followed this lead in their endeavor, among other things, to distinguish between the managerial and entrepreneurial functions. But their studies appear not to have been successful, according to Thomas C. Cochran,[16] in extending received theory. Although, as already noted, the business entrepreneur is only one of many classes of people who are engaged in equilibrating processes, it is inexplicable that Schumpeter's contribution has not become an integral part of received theory.

Israel M. Kirzner presents a perceptive analysis of the state of economic theory with respect to the entrepreneur.[17] He sees clearly the omission of the entrepreneur in received equilibrium theory, but he persists in holding fast to the zero profit concept in that theory and, as a consequence, fails to see the economic rewards that accrue to those who bring about the equilibrating process.

It bears repeating that the standard economic concept of the function of laborers does not include their role as entrepreneurs in allocating their own time and their ability to do this successfully under changing economic conditions. Similarly, the entrepreneurial role and ability of housewives in managing household production and of mature students deciding how to invest in themselves, are omitted in most economic studies.

The human capital approach in analyzing the useful abilities of people represents a marked advance in that it specifies the various skills of people and specifies the manner in which the skills are acquired. At the outset, this approach was restricted empirically to individuals who enter the labor market (where data on earnings could be had). The more recent developments of a theory of the allocation of time[18] and of the household production function have extended the analysis to determine the economic value of the human abilities in this large and long neglected nonmarket sector. This broadened approach is proving useful also in analyzing the capabilities of human beings to do work for hire, or for themselves, or to carry out household activities, or to use their own time in investing in themselves.[19]

6   Elements of a Theory

In analyzing the equilibrating activities of people, we postulate that there are economic incentives to reallocate resources, that people respond to these incentives to the best of their ability, and that the difference in their performance is a measure of the difference among people with respect to the particular type of ability that is required. In accordance with this postulate, there is a type of ability that is useful and whose value is some function of the demand for and the supply of that ability. This particular ability, as noted at the outset, represents the competence of people to perceive a given disequilibrium and to evaluate its attributes properly in determining whether it is worthwhile to act, and if it is worthwhile, people respond by reallocating their resources. The realized gains[20] from such reallocations are the observable rewards.

The expected gains are the economic incentives to enter upon these equilibrating activities. Since the gains that are realized represent an improvement in income, it obviously is not the "zero profit" result derived from general instantaneous adjustments in equilibrium theory. These gains are exemplified by the profitability of the adoption of hybrid corn.[21] In household production, it is exemplified by the gain in utility from using the sewing machine over hand sewing. It is also evident in the gains in income that laborers derive from geographical migration to better jobs, and by the improvement in earnings that students realize by adjusting their studies to changes in the market for college educated personnel.

The demand for the services of these abilities is determined by the characteristics of the disequilibrium. Accordingly, the demand is some function of the particular economic disequilibrium under investigation. For a given disequilibrium there may be a demand schedule in the sense that the incentive to act is high at the outset and as resources are reallocated the incentive to make further adjustments declines.[22]

In searching for the factors that determine the various classes of disequilibria and in ascertaining their respective incentives for resource reallocation, there are strong reasons for distinguishing between the disequilibria that firms, households, and individuals (laborers, students) face. The incentive associated with an advance in knowledge pertaining to nutrition, for example, is easier to perceive and to act upon in feeding poultry and livestock than it is in rearranging the diet pattern in a household. Young people facing the need to change the investment they make in themselves are confronted by a much more complex set of future rewards than most firms are required to reckon with when they alter their investment in structures and equipment.

The supply of services from these abilities depends upon the stock of a particular form of human capital at any point in time and on the costs and the rate at which the stock can be increased in response to the rewards derived from the services of these abilities. The amount of such human capital may be small *per* person, but it is never zero. Regardless of how poor people are, how long they have lived under "stationary" conditions, how limited their experience, and how much they lack in literacy, they are neither indifferent to, nor wholly unresponsive to, opportunities to improve their economic lot.[23] The supply of the services from these abilities in a particular area (sector) can be augmented by the inmigration of individuals with a relatively large component of these abilities who move in response to incentives created by the disequilibrium. A case in point is the response in parts of North India to the high profitability of the new wheat varieties where no small number of well-qualified nonfarm people sought entry into farming. The existing stock of these abilities can be complemented (made more effective) by various forms of extension activities. Over a longer span of time, if the incentives persist, the supply can and will be increased by learning from experience the art of dealing with changing economic conditions and by making investments in this form of human capital by training and schooling.

The effects of education in this connection can be tested empirically, and it is proving to be a strong explanatory variable. It is important to find out what features of education augment the supply of the services from these abilities. The presumption is that education – even primary schooling – enhances the ability of students to perceive new classes of problems, to clarify such problems, and to learn ways of solving them. Although the problem-solving abilities that students acquire pertain to classroom work, the abilities that are developed by this work seem to have general properties that contribute measurably to their performance as economic agents in perceiving and solving the problems that arise as a consequence of economic changes.

7   Interpreting the Evidence

We begin by limiting the implications to the optimizing behavior of individuals, followed by a comment on difficulties inherent in the data, and then turn to insights derived from some general observations and from specific studies.

7.1   *Limiting the Implications*

We are not searching for evidence to explain why disequilibria occur. Instead, given a disequilibrium, we are concerned with the ensuing behavior that is induced by the incentive to reallocate resources. Over time this stock of allocative abilities can be enhanced by various means. Our analysis, however, will be restricted to the existing stock of such human capital, although we shall point out that students also differ in their allocative ability, which in turn affects their efficiency as they invest in education.

The hypotheses that are most readily subject to empirical analysis are that the effects of education and of experience are positive and important in their contribution to the rate at which resources are reallocated. Education in fact has both an income and a price effect. The earnings of individuals tend to rise with their education, and as their earnings increase, the value of their time rises, the consequences of which are revealed as price effects.

7.2   *Difficulties*

Risk and uncertainty are ever present in the optimizing behavior here under consideration. How much of the observed difference in responses is a consequence of the difference in risk and uncertainty (including the difference in preferences to bear them) is very difficult to determine. The allocative efficiency attributed to education presumably affects the costs of searching for information. But the data are as a rule too crude to analyze this interaction. There is no easy way of identifying and measuring the incentives to reallocate resources that are strictly a consequence of a particular disequilibrium, although some progress has been made on this score. For small firms, i.e., farms and households, and for individuals who are laborers or who are students investing in themselves, it is less difficult to get usable data than it is for large complex firms. However, studies by Edwin Mansfield, et al. of the research and innovation behavior of the modern corporation find that the difference in education influences the ability of corporate executives in this context.[24] The specific studies to which I shall refer are restricted mainly to small firms. Finis Welch in a pioneering study of the role of education in modern agricultural production presents estimates of the "worker effects" and of the "allocative effects" attributed to education.[25] In economics, however, there is no decisive test.

7.3   General Observations

Historically, the economic development of agriculture is replete with examples of the positive effects of education on economic performance of farmers. Although there is as a rule both a worker effect and an allocative effect, it seems fairly obvious that a substantial part of the successful performance is a consequence of the ability associated with education to deal with changes in economic conditions. The marked difference in the economic performance between the second generation California farmers of Japanese and those of Mexican heritage is in considerable part explained by a difference in education. Among the European immigrants who entered US agriculture, those who had been lowly peasants or hired farm workers and who had little schooling were in general less successful during the first generation than immigrants from settlements that consisted of a complete community of people with a relatively high average level of education, for example, the settlements of the Dutch in parts of Iowa. Very rapid modernization of US agriculture following World War II has more than halved the number of farms; in the ensuing competition to survive and remain in agriculture, the effects of education on the ability to cope with changes in agricultural production are strongly positive in determining who has been able to survive.[26]

Similarly, in Brazil there is the impressive agricultural success of the Japanese immigrants who entered with more education and with more experience in dealing with agricultural modernization than most

Brazilian farmers. The performance of the Huguenots in Canada and those who became farmers in the United States also exemplify the positive effects of education. In the rapid development of agriculture in Israel, occidental immigrant Jews have been much more successful than the oriental Jews; here too, the difference in education appears to be a strong explanatory factor.[27]

We have had and continue to have a vast amount of internal migration by members of the labor force who have been adjusting to changes in job opportunities. Here, too, in terms of economic performance, those with 16 years of education are more successful than those with 12 years, and the latter do better on this score than those with 8 years of schooling. The difference in ability to deal with these job disequilibria is apparently related to education.

7.4 Specific Studies

Regardless of the method of analysis, there is always room for doubts. Models that are manageable and useful in empirical analysis do not specify the economic system in its entirety, and the data that are used in testing the implications derived from these models are as a rule far from adequate. Our confidence is heightened, however, by the consistency of the results from such studies and those from general observations. We need to be mindful of the fact that the classical principles of economics were developed by economists who were endeavoring to explain what they perceived as general observations of actual economic behavior. With increasing specialization, however, we tend all too often to settle for less. Our sophisticated economic journals today would undoubtedly reject papers by Smith, Ricardo, or Malthus, or even by John Stuart Mill.

Let me begin with *household production*. As already noted, households have long been beyond the pale of economics. They were deemed to be "unproductive" on the grounds that they were not producing for the market; whatever households are doing was considered as consumption. The study by Margaret Reid is an early exception; for it features the economics of household production.[28] In 1953, I treated "the household as a producing unit which handles, stores, processes, and combines food elements to increase their value in satisfying the preferences of the individuals it serves".[29] Households are viewed here as economic enterprises that are, among other things, dealing with changes in economic conditions as modernization proceeds. The prices of their purchased inputs, the value of the time of housewives, and the techniques of household production are all changing over time and each change generates an incentive to alter the resources entering into household production. There are shifts in incentives to purchase household durables, to acquire more nutritious foods, to employ child-care services in order to take "work for pay" and to substitute quality for numbers of children as the value of the time of women increases.

Although it is obvious from everyday observations that households do reallocate the resources at their disposal upon perception of disequilibria, it is not obvious that they differ widely in their performance nor that much of this difference is explained by the difference in the education of housewives. We can see the effect of schooling, however, in the different rates at which "the contraceptive pill" was adopted in the United States during the 1960s. It is more difficult to identify and measure the effects of education on the rate at which housewives take advantage of advances in knowledge pertaining to nutrition. The main contribution of the new studies of household production has been in determining the allocative effects of increases in the value of time of housewives attributed primarily to the differences in their education. Thus, it is the price effect of value of the time that is devoted to household production, and it is undoubtedly true that the price effects of education in this context are pervasive.[30] Education affects the choice of mates in marriage. It may affect the preference for children. It assuredly affects the earnings of women who enter the labor force either part or full time. It evidently affects the household productivity of housewives. It probably affects the incidence of child mortality and it undoubtedly affects the ability of women to control the number of births.

At best these studies of household production give us clues to the behavior that concerns us here, though they are not designed to separate the "worker effect" from the "allocative effect" of education. What is specified and identified is treated as the worker effect, and for this reason the estimates would appear to overstate the pure worker effects. Robert T. Michael finds support for the implication that education increases the efficiency of households.[31] His data did not, however, permit him to get at the difference in the rates at which households dealt with changes in economic conditions; nevertheless, his study suggests at several points that the more educated perform better in this respect than the less educated.

More pertinent data come from studies of the incentives and the responses in adopting new and better contraceptive techniques. Estimates of the difference in the success at using them show a positive influence of education. In another study Michael deals explicitly with education and fertility control.[32] He reports a series of analyses that reinforce each other in showing that the more educated women are more successful in adopting and in using the more effective techniques in controlling fertility than are the less educated. Reid makes the point that the observed differential effects of education "on the efficiency of fertility control due to knowledge and use of new techniques of contraception" will be temporary in view of the fact that the "diffusion of knowledge has been rapid."[33] Since then, Norman B. Ryder has presented evidence on this point,[34] and it strongly supports the perceptive insight of Reid.[35] Ryder concludes that "The upper-education category leads the middle category by eight months, and the lower category by 22 months (using the date when 20 percent was first achieved). . . . It took blacks 27 months longer than whites to reach the level of 20 percent using. One consequence of the lag for interpretation of fertility differentials during the 1960s is that, although the percent using the pill at the end of the decade was the same for blacks as for whites, the proportion using in the decade as a whole was 14.5 percent for the former but 20.7 percent for the latter." Here we have direct and strong evidence that more schooling for wives increases their ability to promptly perceive and to act in dealing with a particular disequilibrium.

Consider next *labor services* and think of each person as having an ability to render labor services for hire or for himself and also as having an ability to reallocate his labor services whenever it is to his advantage to do so. We need to distinguish between these two abilities in order to see how much each contributes to the supply of labor services. Our national income accounts imply that the overall income attributed to labor services is about three times as large as that of nonhuman capital. Within this economically important rubric of labor services, we want to know how much of it is a consequence of the successful reallocation by laborers and what the effects are of education and experience on this behavior. Clearly the value of a man's labor services is affected by many different types of disequilibria occurring during his lifetime: changes in the rate of unemployment for the class of jobs for which a person can qualify, geographical and occupational shifts in job opportunities, changes in incentives for transfer to a better-paying job in the same occupation, changes in opportunities between self employment and working for wages (salaries), and changes that alter the value of the time from earnings relative to that devoted to investment in one's own human capital. Furthermore, after retirement there are geographical changes in consumption opportunities. The foregoing list is far from all-inclusive. Although it is fairly obvious that the people who are affected do respond to these disequilibria, how successfully they respond, and the extent to which their success is determined by education and experience, calls for specific evidence.

Studies of migration, some of which include changes in occupation, provide some indirect information. Most of these studies tend to attribute the differences in the performance of migrants to differences in the costs of information and in the risk and uncertainty that migrants face. There are several studies, however, to which I shall refer, that indicate that these geographical relocations of human resources are responses to incentives that arise as a consequence of disequilibria and that education increases the efficiency of migrants in relocating themselves.

In migration out of agriculture, Dale E. Hathaway and Brian E. Perkins had access to a unique set of data from the Social Security Administration that gave them a continuous register for the period from 1957 to 1963 for each person entering into the analysis.[36] Although the sample has no information on education, in view of other studies of this population, the income differences are a useful proxy for the approximate difference in education. Because of the richness of the data on important variables that are usually omitted for lack of data and the depth of the analysis, the results of this study are strong in showing that the migrants who came from the higher income areas, and from the higher income farms, *were more successful in changing their occupation than were those who came from disadvantaged backgrounds in agriculture.*[37]

Samuel Bowles, using the human investment approach in analyzing the migration out of the US South between 1955 and 1960, concludes, "that part of the monetary return to schooling arises because people with more education adapt more successfully to economic disequilibria."[38] Bowles then remarks on the insufficiency of an equilibrium framework for the analysis of the return to schooling that accrues to individuals as a consequence of its contribution to the equilibrating process.

The human investment approach to migration has been useful in explaining important aspects of this behavior. The first study to use this approach is by Larry A. Sjaastad.[39] Aba Schwartz followed, and in this, his first study, he shows that the prospective differentials in lifetime earnings provide a better explanation of migration than do differentials in current earnings and that the response to differences in lifetime earnings is lowest for the least educated persons and increases monotonically with education.[40] He then finds that the higher the education, the more efficient the migration process, which in turn eliminates (faster) regional disequilibria.[41] June O'Neill makes an additional contribution, for she takes into account explicitly the effects of education on migration in responding to consumption opportunities.[42] In a study of migration in Canada, Thomas J. Courchene finds that the trade-off between income and distance increases sensitively with education.[43] With respect to internal migration in Colombia between 1951 and 1964, T. Paul Schultz finds that the availability of rural schools postpones the migration of school-aged children and of their parents, but schooling accelerates the out-migration rates of older youth who normally constitute the majority of migrants.[44] The schooling of migrants equips "them to better evaluate and respond to employment opportunities in the city" and the migration follows "predictable lines, reducing the disequilibrium between regional markets."

We turn now to *investment in human capital*. Our purpose is not to explain increases in the supply of allocative ability, but to show that the stock of such abilities that students possess influences their efficiency in responding to changes in the economic value to be derived from an education. Investment opportunities in education to which students respond are changing constantly: the demand for educated personnel booms and then stagnates, large shifts occur in the demand for different classes of skills, the costs of educational services change over time, and changes in earnings foregone by students also affect these investment opportunities. As a consequence, the actual behavior of students is occurring under conditions that are beset by all manner of disequilibria in terms of investment opportunities. How successful are students in dealing with these disequilibria and to what extent does their experience and level of education affect their performance? Richard B. Freeman's study of the economics of career choice, shows that the responses of students to changes in the market for college-trained person-nel are strongly positive.[45] It is reinforced in his more recent analysis of the high rate of response of college educated blacks in entering new career fields as these have become open to them since the mid-1960s.[46]

Becker estimated the private rates of return (for white males) from college and from high school education, during the first part of the post-World War II boom in education.[47] My interpretation of his findings is that the responses of college students were close to sufficient to keep the rates of return at what would appear to be approximately equilibrium levels. The responses of high school students on the other hand, large as they were in terms of enrollment increases, were not sufficient by this test. Private rates of return between 1949 and 1961 for college graduates stayed somewhat below 15 percent, and they did not vary significantly. The rates of return accruing to high school graduates rose from the already high level of 20 percent in 1949 to slightly more than 28 percent by 1961.[48] The inference is that students who have had a high school education and who then also graduated from college are substantially more successful (i.e., there is less fluctuation, including growth, in the rates of return) in dealing with disequilibria in the educational sector than are the students who have had elementary schooling and who then graduate from high school.

In an essay on the optimizing behavior of students as they invest in college instruction, I examined in some detail the benefits that students derive from their own allocative abilities while they are acquiring their education.[49]

I have left *agricultural production* until last because it provides the best available evidence. Farmers normally are both self-employed workers and entrepreneurs. Censuses provide production data that can be matched with the age, experience, and education of farmers. Furthermore, special sample surveys designed to obtain the required data are at hand. In analyzing these data several economists have been ingenious in estimating the economic value of education revealed by its worker effects and allocative effects. Studies in this area owe much to Welch[50] and to the original work of Griliches for his basic measurements of agricultural inputs including the quality of farm labor.[51] D.P. Chaudhri in a study of Indian agriculture was among the vanguard in this area.[52] On farmers in Japan we have Bruce R. Harker,[53] for small farmers in Kenya a study in depth by Peter R. Moock,[54] and for Taiwan the research of Craig C. Wu.[55] In getting at the effects of schooling on the allocative ability of farmers, studies by Thomas E. Haller of farmers in Colombia[56]and Wallace E. Huffman of farmers in the US Corn Belt[57]have made major contributions.

It is increasingly clear that the value of schooling in farming depends on the opportunities that farmers have to modernize their production. There are many poor communities in the world, however, where such opportunities are lacking; these are communities in which farming tends to remain "traditional agriculture" of the type described in section 4 above. In such communities there are no significant gains in output from schooling. In my *Transforming Traditional Agriculture*, I was restricted to two sets of anthropological data from communities in which the people had little or no schooling.[58] I was unable to identify any significant departures from an optimum allocation of the factors of production in agriculture in them. The data in *Penny Capitalism* by Sol Tax indicate that farmers in Panajachel, Guatemala, *are very poor but efficient.*[59] Similarly the data for Senapur, a village in India, from a study by W. David Hopper indicate strongly that farmers in this village were, of course, poor but they were efficient in using the resources available to them.[60]

Chaudhri found that agricultural production in India was already by 1960 significantly influenced by the level of schooling and that farm people with schooling were in the vanguard in the use of chemical fertilizer. Chaudhri's results imply that there were gains in productivity before the event of the so-called green revolution associated with imported high-yielding wheat and rice varieties, which is consistent with the findings of Robert Evenson.[61]

The study by Haller is a major advance analytically. He compares the performance of farmers using traditional farming methods with those in the same country who are at an early stage in modernizing production. He designed his study to get both the work effects and the allocative effects of schooling in four regions of Colombia. In three of these regions, farmers were using traditional techniques, and in the fourth, some modernization was evident. He then collected the data that his model called for directly from farmers. His results show no worker effects, but they show positive allocative effects of schooling in his fourth Region, the one that had arrived at an early stage of modernization. "The difference in the number and complexity of the decision alternatives in respect to the use of inputs makes a difference in the extent of schooling's allocative effects . . . This finding is based on the positive results found for Region 4".[62] Haller also obtained the costs of schooling borne by the government and the private costs incurred by the student's family (of which over 80 percent consist of earnings foregone). The benefits from schooling that could be identified and measured are restricted to Region 4, and his estimates of the rates of return to schooling are confined to that Region. In the first three grades the average rate of return in his "basic" estimates in 68 percent and for the five grades as a whole it is 38 percent. He reports that the rate of return to investment more generally in Colombia was about 15 percent. The implication of Haller's study is that none of the benefits from schooling were from its work effects and that the benefits in Region 4 that account for the 38 percent rate of return to five years of schooling were from the ability to deal successfully with the disequilibria associated with early modernization.[63]

In the search for an explanation of the productivity gains in US agriculture, we began to see by the mid-fifties that schooling and the quality of the labor services of farm people were among the major factors accounting for hitherto unexplained gains in productivity.[64] The systematic approaches developed by Griliches[65] gave us new measurements of the inputs including estimates of the effects of education on agricultural production, although the worker effects and the allocative effects of education were not dealt with separately. Welch was the first to design a study that distinguishes between work and allocation.[66] His evidence is for US agriculture as of 1959, a time when agricultural inputs were improving at a rapid rate. Welch was confronted by a puzzle. The proportion of US farmers who had acquired a college education was increasing, while the economic incentives for the college education to engage in farming seemed unexplainable solely in terms of worker effects. Although the highly modernized agriculture of the US called for some additional skills, it was not plausible that the additional skills of college graduates could account for all of the very considerable increases in their labor-service earnings – which in Welch's study came to 62 percent more than that of farmers who were high school graduates. Welch's closing comment both summarizes his results and in large measure resolves the puzzle. "The information presented here is important in explaining the growth in demand for college graduates. Consider the effects of research. Research expenditures per farm were $4.30 in 1940 and $28.40 in 1959. Based on coefficient estimates in [his] table 5, if research were to fall from $28.40 to $4.30, holding factor ratios constant, the relative wage of college to high school graduates would fall from 1.62 to 1.43, indicating that about one-third of the wage differential would disappear".[67] Welch's analysis does not tell us the difference in the rates at which college and high school graduates dealt with disequilibria over time arising out of the improvements in agricultural inputs. What he found was that in terms of where they had arrived in 1959, college graduates were substantially more successful than high school graduates. Under the assumption that in general the rate of return to college education was about 15 percent, my interpretation of Welch's results is that at least a third of it, i.e., 5 percentage points, represents the return to their additional allocative ability.

An equilibrium model, however, applied to cross-sectional data of a given date is not sufficient in analyzing the equilibrating capacities of farmers in dealing with new input opportunities. We want to know who is first and who is fastest in arriving at the new equilibrium. The ability to be among the first to act appropriately and to proceed most promptly in completing the reallocations has an economic value. To get at this component of adjustment requires an equilibrating model and data of the behavior, in this case, of farmers in adopting the more profitable new inputs. It is in this connection that the study of Huffman is an important contribution.[68] Huffman began his analysis to determine the rate at which Corn Belt farmers responded to the real decline in the price of nitrogen fertilizer. He obtained county data in five states (Illinois, Indiana, Iowa, Minnesota, and Ohio) for the period from 1950–54 to 1964 during which the quantity of nitrogen fertilizer applied to all crops in these states increased five fold. He soon discovered that the availability of cheaper fertilizer induced the hybrid seed companies and the agricultural experiment stations to develop and make available new varieties of hybrid seeds that were more responsive to fertilizer and to provide new farm practices for increasing yields. His adjustment model specifies and his treatment of the data takes account of a number of important variables heretofore neglected in analyzing the worker and the allocative effects of the education of farmers.[69]

Huffman finds a positive and significant relationship between adjustment to disequilibria and the level of education. From one additional year of schooling (from 10 to 11 years in his sample) "the profit per farm would have been $52 higher due to this one dimension of improved allocative efficiency *in one farming cativity*, i.e., using nitrogen in corn production"[70] (italics are mine).

8   In Summary

There is enough evidence to give validity to the hypothesis that the ability to deal successfully with economic disequilibria is enhanced by education and that this ability is one of the major benefits of education accruing to people privately in a modernizing economy. We see it in the equilibrating performance of housewives, laborers, students, and farmers. There is no reason to suppose that it is not important in the case of businessmen, although as yet the necessary evidence is lacking. Unless we develop equilibrating models, the function of this particular ability can not be analyzed. Within such models, the function of entrepreneurship would be much extended and the supply of entrepreneurial ability would be treated as a scarce resource.

There are many unsettled questions. Is it the cognitive ability as perceived by psychologists that accounts for what we attribute to education? If it is, what are the sources of the differences in cognitive ability? Is it a general ability in the sense that it is revealed in many different types of human performance? Since the supply of it is a scarce resource that can be augmented, what is the supply response to increases in its economic value? In this study we have taken the first step on what appears to be a long new road.

Notes and References

1   The controversy in biology between those who argue for reductionism, the essence of which is the belief that all of life can be reduced to fundamental laws of physics and chemistry, and those who argue for hierarchies and integration in biological systems, is instructive on this basic issue.

2 In ascertaining the value of an ability that is embodied in a person, both the psychologist and the economist are dependent upon observable acts which are assumed to be the effects of the ability being analyzed. The psychologist may thus look for cognitive ability, the knowing activity of the mind by means of which a person becomes aware of events and the manner in which he perceives them. I am looking for the ability to perceive and interpret correctly economic events, which may be aparticular type of "cognitive ability."

3 K.J. Arrow, "General Economic Equilibrium: Purpose, Analytic Techniques, Collective Choice," *American Economic Review*, 64(3) (June 1973), 253–72.

4 K.J. Arrow, "Limited Knowledge and Economic Analysis," *American Economic Review*, 64(1) (Mar. 1974), 1–10.

5 M. Nerlove, "Lags in Economic Behavior," *Econometrica*, 40(2) (Mar. 1972), 221–51; also "Household and Economy: Toward a New Theory of Population and Economic Growth," *Journal of Political Economy*, 82(2) (Part II, Mar./Apr. 1974), S200–18.

6 Theodore W. Schultz, "The High Value of Human Time: Population Equilibrium," *Journal of Political Economy*, 82(2) (Part II, Mar./Apr. 1974), S2–10, reproduced in Theodore W. Schultz, *The Economics of Being Poor* (Blackwell, 1993), Part III, No. 5.

7 L. Robbins, "On a Certain Ambiguity in the Conception of Stationary Equilibrium," *Economic Journal*, 40 (June 1930), 194–214.

8 Mill put it thus: "I am inclined to believe that it [stationary state] would be, on the whole, a considerable improvement on our present condition. I confess I am not charmed with the ideal of life held out by those who think that the normal state of human beings is that of struggling to get on; that the trampling, crushing, elbowing, and treading on each other's heels, which form the existing type of social life, are the most desirable lot of human kind, or anything but the disagreeable symptoms of one of the phases of industrial power"; J.S. Mill, *Principles of Political Economy*, edited with an introduction by Sir W.J. Ashley (Longmans, Green and Co., London, Toronto and New York, 1909, as reprinted 1926), Book IV, chapter vi, p. 748.

9 Among the "advantages" of the idea of the stationary state, Mill did not anticipate that "general equilibrium theory" would become the analytical core of economics and that it would postulate that economic conditions were given. Robbins ("On a Certain Ambiguity," p. 202) makes the point that the first paragraph of Book IV of Mill's *Principles of Political Economy* opened the door for many ambiguities by his "adding a theory of motion to our theory of equilibrium the dynamics of political economy to the statics." Robbins continued to hold fast to equilibrium theory and expressed the belief that it cannot be extended to cope with economic development: see his *The Nature and Significance of Economic Science* (Macmillan, London, 2nd edn, 1935).

10 A. Marshall, *Industry and Trade* (Macmillan, London, 1919), p. 195.

11   There are studies by anthropologists of isolated "primitive" communities that show the rewards to the factors of production are fixed by custom.

12   This is the foundation of my analysis of the allocative efficiency of farm people in traditional agriculture: Theodore W. Schultz, *Transforming Traditional Agriculture* (Yale University Press, New Haven, Conn., 1964). As a matter of historical fact, however, it would be rare indeed to discover a situation and a period during which farm people were in "perfect" equilibrium for reasons that I noted with care in the 1964 book.

13   Gary S. Becker, *Economic Theory* (Alfred A. Knopf, New York, 1971), pp. 122–23.

14   B.F. Hoselitz, "The Early History of Entrepreneurial Theory," *Explorations in Entrepreneurial History*, 3 (Apr. 1951), 193–220.

15   J.A. Schumpeter, *The Theory of Economic Development*, trans. R. Opie 1911 (Harvard University Press, Cambridge, Mass., 1934; 3rd edn, 1948).

16   T.C. Cochran, "Entrepreneurship," in *International Encyclopedia of the Social Sciences*, vol. 5, ed. D.L. Sills (Macmillan and The Free Press, New York, 1968), pp. 87–91.

17   I.M. Kirzner, *Competition and Entrepreneurship* (University of Chicago Press, Chicago, Ill., 1973).

18   Notably beginning with Gary S. Becker's paper, "A Theory of the Allocation of Time," *Economic Journal*, 75 (Sept. 1965), 493–517.

19   I have sketched the economic logic of the effects of increases in the value of time upon pure consumption, the plausibility that improvements in the technical arts are of little or no avail in economizing on time in consumption, and the implication that the time required in consumption may hold the key to the upper limit of material economic growth in Theodore W. Schultz, "The High Value of Human Time."

20   For people to have gains from their resource allocations does not imply that they are necessarily better off than they were prior to the disequilibrium, but it does imply that their economic position has been improved relative to what it would be if they had stayed in disequilibrium.

21   See Zvi Griliches: "Hybrid Corn: An Exploration in the Economics of Technological Change," *Econometrica*, 25(4) (Oct. 1957), 501–22; "Hybrid Corn and the Economics of Innovation," *Science*, 132(3422) (July 1960), 275–80.

22   The part of this demand schedule that matters in analyzing observable behavior lies substantially above a zero gain, because if it were very small that incentive that directs the equilibrating process would become too weak to warrant proceeding to the perfect equilibrium point. The disequilibrium associated with the event of hybrid corn is instructive. It became available in the early 1930s and it spread rapidly throughout the Corn Belt. There were marked geographic differences, however, in the rate at which hybrid corn was adopted. These differences in the rate of adoption were a consequence of the wide differences in the profitability from the increases in yield that could be obtained from the available hybrid seed. In Iowa in five years the

percentage of the total acreage planted with hybrid seed increased from 10 to over 90 per cent, whereas in Wisconsin during the same period it reached the 60 percent level (see Griliches, ibid.).

23 Although they may be relatively slow in perceiving and taking the appropriate action, their performance in response to strong incentives leaves little room for doubt that there is a component of this ability in the most disadvantaged of the world's population. The fairly rapid adoption of new, highly productive, wheat varieties by the small, financially poor, uneducated farmers of India, associated with the green revolution, is strong evidence of this point.

24 E. Mansfield et al., *Research and Innovation in the Modern Corporation* (Norton, New York, 1971), p. 199.

25 Finis Welch, "Education in Production," *Journal of Political Economy*, 78(1) (Jan./Feb. 1970), 35–59.

26 See G.S. Tolley, "Management Entry into US Agriculture," American Journal of Agricultural Economics, 52(4) (Nov. 1970), 485–93.

27 See Ezra Sadan, Chaba Nachmias, and Gideon Bar-Lev, "Education and Economic Performance of Occidental and Oriental Family Farm Operators," unpublished paper (Lima, Peru, Oct. 11 1974).

28 Margaret R. Reid, *Economics of Household Production* (Wiley, New York, 1934).

29 Theodore W. Schultz, *The Economic Organization of Agriculture* (McGraw-Hill, New York, 1953).

30 See Theodore W. Schultz (ed.), *Family Economics: Marriage, Human Capital and Fertility* (University of Chicago Press, Chicago, Ill., 1975).

31 R.T. Michael, *The Effect of Education on Efficiency in Consumption*, Occasional Paper 116 (National Bureau of Economic Research, New York, distributed by Columbia University Press, 1972).

32 See R.T. Michael, "Education and the Derived Demand for Children: New Economic Approaches to Fertility," *Journal of Political Economy*, 81(2) (Part II, Mar./Apr. 1973), S128–64. He reviews the substantial literature on this topic, presents estimates of the effectiveness of 10 different contraceptive techniques, and analyzes the US 1965 National Fertility Survey data to determine the effects of education.

33 See Michael, cited in Margaret G. Reid, "Education and the Derived Demand for Children: Comment," *Journal of Political Economy*, 81(2) (Part II, Mar./Apr. 1973), S165–67.

34 N.B. Ryder, "Time Series of Pill and IUD Use: United States, 1961–1970," *Studies in Family Planning*, 10 (Oct. 1972), 233–40.

35 The differences in the rates of adoption of the pill between 1961 and 1970, by wife's years of schooling completed, reveal a pattern very similar to that of farmers by states in the adoption of hybrid corn.

36 D.E. Hathaway and B.E. Perkins, "Occupational Mobility and Migration from Agriculture," in *Rural Poverty in the United States*, President's National Advisory Commission on Rural Poverty (US Government Printing

Office, Washington DC, 1968), 185–237.

37 Ibid., pp. 211–12. This study challenges several conventional beliefs. The authors find that other things equal, mobility rates from farm to nonfarm employment are lower for both Negroes and Whites from low income than from high income rural areas, that long-distance migration has no economic advantage, and that the back movement into farm employment in low income areas is higher than for the more prosperous areas largely because a majority of the individuals in low income areas lack the requisites for success in nonfarm employment.

38 S. Bowles, "Migration as Investment: Empirical Tests of the Human Investment Approach to Geographical Mobility," *Review of Economic Statistics*, 52(4) (Nov. 1970), 356–62; see p. 362.

39 L.A. Sjaastad, "The Costs and Returns of Human Migration," *Journal of Political Economy*, 70 (Part II, Oct. 1962), 80–93.

40 A. Schwartz, "Migration and Lifetime Earnings in the US," unpublished PhD dissertation (University of Chicago, 1968).

41 A. Schwartz, "On Efficiency of Migration," *Journal of Human Resources*, 6(2) (Spring 1971), 192–205.

42 J. O'Neill, "The Effects of Income and Education on Inter-Regional Migration," unpublished PhD dissertation (Columbia University, 1969).

43 T.J. Courchene, "Inter-Provincial Migration and Economic Adjustment." *Canadian Journal of Economics*, 3(4) (Nov. 1970), 550–76.

44 T. Paul Schultz, *Population Growth in Internal Migration in Colombia* (RAND, RM-5765/RC/AID, Santa Monica, California, 1969).

45 R.B. Freeman, *The Market for College-Trained Manpower* (Harvard University Press, Cambridge, Mass., 1971).

46 R.B. Freeman, "Decline of Labor Market Discrimination and Economic Analysis," *American Economic Review*, 63(2) (May 1973), 280–86.

47 Gary S. Becker, *Human Capital* (National Bureau of Economic Research, New York, 1964): see table 14 and pp. 128–30.

48 Between 1940 and 1957 the percentage of the population that were high school graduates rose from 12 to 22; for college graduates it increased from 5 to 9 percent of the population. See Becker, *Human Capital*, table 15.

49 Theodore W. Schultz, "Optimal Investment in College Instruction: Equity and Efficiency," in *Investment in Education: The Equity-Efficiency Quandary* (University of Chicago Press, Chicago, Ill., 1972), pp. 12–30.

50 See Welch, "Education in Production."

51 Zvi Griliches, "The Sources of Measured Productivity Growth: United States Agriculture, 1940–60," *Journal of Political Economy*, 71(4) (Aug. 1963), 331–46; "Research Expenditures, Education, and the Aggregate Agricultural Production Function," *American Economic Review*, 54(6) (Dec. 1964), 961–74; "Notes on the Role of Education in Production Functions and Growth Accounting," in W.L. Hauser (ed.), *Education, Income, and Human Capital* (National Bureau of Economic Research, New York, 1970),

pp. 71–115.

52 D.P. Chaudhri, "Education and Agricultural Productivity in India," unpublished PhD dissertation (University of Delhi, 1968). See also his "Rural Education and Agricultural Development: Some Empirical Results from Indian Agriculture," in P. Foster and J.R. Sheffield (eds), *World Year Book of Education 1974* (Evans Brothers, London, 1973), pp. 372–86.

53 B.R. Harker, "Education, Communication, and Agricultural Change: A Study of Japanese Farmers," unpublished PhD dissertation (University of Chicago, 1971); "The Contribution of Schooling to Agricultural Modernization: An Empirical Analysis," in Foster and Sheffield, *World Yearbook of Education 1974*.

54 P.R. Moock, "Managerial Ability in Small-Farm Production: An Analysis of Maize Yields in the Vihiga Division of Kenya," unpublished PhD dissertation (Columbia University, 1973).

55 C.C. Wu, "The Contribution of Education to Farm Production in a Transitional Farm Economy," unpublished PhD dissertation (Vanderbilt University, 1971); also "Education in Farm Production," paper presented at Eastern Economics Association meetings (Oct. 1974).

56 T.E. Haller, "Education and Rural Development in Columbia," unpublished PhD dissertation (Purdue University, 1972).

57 W.E. Huffman, "Contributions of Education and Extension to Differential Rates of Change," unpublished PhD dissertation (University of Chicago, 1972).

58 Schultz, *Transforming Traditional Agriculture*.

59 S. Tax, *Penny Capitalism*, Smithsonian Institution Publication No. 16 (US Government Printing Office, Washington DC, 1953, reprinted by University of Chicago Press, 1963).

60 D.W. Hopper, "The Economic Organization of a Village in North Central India," unpublished PhD dissertation (Cornell University, 1957).

61 R. Evenson, "Research, Extension and Schooling in Agricultural Development," in Foster and Sheffield, *World Year Book of Education 1974*, pp. 163–84; see also "The 'Green Revolution' in Recent Development Experience," Agricultural Economics Workshop paper (University of Chicago, Jan. 17 1974).

62 T.E. Haller. "Education and Rural Development in Columbia."

63 With respect to the value of schooling, Chaudhri's results are consistent with, and Haller's provide strong support for, the analysis of this early stage of agricultural development in Theodore W. Schultz, "The Education of Farm People: An Economic Perspective," in Foster and Sheffield, *World Year Book of Education 1974*, pp. 50–68.

64 Theodore W. Schultz, "Reflections on Agricultural Production, Output and Supply," *Journal of Farm Economics*, 38 (Aug. 1956), 748–62.

65 Griliches, "Hybrid Corn," 1957 and 1960.

66 Welch, "Education in Production." In an unpublished paper, "Education, Information, and Efficiency (National Bureau of Economic Research, New

York, June 1973), Welch includes a somewhat extended version of the 1970 paper along with a major section on theoretical aspects of the value of information, a Bayesian learning model, and steps toward applications. This paper also contains a perceptive review of the analyses and contributions of the studies by Nabil Khaldi, "The Productive Value of Education in US Agriculture, 1964," unpublished PhD dissertation (Southern Methodist University, 1973); by George Fane, "The Productive Value of Education in US Agriculture," unpublished PhD dissertation (Harvard University, 1973); and by Huffman, "Contributions of Education." The final section is devoted to the returns to scale in US agriculture.

67 Welch, "Education in Production," p. 55.
68 Huffman, "Contributions of Education:" see also "Decision Making: The Role of Education," *American Journal of Agricultural Economics*, 56(1) (Feb. 1974), 85–97.
69 As a consequence of rapid changes consisting of the decline in relative price of nitrogen fertilizer, of improved hybrid seed corn varieties including single crosses that are more responsive to fertilizer than earlier varieties, and of new crop rotations moving toward continuous corn with more plants per acre, the economic average optimal level of nitrogen application, for example in Iowa, doubled. The county average optimal nitrogen level in Iowa was 81 pounds per acre in 1959, and 166 pounds per acre in 1964. The average amount used on all corn acres planted in 1959 in Iowa was 213, and in 1964 it had risen to 39 pounds per acre. By 1969 the actual use of nitrogen in Iowa had reached approximately 101 pounds per acre.
70 Huffman, "Decision Making," pp. 94–5.

4

*Increases in the Value of Human Time**

What have our ideas and institutions contributed to the high value we place on human beings and to the remarkable increases in the value of human time? While it is fitting and proper during this bicentennial year to celebrate our achievements as a nation, it is much more important to examine critically and to reassess the social, political, and economic ideas embodied in our institutions. Because of the influential books, pamphlets, and documents that appeared in 1776, it is convenient to date these ideas accordingly. Although these ideas are a critical part of our social heritage, it will no longer suffice to take them for granted. It is a heritage that is being eroded for lack of support against strong alternative social, political, and economic ideas.

The Economic Research Service bicentennial lectures afford an opportunity to examine the interplay between social thought and political economy – presumably with special reference to the economic history of agricultural productivity; the decline in the social, political, and economic influence of the owners of land; and the rise in the economic value of human time.

What people do privately and collectively over time is constrained by the consequences of the interactions between ideas and institutions consisting of observable responses of one to the other. In this context, ideas are embodied in social thought, and the social, political, and economic order is maintained by institutions. The response of ideas to the institutionalized order is of two historical types: those that rationalize and contribute to the codification of the prevailing order, and those that arise in protest to the established order which become embodied in social

* First published as "The Economic Value of Human Time Over Time" in *Lectures in Agricultural Economics*, US Department of Agriculture, Bicentennial Year Lecture sponsored by the Economic Research Service (June 1977), 1–24.

thought and then become strong enough to induce a real alteration in the prevailing institutions.

From the point of view of economics, the consequences of the interactions between ideas and institutions differ markedly from one period to another. It is useful to think in terms of four periods: the mercantile period preceding 1776; the era of economic liberalism that followed; the more recent forms of neo-mercantilism ranging from centrally planned economic development to a system of command economics; and a nascent, neo-liberalism emerging in protest to the various centralized and authoritarian institutionalized orders.

The mercantile system that prevailed for decades, for example in England, prior to 1776 was rationalized by economic ideas. These ideas provided support for governmental restrictions on trade, on internal prices and wages, and on migration. The social and political order was buttressed by the established Church and by the Law.

In protest to the adverse social and economic effects of the then prevailing institutionalized order, 1776 was an extraordinary year in terms of the various intellectual publications that laid the foundation for liberalism. An open competitive economy with people responding to market prices that are not fettered by monopolies in a political order in which the functions of the state are greatly restricted – this was the classic contribution of Adam Smith. Smith's economic ideas complemented the more general liberal thought of his day, which over the decades that followed profoundly altered the institutionalized functions of the government.

Liberalism, because of its accommodation of the economic attributes of capitalism as seen in the adverse social effects of industrialization, led in turn to a wide array of protests. The ideas that emerged from these protests prior to those of Karl Marx called for various forms of socialism. The contributions of Marx, however, came to dominate the political and economic foundations that are required for socialism. The response to Marxian ideas altered greatly the institutions of many nation states. The economic functions of government are much enlarged into a new form of neo-mercantilism.

In protest to socialism there now emerges a neo-liberalism. Because of the dependency of socialism on a vast increase in the functions of government, which in some countries consists of extreme authoritarian nation states, and because of the now widely observed adverse effects of the governmental institutions on personal freedom, protests akin to those of two centuries ago are once again the order of the day.

The core of the argument of this lecture does not deal directly with the ideas and institutions of these various economic systems. The historical evidence, however, which I am about to present, does provide some indirect information that gives rise to doubts about the adequacy of classical theory and of the economic theory of socialism. The economic history to which this paper appeals supports four major propositions that are not at home in either of two long established sets of theories.

The first arises out of the fact that wage and salary workers in high-income countries, and especially in the United States, have become capitalists as a consequence of their large investments in their own human capital. The opportunities and incentives to which workers respond in their investment in human capital is not a part of the theory advanced by Ricardo or of Marx. Nor is it an integral part of Keynesian economics.

Secondly, contrary to the core of classical economics built on the assumption of the dominating effects of Ricardian Rent on personal income shares, the economic and the associated social and political importance of landlords has in fact declined markedly over time in high-income countries.

Thirdly, contrary to Marx and not anticipated in classical theory, changes over time in the functional distribution of income have had a major effect in reducing the inequality in the personal distribution of income.

Fourthly, given the imprint of Malthus, theory until very recently has been silent on the economics of the decline in fertility in high-income countries. There is still another major implication that is not featured in this paper, namely the extraordinary decline in the labor force required to produce agricultural products in high-income countries. Regardless of the source or the mode of received theory, this important historical economic development cannot be derived from theory.

I first present the elements of an economic approach; I then turn to the measurement of the increases in the price of human time and to the secular trend in the prices of natural resource materials and rent. Lastly, I consider some of the implications of the high price of human time.

1   An Economic Approach to the Price of Human Time

Value and capital are the core of economics. Events and human behavior alter the scale of values and the stock of capital. Alterations that enhance the scope of choices are favorable developments. The various forms of capital differ significantly in their attributes. Natural resources are not reproducible; structures, equipment, and inventories of commodities and goods are physical entities that are reproducible; and human beings are productive agents with the attributes of human capital. Human beings are also the optimizing agents and, in a fundamental sense, it is their preferences that matter in the use that is made of the various forms of capital. The concept of human capital, its development and its usefulness, is a recent innovation. In high-income countries, the rate at which human capital increases exceeds that of nonhuman capital.

Despite unfavorable events from time to time, human behavior in high-income countries has brought about a secular increase in the personal stock of human capital, and the increases in it have gone hand-in-hand with the rise in the value of human time. A part of the analytical task is to extend the core of economics to explain the formation and the functions of human capital in the changing context of secular time.

Our knowledge of the economics of the processes that alter the supply of human capital has been advanced during the last two and a half decades. Schooling, higher education, on-the-job experience, migration, and health all contribute to the personal supply. But changes in the supply of human capital are only one of the two major parts of the story in explaining the increases in the economic value of human time. The value that is revealed in the price of human time is the intercept of the prevailing supply of, and the demand for, the market and nonmarket services and for the direct personal satisfactions that people derive from their human capital. Our knowledge of the economic processes that alter the demand for human capital is not nearly as satisfactory as it is with respect to the supply.

To acquire an historical perspective on the unsettled issues pertaining to the price of human time, it is necessary to go beyond current events and recent economic growth. It is useful to recall that the early English classical core of economics rested on the following propositions: a highly inelastic supply of land (natural resources) resulting in Ricardian Rent, population growth resulting in constant (subsistence) wages over time, and productivity attributed to additional nonhuman capital and advances in useful knowledge (state of the productive arts) resulting in a larger population and in increases in Ricardian Rent. All household activities were assumed to be unproductive. Accordingly, the economic activities that mattered were confined to market-oriented production activities.

We shall appeal mainly to seven decades of economic history to establish the fact that the price of human time has risen markedly in countries that have developed a modern economy, and then establish the additional fact that the secular trend of the real price of the services of natural resources, of both renewable and nonrenewable natural resources, has been essentially horizontal. As a consequence, the economic importance of the price of human time has risen greatly relative to the price of the services of natural resources.

In view of this historical development, how can the following issues be resolved? Why has Ricardian Rent lost its economic sting in high-income countries? Why have real wages increased so markedly despite population growth? Closely related, why has the demand for human time increased more than the combined quantity and the quality of the supply?

Although it is obvious that the high price of the services of labor cannot be explained by a theory of subsistence wages, nor by a theory of labor exploitation, and, in spite of the fact that a very large share of our national income accrues to labor, a labor theory of value will not suffice. The extension of the economics of labor that is made possible by the development of the concept of human capital explains in large part the increases in the supply of valuable acquired abilities, including skills by means of investment. But this extension of labor economics, already implied above, does not explain the increases in demand for the services of human capital that become embodied in our population.

We begin with an appeal to general theory and proceed to build on the proposition that the value of the services of capital holds a key to the explanations we are seeking. We require an all-inclusive concept of capital. Reproducible tangible wealth is only one category of capital. Although natural resources are not reproducible, they are treated here as another category of capital. Human agents are the most important category in this all-inclusive concept of capital consisting of the economic attributes of human capital.[1] The value placed on services of these various categories of capital is revealed in human behavior. A closely reasoned economic theory to explain this behavior rests on two basic concepts: the human being is an optimizing agent whose behavior is governed by constraints that are in part peculiar to him, and the market provides the auction at which all individual offers are acknowledged and the terms of trade are established for equalizing supply and demand.[2]

Our approach to the increases in the value of human time concentrates on the changes in the supply and demand intercepts over time. The variables that alter the supply of human time are fairly clear: total hours devoted to market and nonmarket activities, including hours allocated to consumption; composition of the hours of the population that engages in these various activites; and quality of these hours. These supply variables are inter-dependent in their responses to the hourly price and to the income effects of that price.

Given the state of economics, the variables that alter the demand for human time are not wholly clear. The amount and the price of the services of natural resources and the effects of this price on wages have been integral to economics since the early classical period. They form one of the variables that matters, though not behaving in accordance with that theory. Moreover, effects of the rent derived from natural resources on the demand for human time are small in high-income countries. The stock of nonhuman reproducible capital, the price of its services, and the forms of this capital constitute a major variable in their influence on the demand for human time. The effects of the income from this category of capital on the demand for human time are still substantial even though the income from this source has declined relative to the income earned by labor. Another variable of increasing importance over time is the demand for the personal services of professional and competent technicians by families who derive their income from wages and salaries.

The approach advanced here requires an additional critical variable. It consists of changes in the arts of production and consumption that occur as a consequence of advances in useful knowledge. This variable has two important specific economic attributes. In the case of natural resources it consists of new *man-made substitutes* for such resources. In the domain of reproducible physical capital it consists of new forms of such capital which are *complementary* with high human skills, which increase the demand for such human capital and the value of human time.

We now turn to the task of marshalling some of the historical evidence on the extent of the secular rise in the price of human time, concentrating on the period since 1900.

2 Measurement of the Price of Human Time

For most people throughout the world, economic conditions are such that the value of their time is very low. Labor earns a pittance. Work is hard; life is harsh. Countries with low earnings cover most of the world's map. In a few countries, however, the value of the time of the rank and file of people is by comparison exceedingly high. The high price of human time that characterizes these exceptional countries is, from the viewpoint of economic history, a recent development. In Ricardo's day, land rents were indeed high relative to wages. During Marshall's period real wages were a small fraction of what they have become since then. In the United States, for example, between 1900 and 1972, the *real* hourly "wages" in 1967 dollars in manufacturing rose from about 60 cents to $3.44.[3]

We begin with an overview of the secular increases in the economic value of human time. The direct evidence consists of estimates of real wages covering the period since 1900 by decades. Starting with the United States, we use Rees' NBER (National Bureau of Economic Research) estimates of the compensation *per hour* at work for manufacture production workers as a proxy of the price of human time in the market sector. The real hourly price rose during each of the decades. By 1972 the real compensation per hour had risen more than fivefold. As would be expected, the annual estimates show several years when a decline occurred. There were 3 such years before World War I and 8 since then.[4] The marked upward trend, however, is shown in table I.4.1.

The upward trends in real wages in industry in France, Germany. Sweden, and the United Kingdom (table I.4.2) are, in general, much like that of the United States. They differ somewhat, however, in that the rate of increase is higher in Sweden and the United States than it is in the other three up to about 1960, except for the United Kingdom which did not stay abreast of the rest. There are also other country differences in the movement in real wages that are noteworthy. France and the United Kingdom show no increase between 1900 and 1910. As of 1925, Sweden and the United States were substantially ahead of the other three countries (was it a consequence mainly of differences in the effects of the aftermath of the war?). Sweden and the United States maintain their advantage over the others up to 1960 with the United Kingdom losing ground relative to the rest. Lastly, during the decade of the 1960s, France and Germany join Sweden and the United States in showing approximately a fourfold increase in real wages over the period from 1900 to 1970, whereas the increase for the United Kingdom is threefold.

The fact that real wages rose as much as they did implies strongly that the various prices, other than the price of human time which enter into the deflator of actual wages, declined relative to wages. Because of the stress placed on land rent rising as capital is accumulated, population increases over time in classical theory, and the concern about the "unearned" income of landlords in both liberal and socialist thought, we turn to the trend in the prices of the services most dependent on natural resources along with a comment on Ricardian Rent on farmland.

3 Prices of Natural Resource Materials and Rent

We now present evidence on the trends in the prices of these materials. We shall concentrate on the commodities that are most closely identified with natural resources because of the widely held belief that natural

Table I.4.1 Total work compensation per hour of manufacturing production workers, United States, 1900–1972

Year	Rees' wages	1900 = 100
	1967 dollar	Index
1900	0.60	100
1910	.70	117
1920	.92	153
1930	1.06	177
1940	1.60	267
1950	2.15	358
1960	2.85	475
1970	3.27	545
1972	3.44	573

Source: Albert Rees, *Long Term Economic Growth, 1860–1970* (US Bureau of Economic Analysis, Washington DC, 1973), app. 2, B70, pp. 222–23. Note: Estimates for 1970 and 1972 are derived using a similar method. Rees' estimates are adjusted from 1957 to 1967 dollars.

resources are the critical limiting factor available to the economy. We consider renewable natural resources (agriculture and forestry) and nonrenewable natural resources (mining including mineral fuels), and we examine the trends in the prices of the commodities from these sources. We shall refer to this natural resource complex as the extractive industries. The commodity prices that we present are of course not pure material prices; far from it, for they embody in various combinations the productive service of labor and of reproducible capital along with the material component.

Accordingly, our concept of the extractive industries includes mining (of which metals and mineral fuels are the dominant components) and agriculture and forestry. Most of the commodities produced by these industries tend to remain quite constant over time in their physical, chemical, or biological attributes. A bushel of wheat, for example, produced in 1900 differed little from a bushel produced in 1970. Similarly constant are such commodities as lead, copper, or sulphur. Quality changes occur, however, in such commodities as milk and other livestock products. Historical records of these commodity prices are, in general, more reliable than that of final and intermediate goods. For the United States, we have the excellent study by Potter and Christy[5] of commodities produced by extractive industries covering the period beginning soon after the Civil War with annual estimates up to the mid-1950s. The Potter-Christy study has been updated by Manthy.[6]

Table I.4.2 Indexes of real wages in industry in France, Germany, Sweden, United Kingdom, and the United States, 1900–1970

Year	France	Germany	Sweden	United Kingdom	United States
		1890–99 = 100			
1900	112	108	110	104	110
1910	112	116	131	104	210
1925	135	127	158	113	160
1930	138	156	183	124	160
1938	142	155	190	133	203
1950	168	174	252	169	292
1960	290	282	343	219	381
1970	442	482	473	301	446

Source: E. H. Phelps Brown, "Levels and Movements of Industrial Productivity and Real Wages Internationally Compared, 1860–1970," *Economic Journal*, 83, 58–71. Based on tables III and V of the appendix. Note: In interpreting the increases in real wages shown in table 2, it should be borne in mind that we are now dealing with real annual wages in industry. They are not hourly wages. They are less complete in getting at the total compensation of employees than the estimates by Rees. Accordingly, Rees' estimates show a higher rate of increase than Brown's. Thus, for the United States during the period from 1900 to 1970, Brown's real wages show a fourfold increase and Rees' real hourly "wages" a strong fivefold rise.

The empirical story as told in table I.4.3 is that the trend of the deflated natural resource commodity prices over this period was not upward but slightly downward[7] compared to the more than fivefold rise in real hourly wages shown in table 1. Within agriculture, the deflated prices of all crops declined about a third despite various government price supports during parts of this period. The index for all livestock closes out this period at the level where it began (table I.4.4). In general, the costs of producing livestock products have been affected more by the increase in the price of human time than have the costs of producing crops. The deflated prices of mineral fuels shown in table 5 tell us that, whereas the deflated price index for all mineral fuels was about a fourth less at the end of this period compared to 1900, the price of bituminous coal rose and that of petroleum fell. It is undoubtedly true that the rise in real wages accounts for a good deal of the increase in coal prices.

We have not used economic theory in mapping the course of natural resource commodity prices. Nor have we used theory to gain plausibility or to derive testable hypotheses, nor to validate the reported behavior of these prices over time. Our reason for this apparent non-theoretical approach to the factual data is that there is no general economic theory

Table I.4.3 Indexes of deflated commodity prices of the extractive industries, United States, 1990–1972

Year	All commodities	All agriculture	All forestry	All metals
		1900 = 100		
1900	100	100	100	100
1910	99	126	99	76
1920	109	111	97	66
1930	76	90	56	45
1940	77	86	87	60
1950	108	131	99	68
1960	87	95	90	75
1970	79	88	74	76
1972	83	92	84	71

Sources: N. Potter and F.T. Christy Jr., *Trends in Natural Resource Commodities* (Johns Hopkins Press for Resources for the Future, Baltimore, 1962). Actual prices are weighted by the value of output, updated using 1967 weights by Robert S. Manthy, Mich. State Univ. Indexes of actual prices are deflated by the consumer price index, 1967 = 100.

that encompasses the type of development here under consideration. There are conflicting theories of the substitution among capital, labor, and natural resource commodities used by the industrial sector.[8] There are some studies of the value of the amenity services relative to the value of commodities from the same natural resources.[9] Going back, there is what was then considered to be a general theory with built-in Ricardian Rent.

Received theory at the turn of the century predicted that the price of natural resource commodities would rise relative to wages and that the rental income accruing to the owners of natural resources would become an increasing share of national income. No less an authority than Marshall presents this prediction cogently and strongly in the preface to the 8th edition of his *Principles of Economics*. The observed course of natural resource commodity prices, including the price of food produced by agriculture, is obviously not consistent with Marshall's prediction. Furthermore, as we show presently, his prediction with regard to rentals on agricultural land is also inconsistent with the evidence since his day.

There is no general theory for the task at hand. Our recourse is, at this point, limited to partial theories of the demand for and supply of natural resource commodities and of the amenity services derived directly from nature. A good deal is known empirically about the income elasticity of consumer demand for various farm goods, for material goods, and for

Table I.4.4 Indexes of deflated agricultural commodity prices, United States, 1900–1972

Year	All agriculture	All livestock	All crops
		1900 = 100	
1900	100	100	100
1910	126	127	118
1920	111	118	87
1930	90	99	73
1940	86	95	73
1950	131	141	110
1960	95	101	75
1970	88	100	66
1972	92	104	69

Sources: See table I.4.3.

Table I.4.5 Indexes of deflated commodity prices of metals and of mineral fuels, United States, 1990–1972

Year	All metals	All mineral fuels	Petroleum	Natural gas	Bituminous coal
			1900 = 100		
1900	100	100	100	100	100
1910	76	48	42	–	93
1920	66	118	131	118	146
1930	45	61	59	114	79
1940	60	59	57	80	104
1950	68	81	84	68	156
1960	75	79	79	119	125
1970	76	72	68	111	125
1972	71	73	67	112	143

Sources: See table I.4.3.

some of the amenity services of nature. Theory and evidence about price elasticities of the demand are not especially useful in analyzing developments that occur over decades.

In thinking about nonrenewable natural resources, the common sense perception of their eventual exhaustion or permanent impairment as a source of amenities is not in dispute. With regard to renewable natural resources, the ultimate limits of the surface of the earth suitable for growing crops and trees on which agriculture and forestry depend are also not being called into question. The critical unsettled economic question in this connection pertains to the changes over time in the substitution possibilities among natural resources, labor, and reproducible capital.

In dealing with this question, a specific theory of these substitution possibilities for each of the following classes of activities would be of some help: direct substitution of capital and labor for natural resources in the production of natural resource commodities and in providing amenity services; substitution of capital and labor for natural resource commodities in industrial production; likewise in household production; and natural resource-saving adjustments in what is finally consumed. But to reckon fully with these various substitution possibilities, we would also have to know the changes that occur over time in the technical possibilities to substitute.

In retrospect, a wide array of man-made substitutes for natural resources have been developed; namely, substitutes for land in agricultural production, for natural resource commodities in industrial and household production, and in what is finally consumed. These man-made substitutes of the past can be identified and their supply effects can be determined, but it is fair to say that economic theory is yet incapable of predicting the supply of additional, new man-made substitutes for natural resources. The lack of such a theory does not mean we are wholly ignorant with regard to future prospects in this regard.

Before considering the course of agricultural land rentals as one of the prices of the services of natural resources, the state of our knowledge about substitution within other classes of economic activities calls for a brief comment. What is known about substitution among capital, labor, and natural resource commodities in US manufacturing is presented succinctly by Humphrey and Moroney.[10] The two main sets of conflicting views are reviewed followed by an appeal to new evidence using two alternative research designs in estimating substitution as it is revealed in manufacturing during 1963. They conclude that regardless of the underlying causes of input substitution, be it technology-induced or price-induced, "... the evidence suggests that labor and, to a lesser degree, capital are substitutable for natural resource products among most of the resource-using product groups of American manufacturing."

There is no comparable study of substitution in household production, in part, no doubt, because the extension of theory to deal with household production and using it in undertaking empirical analysis are very recent advances in economics. There are some useful studies of substitution that occur in the choice of the components that enter final consumption, including the consumption of natural resource amenities.

Our portrait of prices is pleasing to behold; more pay for less work and enough more of nature's commodities at about the same real price in 1970 as in 1900, although the population had grown from 76 to 203 million and GNP had increased nearly ninefold. But is it a true picture? Our deflator is obviously influenced by the rising cost of labor. It may not be the appropriate deflator in the case of natural resource commodity prices. Beyond this, there is an important defect in our treatment of the price effects of natural resources. It arises out of the fact that natural resource rents were a declining part of actual commodity prices. Accordingly, the course of commodity prices which we have presented is biased upward because of the increasing share of the real costs of producing commodities consisting of wages and of reproducible capital costs. Although the output per man-hour of the extractive industries has increased, we find that, in general, the more labor-intensive the commodity the larger is this upward bias. Within agriculture, for example, the deflated price of wheat declined by one-half between 1900 and 1970–72, whereas that of fresh tomatoes doubled between 1920 (the first date for which the price is available) and 1972. I wish we could determine the true price of the services of natural resources.

If we knew the true rent paid for the original properties of farmland, we would have the most important price of the services of natural resources, inasmuch as the value of the output of agriculture dominates the total value of the output of all extractive industries.[11] But the rent we want is very elusive, for here too the rent that is reported is definitely biased upward and increasingly so over time. The farmland rent that is recorded is not Ricardian Rent; only a part of it is rent paid for the original properties of the soil.

A substantial part of the productivity of farmland is man-made by investments in land improvements. There undoubtedly have been circumstances and periods when some disinvestment occurred. In the United States during the 1930s, soil depletion, including water and wind erosion, became a much publicized issue. The New Deal provided government subsidies for soil conservation programs. Although the actual soil depletion was much exaggerated, the soil conservation programs have been, among other things, land-improving public investments.

To acquire a perspective of the extent to which the productivity of farmland is man-made, we turn briefly to other parts of the world on this point. The original soils of western Europe, except for the Po Valley and some parts of England and France, were, in general, very poor in quality. As farmland, these soils are now highly productive. The original soils of Finland were less productive than most of the nearby western parts of the Soviet Union; today, however, those of Finland are far superior. The original farmland of Japan was vastly inferior to that of northern India. Presently, the difference between them is greatly in favor of Japan. Argentina has excellent natural soils for growing corn and it has good wheat land. But its corn productivity is far below that of Iowa and Kansas. Harsh, raw land is what most farmers since time immemorial have started with; what matters much over time is the investment made to enhance its productivity.

In the United States, investments made to improve the raw land with which farmers began are of various forms and the accumulated amount is large. These investments, however, did not occur at a steady rate because the incentives to invest fluctuated widely over time. They were large during most of the first two decades of this century, notably so in drainage in what are now the best parts of the Corn Belt. From 1920 to 1929 and even more so in the 1930s, investments to improve farmland were at a low ebb. Since then, these investments have gone on apace with the government paying much of the bill. Modern earth-moving equipment reduced sharply the costs of terracing, of improving the water run-off courses, and of leveling land. Since the late 1930s, the acreage under irrigation doubled; it now covers 40 million acres and has cost billions of dollars, much of which has been paid by US taxpayers.

In the more arid and extensive farming parts of the Mountain and Pacific States, the cash rent paid for grazing land, which includes the good higher altitude pasture, averaged less than $4.00 per acre in 1970. The market value of farmland per acre in California provides a clue to the implied effects of investments on rents. In 1970, nonirrigated cropland sold on the average for $560 per acre compared to $1,090 for irrigated land used for intensive field crops. Irrigated land used for truck and vegetable crops was priced at $1,670 per acre and irrigated orchards and groves with their investment in fruit-bearing trees were priced at $2,730 per acre.[12]

Lindert's study of land scarcity[13] includes a series of farmland rents extending back to 1900. It is the gross rent per acre of land rented for cash restricted to five Midwest States. The actual gross rent is adjusted by consumer prices. These rents rose nearly 15 percent from 1900 to 1915, declined 30 percent by 1920, and drifted even lower as of 1940. Lindert's series then shows an upward trend beginning in 1950. By

1970 these rents were 6 percent above 1900 but less than in 1915.

Although farmland prices and agricultural commodity prices fluctuate more over time than gross cash rents, the patterns are in general quite similar. But none of these patterns provides any direct evidence on the share of the gross cash rent that is to be attributed to the original properties of the soil. The indirect evidence indicates that the expenditures of landowners, including the value of time they devote to the management of this property, has risen substantially from 1900 to 1970. It also indicates that land improvement investments and investment in buildings and in other structures, especially in a livestock area such as the Midwest, have been large over the period since 1900. My interpretation of this indirect evidence is that the share of gross cash rent attributable to the Ricardian Rent component declined between 1900 and 1970, probably as much as a third for the reasons indicated. If this interpretation proves to be valid, it implies that whereas gross adjusted cash rents were about the same in 1900 and in 1970, the value productivity contributed by the natural land resource declined substantially. Major factors accounting for this decline have been the effects on farmland rents of the development and use of man-made substitutes for farmland.

We have sketched the seven decades to show the marked upward trend in the economic value of human time. In marked contrast, as we have shown, the price of materials most dependent on natural resources during these seven decades has not had an upward tendency. It is also noteworthy, although we are not presenting the data, that real wages rose somewhat between 1860 and 1900. The increase was small, rising between one-half and onefold for the several countries, including the United States, listed in table 2. Going back in history a bit further, back to Ricardo's day, real wages were rising, but here the comparison has to be in terms of the cost of food. A clue is to be had in the change in the price of wheat relative to that of wages. The estimates that follow tell a good deal about economic history using wheat and wages.

	2 weeks of wages in bushels of wheat
Time of Ricardo (1817) England	1
Marshall's time (1890) United States	20
Eighty years later (1970) United States	200
State of being very poor (1975)	
India plowman	3.5
India field laborer	2 or less
	(Ricardian shadow)

4   High Price of Human Time Implications

The social, political, and economic implications are pervasive. The high price of human time is a clue to many puzzles. These puzzles include the shift in institutional support from the rights of property to that of human rights, the decline in fertility, the increasing dependence of economic growth on value added by labor relative to that added by materials, the increases in labor's share of national income, the decline in hours worked, and the high rate at which human capital increases. The human agent becomes ever more a capitalist by virtue of his personal human capital, and he seeks political support to protect the value of that capital. These are some of the major implications of the high price of human time.

The rise in the value of human time makes new demands on institutions. Some political and legal institutions are especially subject to these demands. What we observe is that these institutions respond in many ways to the changes in demands of the economy. The legal rights of labor are enlarged and in doing so some of the private rights of property are curtailed. The legal rights of tenants are also enhanced. Seniority and safety at work receive increasing protection and discrimination in employment is curtailed. Since I have dealt with these institutional issues and with ways of bringing the analytical tools of economics to bear on them elsewhere,[14] I shall not pursue these issues further on this occasion.

5   Labor's Income Share

The interactions between the effective labor force at work and hourly wages on the one hand, and the amount of nonhuman capital and the price of the services of that capital on the other, are exceedingly complex. Kuznets[15] gives us an analysis of these interactions in which he takes account of the increases in the stock of wealth represented by land and of the stock of reproducible producer capital and the changes in the prices of the services of these forms of capital, along with the increases in man-hours worked and the rise in the price per man-hour worked. His analysis implies an increase in labor's income share.

The obverse of the increase in labor's share of national income is the decline in the share accruing to property assets. Appealing once again to the studies of Kuznets,[16] where he takes a fairly long view of the development in western countries, one finds that the share of national income accruing to property assets declined from about 45 to 25 percent, while labor's share rose from about 55 to 75 percent.

By 1970, about three-fourths of the official US national income consisted of employee compensation.[17] The remaining fourth is classified as proprietors' income, rental income, net interest, and corporate profits. These four classes of "property" income include considerable amounts of earnings[18] that accrue to human agents for the productive time they devote to self-employed work and to the management of their property assets. A conservative estimate of the aggregate earnings that accrue to human agents, as employee compensation plus self-employment earnings, and for management of assets within the domain of the market sector, accounts for more than four-fifths of the 1970 US national income.

Measured national income, however, is substantially less than the full income that people acquire from the services of their property and for their time inasmuch as the concept of national income is restricted to the economic activities of the market sector. It excludes the economic value of all household production. The additional income that is realized from household production is in large part contributed by the value of the time of housewives. Also omitted are the earnings that adult students forego in investing in their education, and the wages that members of the labor force forego in acquiring on-the-job training. These and still other income-producing activities are not included in the accounting of national income.

It is clear historically that labor's income share increased as the price of time rose. The development of the US economy from 1900 to 1970 strongly supports this implication. During 1900–1909, using the official concept of national income, employee compensation accounted for about 55 percent of national income compared to 75 percent in 1970.[19] Between 1900–1909 and 1970, the changes in the shares of income other than employee compensation were: proprietors' income declined from about 24 to 8 percent, rental income from 9 to 3 percent, and net interest from 5.5 to 4.1 percent of national income, whereas corporate profits rose from 7 to 9 percent. The latter two income components fluctuated widely over this period as would be expected in view of the uneven performance of the economy over time.

6   Farmland Rent

The reason why Ricardian Rent has lost its economic sting is implied by the increases in labor's income share, in the declines in the income share accruing to property assets, and in the marked decline in the income share attributed to rental income, which fell from 9 to 3 percent between

1900–1909 and 1970. Farmland rent that is attributed to the original properties of the soil has become an exceedingly small part of US national income. As a consequence, the social and political influence of farm landlords has become minute.

7   Time Allocated to Work

Price and income effects of hourly earnings explain a wide array of changes in the allocation of time. When expected future earnings from more education rise, the response of youth is to postpone entering upon work for pay in order to devote more years to education. The advantages of youth in acquiring the additional education are of two parts, namely the wages that youth forego are lower than they are at older ages and there are more years ahead for youth to cash in on the expected higher earnings from additional education.

As wages increase people who earn their income by working can afford to retire at an earlier age because of the larger retirement income that they are able to accumulate during their prime working years. A counter-effect of increases in earnings is in the improvement in health that is purchased which extends the years that individuals may opt for work. The rise in the value of time of women is an incentive to substitute various forms of physical capital for their time in household production, and inasmuch as children are for women labor intensive, the demand for children is reduced, and an increasing part of the time of women is allocated to the market for labor.

The increases in earnings also explain the decline in hours of work or the increase in "leisure" during this century. For the US civilian economy, the average weekly hours declined from about 53 to 37 hours over the period from 1900 to 1970, and the average annual hours per employee decreased from 2,766 to 1,929 hours. The interaction between annual hours allocated to work and earnings shows a decline of 7 percent in hours and a 43-percent increase in annual earnings between 1900 and 1920. For the 1920 to 1940 period these changes were 12 percent and 53 percent respectively, and for 1940 to 1970 there occurred a 13-percent decline in annual hours while real annual earnings increased by 73 percent.

8   Toward a Population Equilibrium

One of the important implications of the high price of human time is its effects on fertility. The argument is that the high price of time in high-income countries accounts in large measure for the observed decline in fertility. High income countries have arrived at birth rates that are at or below replacement rates. The argument setting forth the economics of the process that leads toward a population equilibrium is presented in two papers, one by Nerlove and the other by me.[20]

I began with the question: what have our ideas and institutions contributed to the high value we place on human beings and to the remarkable increases in the value of human time? I have set the stage with a historical view to help us in examining critically our social, political, and economic ideas embodied in our institutions, as we ponder this important question.

Notes and References

1 It will be necessary to distinguish between the concept of human capital when it is restricted to the abilities that people acquire at some costs and the concept of human capital that includes all innate and acquired abilities of human agents. It is the latter concept that is relevant at this point.

2 See Part I, No. 3 above, "The Value of the Ability to Deal with Disequilibria."

3 These are updated estimates by Albert Rees (see table 1) of the total compensation per hour at work of manufacturing production workers in 1967 dollars.

4 The upward trend of real hourly wages, as measured by Rees, rises weakly from 1900 to the middle of the next decade: it then rises sharply during World War I, after which it rises weakly through the 1920s and 1930s. There follows a strong upward trend for two and a half decades, after which it rises weakly once again from the late 1950s to 1970. The years which show a decline are 1904, 1907, and 1908, and then 1914, 1919, 1921, 1922, 1925, 1932, 1945, and 1946.

5 N. Potter and F.T. Christy Jr, *Trends in Natural Resource Commodities* (Johns Hopkins University Press for Resources for the Future, Baltimore, 1962).

6 Professor Robert S. Manthy, Michigan State University, has been most generous in making offsets of his numberous tables available to me. I am much indebted to him.

7 No doubt the reader who is strongly of the belief that the 1973–75 upsurge in prices of the services most dependent on natural resources is the beginning of a new era will be inclined to look upon the indexes of prices in these tables as bygones that are no longer meaningful for the future. The argument against this view is that the events, both natural and man-made, that accounted for this upsurge in these prices are in large part transitory events. The economic processes that account for the observed prices, say from 1960 to 1972, are approximately the more permanent relative prices

that are in general likely to prevail once again instead of the very high transitory prices of 1973–75.

8   David B. Humphrey and J.R. Moroney, "Substitution Among Capital, Labor and Natural Resource Products in American Manufacturing," *Journal of Political Economy*, 83 (1975), 57–82.

9   John V. Krutilla and Anthony C. Fisher, *The Economics of Natural Environments* (Johns Hopkins University Press for Resources for the Future, 1975).

10 Humphrey and Moroney, "Substitution among Capital."

11 Agriculture accounted for 72 percent of the total output of the extractive industries in 1900 and for 61 percent in 1970.

12 *Farm Real Estate Market Development* (Economic Research Service, US Department of Agriculture, July 1972), table 8.

13 Peter H. Lindert, "Land Scarcity and American Growth," *Journal of Economic History*, 34 (1974), 951–84, app. table 1. States included in this series are Iowa, Illinois, Ohio, Wisconsin, and Minnesota.

14 See Theodore W. Schultz, "Institutions and the Rising Economic Value of Man," *American Journal of Agricultural Economics*, 50 (Dec. 1968), 1113–22, reproduced in *The Economics of Being Poor* (Blackwell, 1993), Part II, No. 1, as "Institutions and the Value of Human Capital." See also the useful paper by Vernon W. Ruttan, *Integrated Rural Development Programs: A Skeptical Perspective* (Agricultural Development Council, New York, 1975), reprinted from *International Development Review*, 17 (1975).

15 Simon Kuznets, *Modern Economic Growth* (Yale University Press, New Haven, Conn., 1966). Chapter 4, pp. 181–83 bears directly on this analytical issue. This part of the analysis is restricted to the United States and to the period from 1909–14 to 1955–57.

16 Simon Kuznets' studies of economic growth and the distribution of income are classic contributions to this subject. See: (i) "Economic Growth and Income Inequality," *American Economic Review*, 45 (Mar. 1955), 1–28; (ii) "Quantitative Aspects of the Economic Growth of Nations: VIII Distribution of Income by Size," *Economic Development and Cultural Change*, 11(II) (Jan. 1963), 1–80; (iii) *Modern Economic Growth*; and (iv) *Economic Growth and Nations* (Harvard University Press, Cambridge, Mass., 1971).

17 US Bureau of Economic Analysis, *Long Term Economic Growth, 1860–1970* (Washington DC, 1973), p. 22. Compensation of employees includes income accruing to persons in an employee status such as wages and salaries, tips, bonuses, commissions, vacation pay, and payments in kind. Also included are supplements and fringe benefits such as employer contributions to private pension, health and welfare funds.

18 We shall restrict the concept of earnings to the income that accrues to human agents as compensation for their productive services. The income accruing to the owners of property assets for the productive services of their property will be referred to as *property income*.

19 US Bureau of Economic Analysis, *Long Term Economic Growth*.

20 Theodore W. Schultz (ed.), *Economics of the Family: Marriage, Children,*

and Human Capital (University of Chicago Press, Chicago, Ill., 1975). See Marc Nerlove, "Toward a New Theory of Population and Economic Growth," pp. 527–45; also Theodore W. Schultz, "Fertility and Economic Values," part II, pp. 14–20, deals specifically with "the high value of human time: population equilibrium."

Part II

Less Dependency on Natural Resources

Part II

Less Dependency on Natural Resources

1

The Declining Economic Importance of Agricultural Land*

In representing the circumstances of his period, Ricardo assigned a major role to agricultural land, and quite properly so in view of the fact that most households in England were spending most of their income for food. It is a long step to R.F. Harrod, who, in 1948 in selecting the economic variables for his *Dynamic Economics*, saw fit to leave land out altogether[1]. While it is true that Ricardo sought mainly to determine the distribution "of the whole produce of the earth" to the various factors during different stages of economic development, and while Harrod endeavored to explain the occurrence of depressions in an economy like that of the United States, each reflected the circumstances of his period, among others, the existing beliefs regarding the place of land in the economy.

Clearly, in particular countries, land is no longer the limitational factor it once was; for instance, in such technically advanced communities as the United Kingdom and the United States and also in many others, the economy has freed itself from the severe restrictions formerly imposed by land. This achievement is the result of new and better production possibilities and of the path of community choice in relation to these gains. This achievement has diminished greatly the economic dependency of people on land; it has reduced the income claims of this factor to an ever-smaller fraction of the national income; and it has given rise to profound changes in the existing forms of income-producing property. The underlying economic development has modified in an important way and relaxed substantially the earlier iron grip of the niggardliness of nature.

* First Published in *Economic Journal*, 61 (Dec. 1951), 725–40. Reproduced by permission of Blackwell Publishers.

Ricardo had in mind a high-food-drain community, while Harrod, the opposite, a difference which may be illustrated by a simple comparison. Take two communities, one representing a situation in which most of the productive effort is required to produce food, a technically undeveloped community with a large population relative to its resources and with a low level of living where rents in agriculture are large relative to total factor rewards. In such a *high-food-drain* community, let us suppose that 75 percent of the income is used for food and in which, say, $33^1/_3$ percent of the cost of food consists of rent (net) for land used in farming. In such a case, one-fourth of the income, at factor cost, would be "spent" for the services obtained from agricultural land. For the second situation, take a *low-food-drain* community, one approximating the United States at its current stage of economic development, and assume that about 12 percent of the disposable income is expended for farm products that enter into food and that about 20 percent of the cost of producing farm products is net rent. Under these circumstances only about 2.5 percent of the income of the community would be spent for the food-producing services of land.[2]

Each of these figures is a significant index of a whole set of attributes of the community from which it is drawn. The social, political and economic differences between a community in which a fourth of the economic rewards go for its productive services of land and one where one-fortieth is for this purpose are so great that it is indeed hard for people living under such diverse circumstances to comprehend what these differences mean. The revolutionary implications of land reform in countries where most of the property consists of land, where this property is held not by the cultivators but mainly by a small group of families who do not farm and where most of the political power and social privileges are vested in those who own land, are, for a person living in a technically advanced community, virtually impossible to grasp. Ricardo's economic logic gave little comfort to landowners, but the case for land reform in high-food-drain communities does not necessarily rest on altering the economic relations within agriculture. Basic social and political issues are usually in the forefront in countries where a transfer of land to existing cultivators would not change the size of the operating units or the type of farming. The production process in agriculture need not be altered in such a case; the reform by means of taxation would absorb the net rent of land because it would simply transfer the rent from private individuals to the state as public revenue.

A century ago it appeared to thoughtful men that land limited greatly the economic fortunes of all communities, and that there was no escape from the restrictions imposed by nature. The classical law of (secular) diminishing returns stands as a symbol of this belief about economic history. But circumstances have altered very much. How has this remarkable change come about? It did not occur by contracting the economy and thus reducing the amount of land required to produce food and thereby making this particular factor relatively more abundant. Such a sequence would be possible if a population were to decline. Yet the record[3] on this score is conclusive; population growth in Western countries was rapid and pronounced during this period, and markedly so during the earlier part, nor has it spent itself.

I shall represent the development underlying the declining economic importance of land in the form of two propositions. The first proposition is restricted to certain changes in the relations between agriculture and the rest of the economy characteristic of communities as they emerge leaving behind their former high-food-drain status. The second proposition relates to changes in the inputs of land relative to other inputs within agriculture. Land is here restricted to agricultural land used to produce farm products, thus leaving aside minerals, sites, recreational and other services obtained from land.

It is my belief that the following two propositions are historically valid in representing the economic development that has characterised Western communities:[4]

1 a declining proportion of the aggregate inputs of the community is required to produce (or to acquire) farm products; and
2 of the inputs employed to produce farm products, the proportion represented by land is not an increasing one, despite the recombination of inputs in farming to use less human effort relative to other inputs, including land.[5]

Whenever these two propositions are in fact valid for a community, it follows that the value added by all agricultural land as an input must necessarily decline relative to the value productivity of all inputs of a particular community. The economic consequences that flow from the first proposition would not suffice, inasmuch as a decline in agriculture by itself would not necessarily mean that the value added by land would fall, because it would be possible under particular conditions for the value contributed by land to rise enough to maintain or even increase its position relative to the aggregate inputs of the community. Also, if the value added by all land were to decline relative to all other inputs in agriculture and if farm products, meanwhile, were to come to claim a larger share of the income of the community, the importance of land, measured in terms of the value added by all agricultural land as an input, could stay constant or even rise. But whenever both of these propositions are valid, land will necessarily decline in importance in the economy. In situations where the first is true and where, in the case of the second proposition, land becomes in fact a smaller proportion of all inputs used in farming, the decline of land, of course, is accelerated.

1   Agriculture Relative to the Whole Economy

Let us look briefly at the empirical evidence supporting the first of our two propositions by touching on the case of the United Kingdom and by considering some relevant data about the United States in a bit more detail before turning to the economic assumptions and logic explaining this development. In England just prior to 1800, when England still had most of the characteristics of a high-food-drain economy, worker families may have spent about 75 percent of their income for food.[6] In 1948 only 27 percent of the expenditures of consumers in the United Kingdom appear to have been for food.[7] While these figures are not entirely comparable, they leave no doubt that a remarkable change has occurred in the proportion of the income required to obtain food.

The historical record of the United States is fairly easy to interpret in this connection because it has been more nearly self-contained throughout. Some insights may be had from crude property data and the occupations of workers. An estimate of all real and personal property in the United States in 1805 places the total value of this property at 2,505 millions of dollars of which 1,661 millions, or about two-thirds, consisted of land.[8] At that time over 70 percent of the labor force was engaged in agricultural pursuits.[9] By 1850, farm-land, including improvements, was a little less than half of the value of all property, while about 60 percent of the labor force was agricultural. The 1880 figures are somewhat more precise, since it is possible to separate agricultural land from improvements. In that year, out of an aggregate of 43,642 million dollars, only 8,158 millions, or less than one-fifth, was agricultural land and about 50 percent of the labor force was in agriculture. The national wealth in 1922 was 321 billion dollars, while agricultural land, excluding improvements, was 41.5 billions, or about one-eighth of the total; and 27 percent of the labor force was engaged in agricultural pursuits.

Another rough check on the first proposition is the downward drift in the proportion of the national income imputed to agriculture. Income estimates for earlier stages of the economic history of the United States are, of course, subject to many limitations and especially for the purpose at hand. The fact that farm families were much more self-sufficient

formerly makes it exceedingly difficult to get at all of the income produced by agriculture at that time compared to more recent periods, and
therefore, these income estimates understate the contribution of agriculture more as one goes back than they do currently. Some insights
are, nevertheless, possible. We have one set of estimates that goes back
to 1799 for the United States based on the realized private produced
income. This series provides the following figures:[10]

Selected year	Total private produced income (in millions of dollars)	Produced by agriculture (in millions of dollars)	Per cent produced by agriculture
1799	668	264	39.5
1849	2,326	737	31.7
1879	6,617	1,371	20.7
1900	14,330	3,034	20.9
1920	60,993	10,569	17.3
1938	47,389	6,140	12.9

National-income estimates for more recent years give us a much better
gauge of the value added by factors used in agriculture, including land
relative to total value productivity of the economy:

Year	Income produced by all industries[a] (in billions of dollars)	Income produced by agriculture[b] (in billions of dollars)	Agriculture as percentage of all industries
1910	30.4	5.2	17.1
1919	68.2	11.8	17.4
1929	87.4	8.4	9.6
1939	72.5	6.4	8.8
1949	216.8	18.1	8.4

[a] US Department of Commerce. The figures for 1910 and 1919 are from the national-
income estimates (old series). The others are from the *National Income Supplement to
Survey of Current Business,* July 1947 and also the July 1950 issue.
[b] US Department of Agriculture, *Crops and Markets,* 1950 ed., vol. 27, p. 139; and the
Farm Income Situation, August 1950. The commerce series on farm income leaves out
rent paid to non-farm landlords, which makes it less useful for our purposes than the
USDA series on which I have drawn.

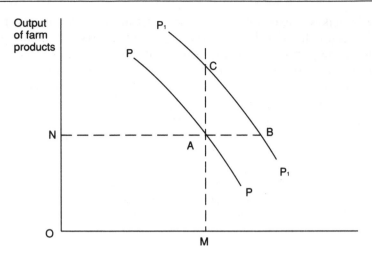

Fig. 1 Output of all other products and services

There is no need to adduce further empirical evidence to support the first of our propositions. The facts, fortunately, are well known and generally accepted. There is, however, no established explanation that is completely satisfactory. I shall endeavor to sketch the essential elements of such an explanation restricted to the kind of economic growth and development that has characterized Western communities.

In its simplest terms the explanation must answer the following query: When the effective aggregate inputs of a community increase as a result of economic development – (1) when does a community find it possible to produce or acquire its farm products with a smaller proportion of its productive resources and (2) why does it choose this possibility? Our task here is not that of explaining the increase in aggregate inputs but the production possibilities and choices that emerge as a result of such changes.

Figs. 1, 2 and 3 are drawn to represent three sets of production possibilities. In each figure the particular community is confronted by the production possibility curve *PP*. The preferred combination of farm products and of other outputs is represented by *A*, with *OM* indicating the non-farm outputs and *ON* the output of farm products.

Fig. 1 represents a situation in which the production-possibility curves are relatively adverse for increasing the output of farm products. Economic development gives the community a new and improved production situation represented by P_1P_1. The triangle *ABC* indicates the range of choices open to the community in going from *PP* to P_1P_1 without going

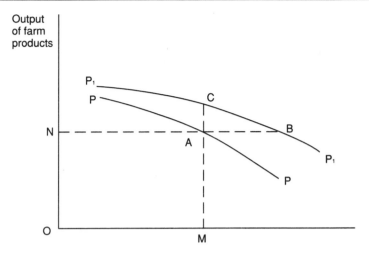

Fig. 2 Output of all other products and services

below the former level of output of either farm products or of non-farm products. The community can now have substantially more non-farm outputs in going from *A* to *B*, provided it chooses to restrict itself to the same amount of farm products it formerly produced. The choice open to the community in the other directions, however, is very slim. It can add only from *A* to *C* to its farm products, even though it foregoes having any more non-farm products than formerly. Let us suppose that along with the new and better production possibilities there were to occur a growth in population which required all of *AC* to provide enough food to keep the *per capita* intake at the old level. In that event, should the community choose to maintain the old level, it would mean stopping at *C* on P_1P_1 with all of the gains in production resulting from the attainment of P_1P_1 being used to produce farm products. This in substance is the Ricardian case.

Fig. 2 is drawn to represent a situation which is the exact converse of that portrayed in Fig. 1. In this case the production-possibility curves are relatively adverse for increasing the output of non-farm products. In going from *PP* to P_1P_1 the triangle *ABC* again indicates the range of choices, and this time farm products are in a much more favorable position than are nonfarm products. No one to my knowledge has advanced the view that this case can represent a real situation, probably because we are unable to rid ourselves of the specter of hunger embedded in our minds by Malthus-Ricardo-Mill. Looking back, it might be said that the early and middle 1930s came close to being a situation of this type;

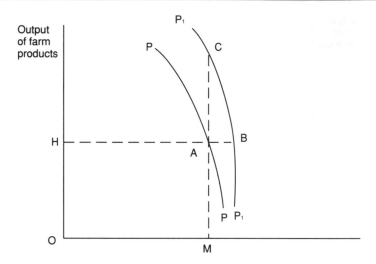

Fig. 3 Output of all other products and services

food-production possibilities improved substantially, while industry appeared to be "stagnant" and, at the same time, the rate of population growth dropped sharply.

When we take the long view, however, it is quite clear that improvements in production have been about as favorable for farm products as for other products and services taken as a whole. American data for the period since 1910 leave little doubt on this point. Figure 3 has been drawn to represent such a situation; it, therefore, should be more instructive than either Figs. 1 or 2 in explaining that aspect of our economic history relevant to the problem under consideration. In Fig. 3 the shape of *PP* indicates that when resources are shifted from agriculture to other industries or the converse, the substitution possibilities are about the same either way. The new and better production possibility curve P_1P_1 also has this attribute; and the triangle *ABC* indicates that the community can now have and thus may choose substantially more farm products along *AC* or non-farm products along *AB*, or some preferred combination of the two on P_1P_1 between *BC*.

With production possibilities like those represented in fig. 3, community choice has considerable room to express itself in going from *PP* to P_1P_1. As new opportunities have presented themselves, it is clear that Western communities have preferred relatively more of the non-farm products and services, or to state this another way, as new and better production possibilities have emerged, the preferred combination has become one in which farm products are a decreasing proportion of all products and services.

Why has the Western community preferred these particular combinations? To explain the path of the community choice, we take recourse to the scale of preferences of the community. Taking the long view, as we have in this study, we shall assume that not only products but also the population is subject to the preferences of people. One possible preference scale, which can express itself given a time span of decades, is more people, enough more to absorb all the gains from new and improved production possibilities. (There is no *a priori* basis for excluding a deterioration in non-farm products and services, that is, the community choosing less of these in order to make possible the production of more food to feed more people.) There is no way of measuring these scales of preferences directly; at best, we infer their contours and positions indirectly from a process in which we can observe certain effects. The history of the growth of population, at least statistically, is an open book. Western communities have not chosen to behave in accordance with the Malthus-Ricardo-Mill model. Moreover, as the income of people has risen, it is clear they have preferred to spend proportionally less of their incomes for food, and especially for the farm products that enter into food. In other words, the income elasticity of farm products has not remained high, as it was when these communities were of the high-food-drain type; it has become less until, under existing conditions, in a community with as high *per capita* incomes as exist in the United States, the income elasticity of farm products is now quite low, probably in the neighborhood of 0.25, with many farm products actually in a position of inferior goods against income.

In explaining the circumstances on which the first of our two propositions rests, we have endeavored to show that it is necessary that the new and better production possibilities which emerge as the economy develops do not exclude improvements in the production of farm products. This condition, in general, has prevailed in Western communities because the advances in techniques, improvements in skills, the use of more capital and improvements in organizations have been about as applicable to agricultural production as to other lines. One of the fundamental consequences of this development has been the favorable choice situation confronting the community. In addition, therefore, it is necessary that the preferences of people, either for more population or for food or combinations of these, do not exhaust the improved possibilities applicable to the production of food. In Western communities it is plain that the preferred combinations underlying the path of community choice that has emerged under these circumstances have called for the production of more non-farm products and services relative to farm products entering into food.

2 Relative Position of Land as an Input in Producing Farm Products

Our second proposition about the course of economic development is that the value productivity of agricultural land has not increased relative to that of all inputs used to produce farm products. The evidence supporting this proposition is fairly conclusive for the United States for recent decades with input estimates now available. But before turning to these data, we need to take account of certain difficulties in getting at the empirical proof.

How can land as an input be measured? In 1910, 1,618 million acres were used for agricultural purposes in the United States; by 1945 this acreage had declined slightly to 1,570 million.[11] During that period, the volume of agricultural production for sale and for home consumption increased 70 percent.[12] From these two sets of facts, we cannot, however, infer either that the aggregate inputs of agricultural land had declined (except in one special and meaningless economic sense, namely that fewer acres were employed) or that the value added by land had declined relative to all inputs used in farming. We are, here, confronted with a series of difficulties, suggested by: (1) What is land? (2) can it be measured and aggregated? and (3) can the other inputs be determined?

It is impossible to standardize land in physical terms; its physical attributes do not permit us to put land into one of several convenient boxes. Land is not only exceedingly heterogeneous physically but also it can be and is altered significantly over time by farming and by nature, even when it is not being farmed. Investment and disinvestment in soil productivity are possible. So what then is land in either a cross-sectional or a secular comparison? Nothing can be salvaged in terms of physical units which are meaningful in determining, say, the supply of land in terms of so many acres, because there is no point whatsoever in adding together the semi-arid, low yielding acres of parts of Arizona and the highly fertile acres of parts of Iowa. We are, therefore, driven to an index weighted by value components, based either on rent or on the price of agricultural land or on other estimates of the value of the productive service of land. These matters are sufficiently important to deserve special investigation; but this is not the place to elaborate on these difficulties or on what can be done about them.

Before turning to American data on the value added by agricultural land, a brief reference to the United Kingdom and especially to France is in order, given the data made available by a recent study.[13] Had the Physiocrats been confronted by modern France, their *Tableau Économique* would have shown a small, unimpressive "net product." Already by 1900 agricultural land claimed only about a fourth of the agricultural income; it has declined to half or less of that figure since then; and the rent imputed to all agricultural real estate has come to represent less than 5 percent of the national income, as the following data for France indicate:

	Agricultural land rent	
Selected years	As percentage of national income	As percentage of agricultural income
1901	7.9	25.5
1906	6.8	21.6
1911	6.5	19.5
1916	5.1	24.0
1921	3.2	11.8
1926	3.4	12.0
1931	3.6	15.6
1936	3.7	16.3
1947–48	(not available)	9.0

The data for the United Kingdom are quite fragmentary, mainly because of the difficulty of disentangling net and gross rent in the way data are reported. Here, again, the study by Thomson shows:

Selected years	Net rent as percentage of net agricultural income[a]
1925	16.8
1938	11.5
1946	5.6

[a] Harkness' figures for gross rent as per cent of net agricultural output in Great Britain are not inconsistent for they indicate a decline from 39% in 1908 to 26.6% in 1930–31. See DAE Harkness, "The Distribution of the Agricultural Income," *Journal of Proceedings of the Agricultural Economics Society,* III (Mar. 1934), 30 table VI.

American data for recent decades permit one to determine the value added by land as an input in farming with considerable assurance. The Bureau of Agricultural Economics has made estimates of the changes in physical inputs employed for agricultural production going back to 1910. These estimates indicate that land as an input has continued to hold about the same relative position throughout, representing somewhat less than a fourth of all inputs used for agricultural production. Agricultural land, that is land in farms, which we shall define below, was 23.6 percent of all the inputs used for agricultural production in 1910– 14 and 24.2 percent in 1945–48. The composition and combination of inputs, including the land component, have, however, changed substantially. While inputs in the aggregate have increased moderately, the amount of labor has declined. In the case of agricultural land the total acres in farms rose from about 880 million in 1910 to 1,148 million in 1948.[14] Meanwhile, farm-buildings and other improvements that are counted as part of the land have come to represent an increasing proportion of the value of agricultural land. The following data summarize the relative size of the various classes of inputs, including agricultural land:

| | *Relative amounts of inputs employed for agricultural production* | |
| | *1910–14*[a] | *1945–48*[b] |
Class of input	*(in percent)*	*(in percent)*
Farm labor	46.0	45.4
Agricultural land	23.6	24.2
Maintenance and depreciation	10.3	9.8
Operation of motor vehicles	0.3	6.0
Interest	9.6	4.9
Taxes	3.2	2.8
Fertilizer and lime	2.5	2.6
Miscellaneous items	4.5	4.3
Total	100.0	100.0

[a] Using 1910–14 cost ratios, from Glen T. Barton and Martin R. Cooper, "Relation of Agricultural Production to Inputs," *The Review of Economics and Statistics*, 30, (May 1948), table 2.
[b] Using 1946–48 cost ratios, from unpublished data made available to the writer by the Bureau of Agricultural Economics.

A word on the meaning of "agricultural land" in the present context seems necessary at this point. It includes cropland, pasture land, other land in farms and buildings. It does not include pasture or range land not in farms[15], but the contribution of this class of land is small; grazing land for which farmers pay fees[16] is a very minor item compared to the net rent of all land in farms; in 1948, for example, it was about one-tenth of one per cent as large. Two major changes in the composition of agricultural land can be measured: (1) as already indicated, the acres in farms has increased about 30 percent during the four decades under consideration and (2) even so, farm buildings have come to represent an increasing proportion of the value of agricultural land, rising from 18 to 33 percent, as set forth below:

Year	Acres in farms (million acres)	Value of all farm real estate (in billions of current dollars)	Value of farm buildings (in billions of current dollars)	Farm buildings relative to all farm real estate (in percent)
1910	880	34.8	6.3	18
1920	956	66.3	11.5	17
1930	987	47.9	13.0	27
1940	1,061	33.6	10.4	31
1950	1,148	63.5	20.6	33

If we assume that the value productivity of farm-buildings was roughly the same per dollar of invested value as it was for land in farms minus buildings, after allowing for maintenance and depreciation, and that about half of the farm-buildings in value terms represented farm-dwellings which we shall, therefore, subtract – the inference is that agricultural land minus farm buildings represented slightly less than 20 percent of all inputs in 1910 and about 16 percent in 1950.[17]

There are gaps, however, in our information about the various capital components that go to make up agricultural land. In a rough way we can take, as we have taken, account of farm-buildings and in doing so separate the buildings used for production from those used for consumption. But there are many other forms of capital embedded and included in agricultural land, for it includes among others such items as fences; windmills, wells and other water facilities; electric lines serving farmsteads; clearing of land, drainage and irrigation structures; and roads. In addition, there are many components related to soil productivity. Existing social accounting, however, does not permit us to make satisfactory estimates of these items. While there is little doubt that for those capital forms not directly related to the productivity of the soil, the tendency has been upwards relative to the aggregate value of the land in farms as in the case of farm-buildings. But it is often alleged that farmers generally have misused the soil, and as a result there has been widespread erosion and depletion, and therefore, in effect, substantial disinvestment of the "natural" soil productivity. The evidence offered, however, does not support the generalization. While there are many particular situations where such disinvestments have occurred, these losses appear, judging from informed opinion, to have been more than offset by improvements on other farms. The productive properties of the soil being farmed in the United States are in all probability substantially better today than they were say, four decades ago, despite the particular soil losses that have occurred.

The following conclusion is warranted: when account is taken of both investments and disinvestments, the input which we have defined as agricultural land has come to an increasing extent to consist of capital components that have been added to the land. We infer, therefore, as a consequence of this development, that the American economy is even less dependent upon the "original and natural properties" of the land than the above figures would indicate.

The proposition that land as an input in agricultural production has not increased relative to all other inputs used in farming appears to be empirically valid for such technically advanced communities as France, the United Kingdom and the United States. The input estimates of the Bureau of Agricultural Economics, on which we have based our analysis, make the case on this point quite conclusive for the United States since about 1910. Is there a satisfactory explanation for this outstanding development?

Before outlining the elements of an explanation, we need to recall that this development with regard to the role and contribution of agricultural land occurred under circumstances from 1910 to 1948 while *farm output* increased from an index of 79 to 141 or 79 percent; *agricultural production* for sale and for home consumption from 79 to 137 or about 73 percent; and *agricultural food* for sale and for home consumption from 75 to 134 or about 80 percent.[18] Also, during this period the largest input, namely farm labor, declined in physical terms and increased in value terms per unit of input sufficiently to keep its relative position as an aggregate at factor costs about the same. The two basic changes underlying this development were technological advances and substitution of other inputs for both labor and land, as is suggested by the following data.[19]

	Amount of inputs expressed in millions of dollars at 1946–48 factor costs		Increase or decrease as percentage of 1910–14
Class of input	1910–14 (per year)	1945–48 (per year)	
Farm labor	12,892.4	11,269.7	−13
Agricultural land	4,680.6	5,999.0	28
Maintenance and depreciation	1,693.4	2,421.5	43
Operation of motor vehicles	19.2	1,489.0	7,655
Interest	1,250.4	1,217.3	−3
Miscellaneous	730.8	1,071.0	47
Taxes	514.8	698.0	36
Fertilizer and lime	226.4	655.0	189
All inputs	22,008.0	24,820.5	13

Leaving aside the difficulties of constructing an index to measure these inputs, since alternative weighting periods and techniques do not change the general results, it is perfectly plain that new and better technique, increasing the output per unit of input, has played a primary role in this development. Roughly, three inputs now produce about as much as four inputs did four decades ago. Meanwhile, because of technical advances, it has become economic to substitute to an increasing extent several classes of inputs for both land and labor, notably motor vehicles and fertilizer and lime.

We realize that land is not for food alone. It is important for other purposes in the community and the economy, purposes which we have neglected throughout this study. The conclusion, however, is firm; the economic developments that have characterized Western communities since Ricardo's time have resulted in improved production possibilities and in a community choice that has relaxed the niggardliness of nature. As a consequence of these developments, agricultural land has been declining markedly in its economic importance. Will it continue to do so? Existing circumstances in the United States indicate a strong affirmative answer. Nor is the end in sight. But can existing high-food-drain communities realize a similar economic development? As yet we do not know.

Notes and References

1   R.F. Harrod, *Towards a Dynamic Economics* (Macmillan, London, 1948), p. 20: ". . . I propose to discard the law of diminishing returns from the land as a primary determinant in a progressive economy . . . I discard it only because in our particular context it appears that its influence may be quantitatively unimportant."

2   A rough gauge for 1949 would be as follows: Disposable personal income, $187 billion; expenditure on food, excluding alcoholic beverages, $50.7 billion; assuming that one-half of the expenditures for purchased meals represent costs of food at retail, the food expenditure figure becomes $44.9 billion, of which about one-half or $22.5 billion is for the farm products entering into food. 22.5 is 12 percent of 187. See US Department of commerce, *Survey of Current Business* (July 1950), pp. 9 and 24 for relevant figures.

3   A stage of the history of Ireland may, however, be cited as an exception to this record.

4   The two propositions can be integrated into a single and more general proposition by simply relating all agricultural land (as an input) to all inputs of the community. Existing statistics, however, are such that it is not possible to get satisfactory data bearing on such a general proposition, while there are some data which permit us to observe the apparent validity of each of the two propositions as I have formulated them.

5   One may, of course, represent the economic importance of land in different ways. Changes in the relative value per unit is one approach, and when rent per acre declines relative to the rewards of other factors it may be said that the economic importance of land is diminishing. Such a representation is, however, not a complete measure of the changes in land viewed as a price-quantity aggregate. We, therefore, turn to the "value added" by all land relative to all other inputs for our measure, difficult as it is to combine and add together various parcels of land used to produce farm products.

6   Sir Frederick Morton Eden, *The State of the Poor* (1797), vols. II–III.

7   United Nations Statistical Office, *Monthly Bulletin of Statistics* (Feb. 1950), p. 3.

8   US Department of Commerce, *Historical Statistics of the United States, 1789–1945* (Washington, 1949), table 1, p. 1. The total valuation is reduced by $200 million when the item covering slaves is subtracted, making it 2.305 million, and when land not adjoining or near to the cultivated land is subtracted the figure for land drops to 759 million, or about one-third of the total.

9   J. Frederic Dewhurst and Associates, *America's Needs and Resources* (The Twentieth Century Fund, New York, 1947), table 215, p. 620.

10 *Historical Statistics of the United States*, Series A 154–64, p. 14.

11 All land in farms plus all nonfarm land grazed by livestock. From L.A.

Reuss, H.H. Wooten and F.J. Marschner, *Inventory of Major Land Uses in the United States* (US Department of Agriculture, Misc. Pub. 663, 1948), table 16.

12   Based on *Consumption of Food in the United States, 1909–48* (Bureau of Agricultural Economics, Misc. Pub. 691, Aug. 1949), table 3.

13   The data appearing below for France and the United Kingdom are from an unpublished study by Procter Thomson, *Productivity of the Human Agent in Agriculture: An International Comparison.* This study was financed by the Rockefeller Foundation as a part of a research programme in Agricultural Economics at the University of Chicago.

14   The earlier acreage figures included all land used for agricultural purposes, while here only land in farms is included. The import of the difference is discussed in the text of the paper below.

15   For a note on the method used in measuring the input of agricultural land, see *Farm Production Practices, Costs, and Returns* (Bureau of Agricultural Economics, Statistical Bulletin 83, Oct. 1949), table 27.

16   These fees are included in the input referred to as "miscellaneous items."

17   For estimates of farm-buildings and of dwellings and of service buildings used for production see *Income Parity for Agriculture* (US Department of Agriculture, Mar. 1941), Part II, Section 5; *The Balance Sheet and Current Financial Trends of Agriculture* (Bureau of Agricultural Economics, Agricultural Information Bulletin 26, Oct. 1950); and *Federal Reserve Bulletin* (Sept. 1950).

18   In each of these measures of production, the increase would probably be somewhat less if 1946–48 price weights were used in place of the 1935–39 weights, but the general picture would remain about the same.

19   Based on unpublished data made available to the present writer by the Bureau of Agricultural Economics.

2

Connections Between Natural Resources and Increases in Income*

My topic is burdened by a heavy intellectual tradition based on a widely held belief that economic progress is severely subjected to diminishing returns of labor and capital against land. The belief persists despite much evidence to the contrary. Clearly the role of land in economic growth is no longer nearly as important as it appeared to Ricardo and his contemporaries. Yet, it is not easy to free ourselves from old ideas, especially so where such ideas have become entrenched behind strong doctrines.

My purpose is simply to clear the deck of these ideas that keep us from seeing the more relevant connections between natural resources and economic growth. I propose to examine three closely related questions: What is the value of natural resources as a factor in production? Are the economic growth possibilities of a country, especially so if it is poor, substantially restricted by its endowment of natural resources? Are we confronted in the case of the services of natural resources by a rising supply price?

Before turning to these questions, I want to pay my respects to the rich intellectual history about natural resources; there is no dearth of literature. There is the well-known concern of the older economists about land as a limitational factor in economic growth. There are also well-developed treatments of particular natural resources in mining, fishing, forestry, and agriculture and of urban uses of land. Then, too, location and transport have received much careful thought. There are now some good estimates of land as a stock of wealth and also as a factor of production. In this respect we enter an old and well maintained vineyard

* First published in Joseph J. Spengler (ed.), *Natural Resources and Economic Growth* (Resources for the Future, 1960) 1–9. © 1961 Resources for the Future.

and our task might be viewed as simply one of gathering the fruit of these intellectual efforts.

But my purpose cannot be achieved by merely building on received knowledge. It does not, as things now stand, place natural resources in their proper economic perspective, because all too little account has been taken of the rise in substitutes, the rise in the quantity and value of other resources, and the dynamic properties of modern economic growth in developing substitutes for ever more classes of natural resources. One's conception of economic growth is not unimportant in this regard. We do well to restrict it to increases in national income that can be identified and measured. Much, however, depends on the sources of these increases in national income. If it were only the result of additions to the stock of conventional reproducible nonhuman wealth and to the number of persons in the labor force, it would be simple. But, we know that this conception leaves most of the increases in national income unexplained. I propose to think of economic growth as a particular type of dynamic disequilibrium, during which the economy is absorbing various subsets of superior resources. They are superior resources in a special sense, namely, they provide investment opportunities with relatively high rates of return; and these relatively high rates of return imply inequalities in the way resources are allocated and a lagged process in bringing these rates of return into equality; moreover, this dynamic disequilibrium will persist to the extent that additional superior resources are developed and absorbed.

1   What is the Value of Natural Resources as a Factor of Production?

There are presently two very different views and treatments of this measure of the economic importance of these resources. One attributes a dominating role to natural resources as is the case in the classical dynamics,[1] and the other attributes to them no role whatsoever, e.g., there is no land in the Harrod models.[2] Harrod said, "I propose to discard the law of diminishing returns from land as a primary determinant in a progressive economy . . . I discard it only because in our particular context it appears that its influence may be quantitatively unimportant."[3]

I leave it to others to decide whether these magnificent growth models are tools or toys. What is clear, however, is that both of them are based on a grand, country-wide, macroconception of a particular economy at a given period in its history. The particular economy under consideration was England in Ricardo's day and the United Kingdom in the present era, respectively. The underlying circumstances were indeed very different, as I have attempted to show in "The Declining Economic Importance of Agricultural Land."[4]

Neither of these contrary views has any general validity. Whether we measure natural resources as a *stock* of wealth or as *flow* of productive services rendered by them, we are in the domain of estimates. For the United States we have Goldsmith's estimates which indicate that between 1910 and 1955 the proportion of national wealth represented by "all land" fell from 36 to 17 percent. Agricultural land dropped from 20 to 5 percent of national wealth.[5]

When we measure the flow of productive services, we would expect natural resources to represent an even smaller fraction of all productive services than they are of the total stock of nonhuman wealth. The "Paley Report"[6] provides a clue, if we assume that there has been a fairly stable linkage between the flow of raw materials produced and the stock of natural resources on which this flow has been dependent. The value of all raw materials consumed in the United States declined, relative to gross national product, from about 23 to 13 percent, between 1904–13 and 1944–50. For agriculture, the income attributed to farm land, excluding capital structures that have been added to such land in the United States, fell from 3.2 to 0.6 of one percent of net national product, between 1910–14 and 1955–57.[7]

There are two general relationships between natural resources as these are traditionally defined and all resources that have strong empirical support (both of these relationships are expressed in terms of the *flows* of the productive services of these resources and not in terms of *stocks* of wealth):

1   When we compare countries as of a particular date, we observe that the proportion of natural resources to all resources employed to produce the income is greater in poor countries than it is in rich countries. (I would venture that the upper limit in the proportion of natural resources to all resources in poor countries is in the neighborhood of 20 to 25 percent and the lower limit in rich countries is about 5 percent.)

2   When a country achieves economic growth that increases its per capita income over time, natural resources become a decreasing proportion of all resources that are employed to produce the income. (It would appear that during recent decades the rate at which this particular proportion has declined has been large.)

2   How Large a Contribution Can Natural Resources Make to the Economic Growth of Poor Countries?

The answer to this question turns basically on the growth possibilities of poor countries. Here, too, we are confronted presently by two contradictory assessments.

There is a widely held belief among economists that primary production – mining and especially agriculture – is essentially a burden on the economic growth of poor countries. Poor countries are over-committed to agriculture. Land is as a rule used intensively and the supply of land is virtually fixed. The marginal returns to labor in agriculture are at or near zero. These conditions are thought to be such that additional effort to increase the production of primary products can add little or nothing to the national product. On the other hand, large gains are to be had from a comparable effort and investment to produce industrial products. Furthermore, according to this view, backwardness is an intrinsic complement of the land-using sectors, notably in the case of agriculture; and, in addition, to add to its economic woes, in producing primary products a country is particularly vulnerable to the economic instability of rich countries. For these several reasons it is held that the natural resources sectors, especially agriculture, are less rewarding than are the sectors that contribute to industrialization on which the economic growth of poor countries, so it is presumed, is basically dependent.

The other assessment of the economic growth possibilities of poor countries holds that the endowment of natural resources in such countries, including farm lands, is a relatively important asset and that differences in stocks of these resources among poor countries are a major variable in determining the growth possibilities of such countries.

This issue is plagued by confusion and by a lack of firm evidence. A part of the confusion arises from a difference in the weight that is given to natural resources. As already noted, they are as a rule more important relative to all resources in poor than in rich countries. Most of the confusion, however, originates from a failure to distinguish between the rate of return to be had from additional reproducible capital of *the existing forms* and the rate of return that can be realized from *new and better forms* of reproducible capital.

There is first the fact that the technical properties of these two forms of reproducible capital are different, and there is the further fact that the economic attributes are also different inasmuch as the marginal rate of return from additional resources of the existing forms is low relative to the rate of return from investments in the new forms of resources. Once this distinction is made between these two forms of reproducible capital, the critical question is whether the new forms of capital are unique in that they have technical specifications that make it impossible to use any of them in primary production.

I have no doubt whatsoever that these new and better forms of reproducible capital are not restricted to industry. Many of them are applicable to agriculture and to other sectors heavily dependent upon natural resources. If the choice were only one of adding another irrigation well, a ditch, a bullock, or a few more primitive tools and pieces of equipment of the type that are being employed in a poor country, the prospects of winning a relatively high rate of return from such additions to the stock of capital would be dim indeed. But this is not the choice, whether it be in agriculture or industry. The choice that can be made and that carries with it the prospect of larger rewards entails new and better forms of reproducible capital both in agriculture and industry.

It has long been an accepted tenet of economic thought that the rates of return on additional capital in poor countries are relatively large. According to this tenet, these returns are large because poor countries have a relatively small supply of reproducible capital to use with their labor and land. The view that these earnings are relatively high has gained support from the vast movements of capital historically out of particular Western countries into many a poor country. These large transfers were in response, so it is held, to the differences between the *low rates* that had come to prevail in some of the comparatively rich countries and the *high rates* that characterized the production possibilities awaiting such capital in poor countries. What has not been made explicit in this assessment is the fact that for the most part these capital transfers were not employed simply to multiply the then existing forms of reproducible capital; instead new forms of capital were introduced into these poor countries as a consequence of these transfers.

It is widely held that the supply price of the productive services of natural resources must rise relative to the prices of the services of the reproducible factors as a consequence of economic growth. We have been taught that this is inevitable as the stock of reproducible capital increases along with the growth in population and production. Lower transport costs and improvements in the arts of production could temporarily hold the rise in the supply price of productive services of natural resources in check but that was the best that could be hoped for. Ultimately, however, diminishing returns of labor and capital against land would always prevail. This economic dictum is clearly at variance with our estimates; it is time that we relegated this dictum to our stock of folklore. But the image of a fixed supply of natural resources and a rising supply price of the products of these resources, persists.

A plausible approach is to treat raw (crude) materials as if they were produced under constant supply price conditions. This is the basic assumption that has made the Paley Report useful. It is a rough approximation to what has been happening, and the projections of the consumption of raw materials in the United States (to about 1975) based on this assumption have been doing quite well thus far.

I am aware, however, that there may be many a slip between the prices of the services of natural resources and the prices of raw materials. Unfortunately, there are all too few estimates of the prices of the services (rents) of natural resources; the studies that have come to my attention stop with raw materials. This led me to undertake some estimates of the

Table II.2.1 US Farm Output and Input Prices, 1910–14 and 1956*

Item	Increases between 1910–14 and 1956 1910–14 = 100	Increases relative to the prices of farm products 235 = 100
1 Prices received by farmers for farm products	235	100
2 Prices of classes of farm inputs		
(1) Farm wage rates	543	231
(2) Building and fencing materials	374	159
(3) Farm machinery	329	140
(4) Farm supplies	279	119
(5) Fetilizer	150	64
(6) Farm land[†]		
a. Price per acre of farm land	158	67
b. Price per constant unit of farm land	181	77
c. Rent per constant unit of farm land	166	71

* Based on table II in Theodore W. Schultz "Land in Economic Growth" see below Part II, No. 3.
† In each of these three estimates I have attempted to exclude the reproducible capital structures that have been added to farm land. Also see Ross Parish, *Trends in the Use of Summer Fallow in Saskatchewan: An Economic Interpretation* (unpublished PhD thesis, University of Chicago, 1959), for estimates that show the price of the services of farm land in Saskatchewan as having decreased substantially relative to the price of wheat and relative to other major farm inputs.

changes in the prices of the services of farm land in the United States.[8]

Although my estimates are subject to a number of qualifications, they strongly indicate that the price of the services of farm land declined substantially between 1910–14 and 1956 relative to farm product prices and even more so relative to the prices of all inputs used in farming.[9] In interpreting these estimates it should be borne in mind that farm product prices receded about 15 percent, both relative to the prices of all commodities at wholesale and relative to prices of all consumer items at retail, between 1910–14 and 1956.

Land as an input in farming is cheaper now than it was just prior to the first world war. This decline in the supply price of the services of farm land in the United States is not a freak event. It did not occur from a contraction of agriculture, because farm output rose about 80 percent between these two dates. Nor is it a consequence of large increases in the amount of such land. On the contrary, crop land harvested actually declined slightly, from 330 million (average for 1910–14) to 326 million acres (1956): see table II.2.1. I shall not enter at this juncture upon an explanation of this decline in the relative price of the services of farm land. Suffice it merely to note that the proposition that price of the services of natural resources must rise relative to the services of reproducible capital over time as a consequence of economic growth, is demonstrably false.

3   Connections between Natural Resources and Economic Growth

Up to this point my purpose has been to show that natural resources at factor costs have been declining in value relative to aggregate value of all resources and that the supply price of the services of these resources has not been rising relative to the supply price of other major classes of resources. Implied in this evidence is the inference that the marginal contribution of natural resources over time has not been increasing. Then, too, although natural resources are mainly an integral part of so-called backward sectors of the economy of most poor countries, it does not follow that the production possibilities of these countries are such that their natural resources act as a burden on their economic growth.

The connections between natural resources and reproducible non-human capital and the labor force are being altered substantially over time by economic growth. The type of economic growth that we have been experiencing represents a form of economic changes brought about by the introduction of new and superior resources. These resources, among other things, have been at many points in the economy effective substitutes for one or more classes of natural resources. To see the process broadly it will be necessary to use a comprehensive concept of capital, a concept that includes both nonhuman and human wealth, in order to take into account additions to stock of capabilities of a labor force that are useful in economic endeavor, capabilities that can be had by investments in man.[10]

We are accustomed to thinking of new and better machines as a substitute for labor. Surely, in agriculture they have become an important substitute for farm land as well as for labor. Johnson's study of grain yields attributes a third of the increase in the yield of corn since 1880 to farm mechanization. Improved seeds have also become a major substitute for farm land, and they appear to have contributed as much to increasing yields as has mechanization.[11] The economic effects of hybrid seed corn are noteworthy in this connection.[12]

Then, too, new forms of capital have entered into the production of fertilizer; these seem to have reduced substantially the real price of fertilizer, so that it has become a strong force not only in holding but in reducing the price of the services of farm land because of substitution. Not least of all have been the improvements in the capabilities of man (in this case of farmers and others in the farm labor force). Some of these new capabilities have also acted as substitutes for farm land.

The long established practice of treating these new and better resources as an *ad hoc* variable under the label of "technological advances," is a convenient way of covering up ignorance. Moreover, it is inconsistent with the economic logic of the properties of a production function. To assert that a production function (say in farming) has improved, or has been shifted to the right, because of an advance in technology, can only mean that at least one new resource (input) has been introduced in production, because a production function can only be derived from the properties of the resources that are employed in that production. If a production function has changed, it always means that at least one additional resource with different technical properties has been introduced in production. The analytical task, therefore, consists of developing concepts and of building models that will permit us to identify and measure the resource that provides the new technical properties and not to treat all or part of the unexplained residual by simply calling it "an advance in technology."

Lastly, the persistent and impressive economic growth that we observe in not a few countries and that we want to understand does not fit into the pattern of traditional thought. It does not fit because not all of the history of economic growth has been an exercise in stationary long-run equilibrium based on land, labor, and capital as these have been traditionally conceived. Diminishing returns, as labor and capital have been increased against a given stock of natural resources (land), is not the only game that history has been playing. In the history we want to understand, the game has been altered as a consequence of a couple more aces having somehow gotten into the deck. New and better production functions have entered from somewhere. The capabilities of labor have been improved, and the line of demarcation between capital and labor has become very blurred by investments in man. And so has the line between capital and natural resources, as new, useful knowledge has entered.

Notes and References

1   William J. Baumol, *Economic Dynamics* (The Macmillan Co., New York, 1951), chapter 2.

2   R.F. Harrod, "An Essay in Dynamic Theory," *Economic Journal* (Mar. 1939). See also *Towards a Dynamic Economics* (Macmillan, London, 1948).

3   Harrod, *Towards a Dynamic Economics*, p. 20.

4   See above, Part II, No. 1.

5   Raymond W. Goldsmith and Associates, *A Study of Saving in the United States* (Princeton University Press, Special Studies, 1956), vol. III, table W-1; and Goldsmith's estimates appearing in the *Thirty-Seventh Annual Report of the National Bureau of Economic Research* (New York, 1957).

6   The President's Materials Policy Commission, *Resources for Freedom* (Washington DC, June 1952). This Commission was appointed by President Dwight D. Eisenhower.

7   See Part II, No. 3 below, "Land in Economic Growth."

8   Ibid.

9   Of the major classes of farm inputs only the price of fertilizer did not rise relative to the price of the services of farm land.

10   See Theodore W. Schultz, "Investment in Man: An Economist's View," *Social Service Review*, 33 (June 1959), 109–17.

11   D. Gale Johnson, "A Study of Increases in Grain Yields in the United States, 1880–1958," University of Chicago (Oct. 1959).

12   See the studies of hybrid corn by Zvi Griliches, including "Research Costs and Social Returns: Hybrid Corn with Comparisons," *Journal of Political Economy*, 66 (Aug. 1958).

3

Land in Economic Growth *

The economic growth of a country consists of increases in national income. This income is viewed as a stream that has its origin in the productive services rendered by resources. These resources consist of stocks, and the augmentation of these stocks is an essential part of the process of economic growth. Land, however, is a resource that cannot be readily augmented. We think of the stock of land as being virtually fixed. What, then, are the implications of this characteristic of land for economic growth? The classical answer, going back to Smith and especially to Ricardo, has been that the supply price of the services of land must rise relative to that of other resources. There is a long-established doctrine on the increasing economic scarcity of land. The principal burden of this paper, however, will be to show that the classical view of the role of land in economic growth is far from satisfactory.

The proposition that the fraction of the national income attributed to land declines with economic growth is now widely accepted. But this proposition does not necessarily rule out land becoming scarcer in the sense that the supply price of the services of land rises relative to the prices of the services of other resources during economic growth. Our findings strongly indicate that in the United States the prices of the services of farmland have not been rising; on the contrary, they appear to have been declining relative to other relevant prices. These findings are perplexing in view of traditional thought.

1 Our Intellectual Heritage with Regard to Land

Economists have long been concerned about the role of land and the claims of rent as they have given thought to economic progress. The early English economists considered land and rent of major importance. Adam Smith devoted well over two-fifths of his famous Book I in *The Wealth*

* First published in Theodore W. Schultz, *The Economic Organization of Agriculture* (McGraw-Hill, New York, 1953).

of Nations to the "Rent of Land."[1] Ricardo's theory of value is keyed to land and no small part of his *Principles of Political Economy and Taxation* is given over to rent, taxes on rent, land tax, and to the doctrine of Smith and the opinions of Malthus on rent. Mill, the great codifier of classical thought, followed suit in his *Principles of Political Economy*; and Book IV concentrates on economic progress, with major attention to the interplay of population and rent. The cleansing winds of controversy continued to blow strong and much dead wood was eliminated. But land and rent were not among the casualties. They were only trimmed and bent by Marshall and continued to carry a heavy analytical load.

Since Marshall – more specifically since 1920, the date of the eighth edition of his *Principles of Economics* – most economists have turned to the problem of economic instability. Mass unemployment was put at the top of the agenda, and Keynesian thinking took shape. Agriculture was not spared, and my effort in *Agriculture in an Unstable Economy*[2] was a part of that period. Time and circumstance have ushered in a new period. Nations everywhere, poor and rich, want to produce a larger national product. Economic development is the fashion. The art of political economy and the skills of economists are in strong demand.

What has happened to land and rent in economic analysis? If one only scans what is being written, one would conclude that they have all but disappeared. A widely used textbook for principles of economics has little to say about land and rent.[3] Nor have agricultural economists and those in land economics altered the course that economic thinking has been taking with regard to land and rent.

We would do well to take stock of our ideas about land. What we need in doing so is a broad historical perspective of the changing role of land. It has dimensions that go far beyond economics. It is not a single lonely hut in the valley of ideas. Our ideas about land are old and encrusted with tradition. Poets and philosophers have had a hand, since time immemorial, in building this tradition. So have statesmen and patriots. What, then, is land? For some it is where people live, where they have their homes and their roots. Without land, there is no country, nor can there be sovereignty. Land, in the minds of some, is nature's endowment to man, our natural resources, ultimately a fixed stock, and, as such, a limitational factor in production. Land consists in the original and nonreproducible properties of nature. Land is what our precepts make it. Some have made it an object to be greatly prized, so much so that a deep-seated hunger for land is deemed to be only natural, and for man to be landless is contrary to natural law. Many traditions indeed are based on the glory of land.

There are, altogether, too many ideas about land for orderly thinking.

As a consequence, we find much confusion, doubt, and even indifference about the subject. There are conflicting doctrines about soils.[4] Major disagreements exist about the economic contributions, political importance, and social functions of land. Old precepts and policies are no longer adequate, and yet they persist because we have neither the will nor the knowledge to change them for the better.

2 Old Ideas Inconsistent with New Facts

Our doubts and confusion come from many new experiences. We are taught that the growth of cities will give rise to a vast pyramiding of urban land values. We observe, however, that the cores of many of our metropolitan areas have been decaying, and land values at these cores have been declining. The rental value of all land is supposed to rise, and the value of the stock of land increases relative to national wealth, as population grows and as the nation becomes a developed and settled country. Instead, we have seen the income from rent become ever smaller, in proportion to the income from other property, and we have seen land become a rapidly declining fraction of our national wealth. Agricultural land, for example, has fallen, since 1910, from one-fifth to one-twentieth of our stock of national wealth (table II.3.1).

One of the early predictions was that once the frontier was gone, farm foods would become dearer. This has not occurred. We have seen the population more than double since the turn of the century. We have data to show that the consumption of food per person has risen substantially. Yet there is more than enough food, and it is not more costly. Red meats, in large and increasing amounts, were once thought to be a luxury reserved for new countries with plenty of grassland, before sod had given way to stubble. We now see clearly that twenty years ago the US reversed the downward trend in per capita consumption of these meats. Consumption per capita has risen by fully a third since then, and already exceeds the very high figures back in 1909 when these data began.

We were taught that there is, among the desires of man, an age-old hunger for land inherent in poor and rich, in both the peasant and the aristocrat. Prof. B.H. Hibbard's lectures at the University of Wisconsin in the late 1920s were abundant in illustrations of this land hunger. First- and second-generation German farm families, for example, sacrificed consumption and gave up education for their children, in order to save and to acquire more farmland. Industrialists who had become rich proceeded to buy and build up impressive estates. But the mainstream of evidence has clearly been running the other way. We have become a

Table II.3.1 Land and Total National Wealth of the United States, 1896–1955, in Current Values*

	Total national wealth	Total land		Agricultural land	
	$ billion (1)	$ billion (2)	% of national wealth (3)	$ billion (4)	% of national wealth (5)
1896	69	26	38	12	17
1900	88	31	35	15	17
1910	152	55	36	30	20
1920	374	103	28	50	13
1930	410	104	25	32	8
1940	424	92	22	24	6
1945	571	128	22	45	8
1949	898	160	19	54	6
1955	1,344	224	17	69	5

* From Raymond W. Goldsmith, Dorothy B. Brady, and Horst Mendershausen, *A Study of Saving in the United States*, Vol. III. Special Studies (Princeton University Press, 1956), table W-1; and Goldsmith's data appearing in the *Thirty-Seventh Annual Report* of the National Bureau of Economic Research (New York, May, 1957).

highly mobile people. We readily pull up stakes, sell our homes to the highest bidder and move elsewhere. Even with the hedge that land affords against inflation, with the favorable income tax treatment of homeownership, and with the vast gains in real income per family, the observed demand for land does not support the land-hunger idea. It would be hard to prove that land is a preferred asset. On the contrary, many people who can afford land seem to prefer to hold other kinds of assets and be landless.

Even so, is there room enough to accommodate the upsurge in population? One needs only to recall the stern warning of that towering and distinguished professor, E.A. Ross, that there would be *Standing Room Only*.[5] But where is the evidence to support the opinion that we are more crowded today than we were three decades ago when this warning was issued? Simply to take our 1,904 million acres and divide by the number of people is hardly relevant. Surely, our farms have not become more crowded with people. The growth of suburban areas and the relative decline of the central parts of our cities point to less crowding than formerly. Through much more travel and the greater use of parks and of the public domain, more people enjoy more space than was formerly the case. We may be becoming more crowded, nevertheless; but relative to what?

Land, however, has still other dimensions. We are a people on wheels, and we move often and travel much. We demand ever more transportation, and require more room. Railways, nevertheless, are of declining importance. But our highways continue to be crowded despite the prodigious effort that this country has put forth to stay abreast of the growing demand. The supply of parking space in cities becomes increasingly scarce. As our airways are presently being managed, our airlanes have become tragically overcrowded. Then, too, room for missiles and other space inventions is no longer science fiction.

Another important dimension of land is its role in the disposal and dispersion of waste. Modern man has an extraordinary propensity to generate waste. This unbridled talent for pollution may ultimately be our undoing. We pollute the soil, the water, and the air about us. The smoke nuisance is an old story and long has served as the classic classroom example to show how social and private interests can diverge. From our travels by air, we have gained a new awareness of the gigantic volume of smoke and fumes and dirt put into the air by our cities, for one often sees the immense tail of polluted air drifting leeward fifty miles and more. Smog is yet another type of air pollution. Fall-out from radioactive materials is an added hazard. Nor is the end in sight. In the case of water, we have come to accept the pollution of many streams and rivers as of the nature of things and, thus, have come to look upon them as mere carriers of wastes. Less seems to be known about the pollution of soils, but this, too, must be a matter of concern.

We may not be far wrong if we infer that there is not enough room in the air, the water, and in the soil for all of the waste we are now generating. If this is true, this particular service of "land" faces a rising supply price, not in the market but in our hard-to-reckon social accounts. But this idea about a rising cost of disposal of waste is fairly new, and it should, therefore, not be confused with those that have been handed down to us.

3 From Ideas to Theory

Ideas are, as a rule, only surface manifestations of deeply held beliefs. Scratch an idea and you will find a theory. The particular ideas about land that we have been considering are not unrelated; in fact, they are all part and parcel of a particular theory of economic growth. This is our classical theory. It is a theory in which land plays a critical part. In this theory any production that requires an appreciable amount of land is subject to a fundamental disadvantage in contrast to production that requires little or no land. According to this theory, land always brings diminishing returns into play. The older economists placed much stress on several implications. They reasoned that, whereas agriculture is necessarily subject to diminishing returns, manufacturing could enjoy increasing returns. The rental values of land must rise as a consequence of economic progress, and the owners of land are, as a result, in a "preferred" wealth and income position.

This theory of economic growth with land and rent and population in the forefront continued to dominate much of our policy. Although it may be considered less compelling in the case of some rich countries, this theory is primary in regard to poor countries. The theory is at the back of most of the current precepts for economic growth, even in the cases in which land is omitted in the construction of new economic models. Growth requires industrialization because industry, so it is believed, can contribute more than agriculture. Agriculture, more likely than not, so runs the current belief, will retard economic growth, because agriculture is so heavily dependent upon land. Various and sundry reasons are given for this idea. Disguised unemployment in agriculture is thought to be widespread in poor countries. Economies of scale are abundant in industry. New techniques and improvements in skills go with industrialization. As one gets beneath the surface of these various ideas, however, one finds a false reliance on the retardation effects of land upon agricultural production.

It is important not to confuse this theory of economic growth with static theoretical analysis and the implications of the variable proportions of factors under static conditions. This theory is based on a particular view of economic history that may be represented as a kind of secular diminishing returns of labor and capital against land. The supply of land cannot, in this view, stay abreast of the supplies of labor and capital. The older English economists became deeply committed to this image of economic progress. The stern, rigorous logic of Ricardo made an indelible mark on the minds of economists and statesmen alike, as he made explicit the basic implications of the population spector of Malthus, the virtually fixed supply of land and the diminishing returns from land as more doses of labor and capital were applied.

Nor was Marshall, with all his gifted insights – as he untangled the short-from the long-run, quasi rents from pure rent, and as he pondered over the contributions of cheaper forms of transportation, the opening of new countries, and the effects of new knowledge useful in production –

able to erase from his mind the dictates of Ricardo's logic. As late as 1920, in the preface to the eighth edition of his *Principles of Economics*, he wrote:

> There have been stages in social history in which the special features of the income yielded by the ownership of land have dominated human relations: and perhaps they may again assert a pre-eminence. But in the present age, the opening out of new countries, aided by low transport charges on land and sea, has almost suspended the tendency to Diminishing Return, in that sense in which the term was used by Malthus and Ricardo, when the English labourers' weekly wages were often less than the price of half a bushel of good wheat. And yet, if the growth of population should continue for very long, even at a quarter of its present rate, the aggregate rental values of land for all its uses (assumed to be as free as now from restraint by public authority) may again exceed the aggregate of incomes derived from all other forms of material property; even though that may then embody twenty times as much labour as now.

The hand of history has been writing quite another record. Although population has continued its upward surge, rental values of land have not risen relative to "the aggregate incomes derived from all other forms of property." The stock of land has continued to decline relative to total national wealth. In Goldsmith's[6] estimates, land represented about 38 percent of the total national wealth in 1896 (this is his beginning date which is six years after the publication of the first edition of Marshall's *Principles*), and in 1920, land was down to 28 percent. By 1956, the stock of all land – agricultural, nonfarm residential and nonresidential, forests and public land represented only 17 percent of our total national wealth. Marshall took Henry George to task, in the first of a series of lectures on "Progress and Poverty," at Bristol, in 1883. He pointed out that, "Mr George seems to think that rent proper – that is, the rent of the inherent properties of the soil, including ground rent, etc. – is larger than it is. So it will be best to put as high an estimate on it as we can, say 75 millions."[7] He then proceeded to place the interest on capital at 250 millions – more than three times as large an estimate. And yet, in 1920, when rent was even less, relative to the income from all other forms of material property, he envisioned the prospects of the rental value of land exceeding that of all other forms of property.

The time has come for us to face up to the evidence in the record of our economic growth. A theory of economic progress of the general type that we have been reviewing will not do. It does not meet any of the tests of a satisfactory theory. If we use it to classify, broadly, economic variables and relationships among them, there is nothing useful that we can do with the classification. If we use it to generate testable hypotheses, we find that, one after the other, these hypotheses are not supported by the evidence. As a theory, it is found wanting. It should be discarded as an analytical tool in studying economic growth. This does not mean it is to be forgotten. It is, and will remain, a part of our intellectual heritage, one of the old mansions in the valley of ideas about land.

4   Supply Price of Services of Land

One may suspect from the preceding arguments that we are less than happy with a theory of economic growth that makes land the limitational factor of progress by vesting it with secular properties of diminishing returns and by authorizing the owners of land to be collectors of a special toll who keep raising their toll as more labor and capital appear. This makes the rental value of land an ever heavier burden that progress must carry. It ranks the potential contributions that the various sectors can make to a nation's economic growth and, in doing so, rates agriculture far below industry. Agriculture is put in the position of a poor second best because it is so heavily dependent upon land. Nevertheless, what I may like or dislike on these scores does not really matter analytically. What is important is the fact that this theory does not work.

5   Increases in National Product and Primary Product Prices

Many nations, rich and poor, old and new, are presently heavily committed to achieving large increases in national product. Among them are old nations who during an earlier period led the way in industrialization and who subsequently lost their forward momentum. Some of these have now shaken their lethargy and have proceeded once again to win for themselves large increases in national product. There are, also, some new nations which are achieving large increases. None, however, appears satisfied with the rate of growth. Meanwhile, ideas on how best to go about the business of winning increases in national product have taken on strong ideological overtones; an economist may hope, nevertheless, that these differences in beliefs and values will not bias his analysis of the role of land in economic growth.

A word or two may be in order on what is meant by economic growth. We have been using it to mean increases in national product. For the purpose at hand, how much the national product increases need not be specified. The increase may be at a low or a high annual rate; it may be at a rate that is less than, or more than, the growth in population; it may exceed, or fall below, the rate at which the physical stock of national wealth is being increased. Accordingly, our concept of economic growth does not rule out national situations in which we find diminishing returns against land as more capital and labor are employed.

On the demand side, it is now well established that the income elasticities of the demand for farm foods and for raw materials generally, are relatively low in countries with high personal incomes, as they are in most of Western Europe, Australia, New Zealand, Canada, and the United States. Because of these low income elasticities and because the prices of these products have not been rising relatively, we have come to expect farm products and raw materials, in general, to represent a declining part of the national product.

We thus have become accustomed to national developments of the kind set forth in the *Report by the President's Materials Policy Commission*.[8] The value of all raw materials[9] consumed in the United States fell from 22.6 to 12.5 percent of gross national product between 1904–13 and 1944–50; the respective figures for all agricultural materials fell from 15.5 to 8.2 percent between these two periods. If we had comparable estimates for other countries with high and increasing per capita incomes, we would be surprised if they did not show a similar decline for raw materials and for farm products.

In explaining a development of this type, we are not at a loss to account for the low and gradually declining income elasticities that our estimates reveal. These do not, however, imply that the demand has not been increasing; and they do not tell us why it is that the relative price of these raw materials has not risen. The demand has continued to increase because the income elasticities, although low, are nevertheless positive and because the growth in population with income to support it has not been small. Meanwhile, the supply schedule of raw materials has been increasing with apparent ease, a development for which there has been no satisfactory explanation.

Looking at quantity, we observe that the total consumption of agricultural materials, and also of all raw materials, virtually doubled between 1904–13 and 1944–50.[10] Looking at price, we observe that those products most dependent upon land in general have declined relative to other major sets of prices. In the United States, between 1947 and 1957, current prices of crude materials at wholesale did not rise at all; however, intermediate materials and components rose 30 percent. Similarly, within the consumer price index, the prices of services have risen more than any of the other major groups of items appearing in that index. If we take a longer view of the drift of prices, a similar pattern emerges. Of the three broad classes of products – primary, secondary, and tertiary – the prices of primary products have been declining relative to the prices of the products and services of the other two sectors. But it is the production of primary products that is most dependent upon land (natural resources). That of tertiary services is least so.

6   Changing Role of Farmland as an Input

I shall concentrate on farmland because the data on land used for mining, roads, residences and other nonfarm uses are less satisfactory for my purpose. Fortunately in this connection the principal use of land is for farming. I shall show that in the United States farmland has not become scarcer in comparison to other resources based on what has been happening to the relative prices of the services of farmland. However, before I examine these prices it may be helpful to look briefly at some aspects of acreage and the income attributed to farmland.

Yields and production have been increasing and the acreage used for crops has been declining. Between 1932 and 1957, for example, the acreage of crops harvested declined from 371 to 326 million acres, off 12 percent. Major crops such as corn, wheat, and cotton have come down much more; they accounted for 55 percent of all crops harvested in 1932 and for only 40 percent in 1957. The reduction in acreage in these three big crops alone, from their respective peaks since 1932, has freed 100 million acres, an area as large as all of the arable land of France, West Germany, United Kingdom, and Denmark combined.

As an input, farmland is being given, as we noted at the outset, an ever smaller weight because the income attributed to it has become a smaller fraction of the various income streams. Farmland for this purpose may be represented by farm real estate and thus it would include all farm structures that have been added or embedded in such land. This concept of farmland may be viewed as a gross measure of the physical capital represented by farmland. A net measure, the one we shall use in the comparisons that follow, is obtained by separating and subtracting farm capital structures. We observe that more and more farm capital structures have been added: In 1910–14 they accounted for about 15 percent of farm real estate and by 1948–49 they had risen to about 32 percent. Our estimate for 1955–57 is an extrapolation of this trend with farm capital structures representing 37 percent of farm real estate.[11]

The estimates below show that the income attributed to farmland, not including that rendered by farm capital structures, fell from 18 to 11 percent of the net income from agriculture, from 13 to 5.4 percent of gross farm income and from 3.2 to 0.6 of one percent of net national product, between 1910–14 and 1955–57.

Income attributed to farmland excluding structures	Net income from agriculture	Percentage (1) is of (2)	Gross farm income	Percentage (1) is of (4)	Net national product	Percentage (1) is of (6)
(1) $ billion per year	(2) $ billion per year	(3)	(4) $ billion per year	(5)	(6) $ billion per year	(7)
1910–11 0.99	5.53	17.9	7.6	13.0	31.0	3.2
1955–57 1.53	16.60	11.1	34.2	5.4	292.0	0.6

What has, however, escaped our attention is the decline in supply price of the services of farmland relative to that of other major classes of inputs, except that of fertilizer. Let me summarize a number of these changes in prices of both products and factors (inputs) as follows:

1   Between 1910–14 and 1956, the prices received by farmers for farm commodities declined about 15 percent relative to the index for consumer prices.

2   Prices of farm products at wholesale also declined about 15 percent relative to all commodities at wholesale between 1910 and 1956. Breaking the period at 1929, one finds that farm product prices rose slightly between 1910 and 1929 relative to all commodities at wholesale and, therefore, the relative decline between 1929 and 1956 was somewhat in excess of 15 percent.

3   Although there are no really satisfactory measures of the rental rates of land in terms of some standard input unit, there is little doubt that the price of the services of farmland has been falling relative to that of all inputs, taken together, used in farming. This is highly probable, if for no other reason than that the price of human effort per hour has been rising markedly relative to other groups of inputs and that human effort bulks large among these inputs.

4   A few figures on the changes in the prices of farm inputs, other than land, between 1910–14 and 1956 may be helpful. The index of prices received by farmers for their commodities gives us two bench marks; this index rose from *100* to *235*. If the price of a particular input rose more than this, between 1910–14 and 1956, it will be represented as having risen relative to farm product prices, and conversely, if the

Table II.3.2 Selected Farm Output and Input Prices for 1956 Compared with 1910–14 in the United States

	1910–14 (1)	1956 (2)	Index for 1956 (1910–14 = 100) (3)	Index for 1956 (index of prices received = 100) (4)
1 Prices received by farmers for farm[a] commodities			235	100
2 Farm wage rates[b]			543	231
3 Buildings and fencing materials[b]			374	159
4 Farm machinery[b]			329	140
5 Farm supplies[b]			279	119
6 Fertilizer[b]			150	64
7 Value of farm real estate per acre (in current dollars)[c]	$41.62	$88.63	213	91
8 Line 7 adjusted to remove farm structures (in current dollars)[d]	$35.38	$55.84	158	67
9 Total value farm real estate divided by quantity of land (in current dollars)[e]	$40.05	$97.80	244	104
10 Line 9 adjusted to remove farm structures (in current dollars)[f]	$34.04	$61.61	181	77
11 Returns on farm real estate capital divided by quantity of land (in millions of current dollars)[g]	$1,252	$2,800	224	95
12 Line 11 adjusted to remove farm structures (in millions of current dollars)[h]	$1,064	$1,764	166	71

[a] USDA, *Agricultural Outlook Charts, 1958* (Nov. 1957), table 19.
[b] USDA, *The Farm Cost Situation* (May, 1958).
[c] USDA, *The Farm Real Estate Market* (May, 1958), table 2.
[d] USDA, *The Farm Real Estate Market* (May, 1958), table 2, with the value of farm structures removed; these structures represented 15 per cent of the value of farm real estate in 1910–14 and 37 percent in 1956, extrapolating Raymond Goldsmith's estimates appearing in Vol. III of *A Study of Saring in the United States*, table W-1.
[e] USDA, *The Farm Real Estate Market* (May 1958).
[f] Adjusted down to remove farm structures as set forth in footnote "d."
[g] USDA, *The Farm Real Estate Market* (May, 1958), table 10.
[h] Farm structures removed as set forth in footnote "d."

input price rose less than did the index of farm product prices. Certain inputs, listed below, have risen more in price, between 1910–14 and 1956, than has the index of farm product prices; farm wage rates have more than doubled relative to the index of prices received by farmers; building and fencing materials have risen about three-fifths relatively; farm machinery, two-fifths; and farm supplies have gone up about one-fifth, relative to the prices received by farmers. On the other hand, the price of fertilizer has fallen about one-third relative to farm product prices.

5   The price of the services of farmland has undergone a change. We have inferred this change from three estimates, two based on farm real estate values and one on the returns to farm real estate excluding in each case the value, or the returns to farm structures. These estimates[13] indicate

(a)   the value of farm real estate per acre, with farm structures removed, has declined 33 percent relative to farm product prices, between 1910–14 and 1956 (line 8 of table II.3.2);

(b)   the value of farm real estate, divided by an index of the quantity of farmland, in which there was a slight rise in terms of acreage, and with farm structures removed, has declined 23 percent in the above context (line 10 of table 2);

(c)   the income attributable to farm real estate, divided by an index of the quantity of farmland, and with farm structures removed, declined 29 percent in relation to farm product prices, between 1910–14 and 1956 (line 12 of table 2).

7   Falling Supply Price of Farmland Service

Could it be possible that the supply price of the services of land has been falling? In the case of the services of farmlands in the United States, leaving farm structures aside, the evidence under review strongly supports this view. The supply price appears to have been falling relative to a weighted average of the prices of all the other inputs used in farming, or to the prices received by farmers for their commodities, or to consumer prices at retail.

How could this have occurred? Had there been a flood of imported farm products replacing domestic production, such a situation could have arisen, but this has not happened. On the contrary, US farm output rose 80 percent between 1910 and 1956. Had there been large new areas added to the supply of farmland, it could have happened; but this, too,

has not been the case. Is it not correct to say that the demand schedule for
farm products has shifted far to the right and that the supply schedule of
the services of farmland has shifted, if at all, only slightly in that direction? Under these circumstances, why has the supply price of the services
of farmland not been rising? Are we involved in some basic inconsistency
and, thus, giving credence to an economic record that is quite impossible
on purely economic grounds? The answer is no; we have developed
effective substitutes for farmland.

8   A Theory of Economic Growth and a Hypothesis

To find that the supply price of the services of land need not rise, but may
even fall, with economic growth, should fill our pores with optimism. It
should be an occasion to celebrate. But it confronts the economist with
a perplexing problem. How is he to explain the fact that the supply price
of the service of farmland does not necessarily rise as the production of
primary products increases?

Let us look again at what is happening. The rise in national product
exceeds the growth in population, and this makes possible a larger per
capita consumption. Although the income elasticities of the demand for
what consumers get from primary products is relatively low, the demand
for primary products keeps increasing mainly because of population
growth. The new families and new members of the labor force earn
income, and the income elasticities, although on the low side, are still
substantially positive. In the United States, the consumption of all raw
materials virtually doubled between 1904–13 and 1944–50.

Enough production has been forthcoming at a declining long-run
supply price despite the fact that products of primary industries such as
agriculture and forestry are more dependent upon land than are the
products and services of secondary and tertiary sectors. We then look to
see what changes have been taking place in inputs and in prices of the
inputs used in producing primary products. We observe, as one would
expect, that the quantity of land has been increasing only a little and,
therefore, much less than has the production of farm products. However,
as one *would not have predicted*, the supply price of the services of this
land has not been rising but declining.

These, then, are the stubborn economic facts to be faced. A theory of
economic growth is needed to cope with these facts. To keep sweeping
them under that old intellectual rug of (historical) diminishing returns of
capital and labor against land, is not only untidy, but is obviously no
solution to the problem at hand.

We already have made it clear that economic growth means increases in national income. Economists and others already owe much to Simon Kuznets for his pioneering and painstaking studies of national income. There are, however, all manner of problems in measuring the national product and the changes in its size. We cannot dwell on these problems here, except to post the warning that it is hard not to overestimate the rate at which the national product is increasing during the stages when much production is being transferred from the self-contained and household areas into the market sectors of the economy. Then, too, there is a basic pricing difficulty with the growth of cities and their higher costs of living gradually seeping into the price weights. Measures of the contribution that agriculture makes to the national product, especially in poor countries, are as a rule far from the mark, because of what is overlooked and because of the all-too-low prices that are used in weighting farm products. Nevertheless, measures of national product represent a major advance in economics, and the errors that plague us in these estimates are indeed small compared with what we are up against in the measures of resources.

9   Underspecification of Resources

The thesis of this study is that economists have not taken into account all of the resources used in production. There have been some new resources among those not considered and some of these have been effective substitutes for land.

Our theorizing rests on the following base: In relating resources to economic growth, we define resources as those components of production that render a service of value in production. From these productive services we obtain income. We place a value on resources because of these services, and, in the case of physical resources (nonhuman resources), we may capitalize and discount the future expected income flow. These resources are of the nature of stocks. Human resources may also be treated as a set of stocks, although under our institutions, with its regard to "free men," they are not capitalized. By adding to the stocks of resources, and by using them we increase the national product. Thus, increases in resources result in economic growth.

We augment the stocks of resources in many different ways. The stocks of some physical resources can be increased much more readily than can others. Land is, by definition, that class of physical resources the stock of which can be increased relatively little. This basic characteristic distinguishes it from other physical resources. When we measure the national stock of physical wealth, there emerges a dichotomy consisting of physical capital, which is reproducible, and of *land*, which essentially is not reproducible.

This is an old story: man can double, treble, and quadruple the number of offices and the number of workers who can be employed, say, in the Loop in Chicago, but he can increase the stock of land on which the Loop is situated only a very little. As economic growth proceeds, the United States can double its steel plants, but it cannot double the area of the Corn Belt. The USSR can build up industrial plants, but it cannot make a corn belt.

Another characteristic of modern economic growth is that wholly new resources are developed and these play an ever increasing role in production. In the main, these new resources are not taken into account in studying economic growth. In our great concern about the details of current production and the little malallocations of resources on farms, in business firms, and by government agencies, we fail to see the big and important allocative decisions that determine the rate at which the national product will increase. We are lost in the maze of details, unable to see that the decisions that really count are the allocations that are made to increase the stocks of particular resources, mainly the development of new resources. The criterion that we get from economics is clear enough in principle: We want to achieve for each and every resource an equalization of the expected real rates of return. We keep looking, however, at conventional physical capital in the area where it may be possible to obtain 5 or even 10 percent returns. We are, so it seems, not even aware of the fact that there are some resources, such as investments in new useful knowledge, producing a much higher return. The very resources that are among the best producers, we either leave entirely out of account in thinking about additions to our stocks of resources and economic growth, and in measuring our national wealth; or, at best, we bring them in through the back door on an *ad hoc* basis.

Resource and income estimates have been diverging. This is a basic finding that has come out of national income and related studies of labor and national wealth. The pioneering work of Kuznets and subsequent work by Abramovitz, Kendrick, and Goldsmith all tell essentially the same story.[14] Over the very long span of years, between 1869–78 and 1944–53, estimates by Abramovitz show that national income increased at an average rate of 3.5 percent per year, whereas resources, consisting of man-hours and the stocks of national wealth, appropriately weighted, increased at a rate of only 1.7 percent per year. Kendrick, in his study of *factor productivity*, found the gains in factor productivity averaged 1.1 percent per year between 1899 and 1919, and then rose at a rate twice as large for the period between 1919 and 1953. The implications of his findings are that the increases in income not imputed to increases in conventional resources ran much higher in the later years than they did earlier.

We offer still another set of figures for a much shorter and more recent period. The data, accordingly, are less fragmentary and also closer to the base year on which the weights of the income components and of the several resources depend. In the United States, between 1929 and 1953, national income fully doubled, rising by 106 percent. Resources, as an index number, rose 33 percent. The two components in resources, manhours and the stock of capital, rose 17 percent and 42 percent respectively. In short, the average rate of increase in income was 3 percent per year, whereas, the rate of increase in resources was only 1.2 percent per year. The increase in land and labor and reproducible capital, taken together, was only two-fifths as great as the rate at which the national income was increasing.

These estimates would seem to indicate that the connection between resources and income has become tenuous over time. The observed divergencies between resources and income may be taken as a measure of the extent to which economic growth falls outside the theory of resource allocation when it is restricted to conventional resources. This divergency may also be viewed as an indication of the underspecification of resources. To recognize some of the underlying issues, it may be helpful to consider the practical policy question: Given this pattern of economic growth in which the increases in national income exceed, by a wide margin, the rate at which man-hours and physical capital increase, what are the appropriate policies and programs to increase the *rate* of economic growth of a country?

Take the United States, for example, and suppose we, the people, wanted to increase the rate at which our national income is being increased, say, from $3^1/_2$ to $4^1/_2$ percent per year. What can economists say about the efficient means to achieve this goal?

This question may be examined in terms of the spectrum of public policy. One might conveniently group such policies into those that would emphasize the role of the public sector and those that would favor the enlargement of the private sector. The first of these might stress the allocation of more resources to government for housing, urban redevelopment, river basin development, land and water conservation, hospital and other health facilities, highways, parks, and other recreational facilities. But where is the evidence to create even a plausible case that the enlargement of the role of the public sector in these directions will increase the *rate* of economic growth substantially? Presumably, each of these measures may be supported for one or more purposes other than for what they may or may not contribute to economic growth. The only issue on which we are focusing is this question: Will these particular public measures, other things remaining the same, increase substantially the *rate* of economic growth? There is no evidence at hand, to my knowledge, that would make an affirmative answer plausible.

Let us comment now on those policies that would enlarge the role and, presumably, the effectiveness of the private sector. To do this, one might increase the incentives of families and firms to save and to invest. It would also entail a reduction of the misallocation of resources caused by existing government programs, for example, in transportation, and in the way some farm products are being priced. Here again, each of these policies may have merits on one or more scores independent of what they contribute to the *rate* of economic growth. But, is there any evidence that would make it plausible that these policies, of themselves, other things equal, would increase substantially the *rate* of economic growth? Again, one must say that no such evidence is at hand.

Suppose the stress were put more directly on two programs. First, adopt policies to reduce the "normal" rate of unemployment one to two percentage points. Instead of having an average of 5 percent of the labor force, as it is presently measured in the United States, unemployed during a business cycle, programs would be undertaken to reduce unemployment to $2^{1}/_{2}$ percent. Second, programs would be undertaken that would increase savings and investments, thus increasing the stock of conventional reproducible physical capital accordingly. The first program would be an appreciable gain. But once this had been achieved, increasing the average employment would no longer increase the *rate* of economic growth. The second program, the increase in the rate of capital accumulation, would and could add in a more continuing sense, but the effect would be small as one now reads the income and resource pattern of growth.

Policies and programs that deal only with the conventional resources, i.e., labor, land, and reproducible physical capital, are not enough, if there is another set of resources holding the key to ways and means of increasing substantially the *rate* of economic growth. Our contention is that this unspecified set of resources has provided us with effective substitutes for land.

10   Underspecification of Resources Hypothesis

We thus envision two sets of resources, one consisting of labor, land, and reproducible physical capital, as these are conventionally treated and measured, and the other consisting of various forms of human and physical capital not included in the conventional set. The second of these two sets is the one not accounted for in the way resources are being specified. Therefore, a hypothesis based on such underspecification would appear to be relevant.

The characteristics of the resources that fall in this second set are as follows: They pertain primarily to improvements in the *quality* of the conventional resources. They are, in the main, of the nature of *human capital* because they largely represent additions to the quality of the labor force and to the stock of useful knowledge. Our hypothesis would be strongly supported if the size of the stock of this second set of resources had been increasing in comparison to that of the conventional set and if the rate of return obtained from the productive services of these new resources had been relatively high.

There is a growing body of evidence to support this hypothesis. Any measure of labor as a resource based on man-hours worked disregards all changes in the quality of human effort. Conventional measures of the stock of physical capital discount most of the changes in the quality of such capital. Meanwhile, many things have been happening to improve the quality of human effort and of the stock of physical capital employed in productive activities.

Education may enhance the quality of human effort although we look upon education, and properly so, as serving cultural purposes, quite apart from the formation of human capital that contributes to economic growth. Let me draw upon a recent paper of mine.

> One may treat the resources used in education as a measure of the capital that is formed in this way. I have attempted to estimate the gross capital formation represented by the four high-school years (ninth, tenth, eleventh, and twelfth years of school) and also that represented by education beyond the twelfth year of school. Both private and public resources used for these purposes were taken into account. My tentative estimates for 1920 and 1956 along with estimates of conventional capital are shown . . . *below*. When we look upon this education as improving the quality of the human agent and treat it as capital formation, one finds that the gross figures have risen much more since 1920 than has the gross capital formation of the conventional types. Also, the totals for education are far from being unimportant, for they were already 7 percent as large as that of conventional capital in 1920 and have risen to 28 percent of that of conventional capital in 1956.
>
> My efforts to get at net capital formation are less complete because of difficulties in obtaining data. But what is clear is that capital embodied in humans has acquired over a period of time a somewhat longer average life, whereas capital in physical forms (nonhuman) has moved in the other direction; its average life has been declining. Accordingly, the increases in

net capital formation have been even more favorable to education relative to conventional capital than that shown above for gross capital formation.

There are, however, many unknowns. All that I want to say is: if the rate of return on this and other capital used to improve the quality of human agents is high, as it seems to be, then the increases in this form of capital may account for a substantial part of the unexplained economic growth considered . . . *above*.[15]

Estimated gross capital formation represented by the four high-school years and by education beyond the twelfth year of school in 1920 and 1956 in the United States

	Gross Capital Formation (Iu Billions of Dollars at Current Prices)	
	1920	*1956*
1 Highschool years	1.0	12.4
2 Education beyond the twelfth year of school	0.6	10.3
3 Total for this education (1 + 2)	1.6	22.7
4 Total conventional capital	23.1	80.6
Percent that gross capital formation in this education is of gross capital formation of conventional type (3 ÷ 4 × 100)	7	28

Are the rates of return obtained on these investments that improve the quality of resources, both human and nonhuman, large enough to give us the kinds of increases in national income that we have been observing? In the case of education, Zeman[16] careful and critical analysis of the effects of color, region, sex, age, city size, and education upon the wages and salaries of urban male workers, indicates that those male workers who had completed 12 years of school earned about 30 percent more than did those who had completed only 7–8 years of school for the ages 25–29, regardless of city size; for ages 30–34, between 34 and 43 percent more, depending on city size; and for ages 35–44, between 37 and 57 percent more, again depending on city size.

There are also many signs that the resources used to find and develop new techniques of production earn high rates of return. I became aware of this in the case of agriculture in analyzing production data for the United States when I prepared Chapter 7 of *The Economic Organization of Agriculture*. Griliches'[17] studies are the first that I know of in which a rigorous attempt is made to estimate the rate of return on all of the resources that have been used to "discover" and to develop a new technique of production. In the case of hybrid corn in the United States, using a 10 percent interest rate, the accumulated past research expenditures, 1910 through 1955, were 131 million dollars and the net accumulated past returns were 6.5 billion dollars. The total current annual returns, as of 1955, were 902 million dollars on an accumulated research investment of 131 million dollars, or about $7.00 earned annually on each dollar so invested. A 700 percent rate of return is the kind of capital to use in building for economic growth!

In table II.3.2 we show that the price of fertilizer has fallen a third in relation to the price of farm products between 1910–14 and 1956. Farmers have responded to this change in prices as one would expect. The price elasticity of the derived demand for fertilizer appears not to have changed over time according to Griliches.[18] For our purposes, what is more relevant are the developments that have reduced the relative price of fertilizer. These underlying factors have not as yet been investigated. There is, however, a strong persumption that here, too, new resources of the kind that fall into our second set, have played a major role in bringing down the relative price of fertilizer.

11 Summary and Conclusions

The role of land in economic growth is turning out to be very different from both the common-sense and the classical image of land. As a factor of production, the economic importance of land has been declining. It has become an ever smaller fraction of the total factor costs of producing the national product. This particular inference was the burden of my paper in the *Economic Journal* in 1951.[19] Goldsmith's study, which has appeared since then, provides evidence that in current values land has been a deelining fraction of the national wealth of the United States. All land represented 36 percent of our total national wealth in 1910 and only 17 percent in 1955. Agricultural land fell much more, for it declined from 20 to 5 percent of the stock of national wealth between 1910 and 1955. The income attributed to farmland has become a very small fraction of the income stream provided by the resources of the United States. In 1910–14 the productive services of farmland, excluding farm structures, represented 18 percent of the net income attributed to agricultural resources, whereas in 1955–57 this fraction had fallen to 11 percent. Taking the economy as a whole, this stream of income attributed to farmland was equal to 3.2 percent of the net national product in 1910–

14 and to only 0.6 of one percent in 1955–57. These estimates strongly support my earlier results.

We have set forth the framework of a theory of economic growth to cope not only with substitutes for land but also with other economic developments that alternative theories have not been able to manage. Our theory proposes two sets of resources, the conventional set (land, reproducible capital, and labor, as these are customarily conceived and measured) and a new set of resources. Our hypothesis assigns particular importance to this new set of resources, which consist of improvements in the quality of resources. In the main, they are in the nature of *human capital*. The stock of these new resources has been increasing relative to the conventional set and the return has been relatively high. This is a testable *hypothesis*. Although much remains to be done, the evidence examined supports this hypothesis.

Notes and References

1 In the Modern Library edition of Adam Smith's *The Wealth of Nations* (Random House, New York, 1938), the first ten chapters of Book I cover 140 pages and the eleventh and last chapter of this book, "Of the Rent of Land," takes up 115 pages.

2 Theodore W. Schultz, *Agriculture in an Unstable Economy* (McGraw Hill, New York, 1946).

3 In the index to the second edition of Paul A. Samuelson's *Economics, An Introductory Analysis* (McGraw Hill, New York, 1951), there is not a single reference to land.

4 See Charles E. Kellogg, "Conflicting Doctrines about Soils," *The Scientific Monthly*, 66 (June 1948).

5 Edward A. Ross, *Standing Room Only* (Century, New York and London, 1927).

6 Raymond W. Goldsmith, Dorothy S. Brady, and Horst Mendershausen, *A Study of Saving in the United States*, vol. iii (Princeton University Press, Princeton, NJ, 1956), table W-1, pp. 14–15.

7 George S. Stigler has reproduced these *Three Lectures by Alfred Marshall* from original newspaper accounts, mimeographed by Stigler, April 1958. Marshall is, of course, referring to Great Britain and the figures are in pounds, not in dollars.

8 *Resources for Freedom*, Washington DC (June 1952).

9 Gold is not included.

10 From the *Report by the President's Materials Policy Commission*: the consumption of all raw materials, except gold, rose from $9.9 to 18.6 billions, 1935–39 prices, and that for all agricultural materials rose from $6.8 to 12.2 billions between 1904–13 and 1944–50.

11 Raymond Goldsmith's estimates in *A Study of Saving*. Table W-1 places farm structures at $5.6 billion and agricultural land at $31.4 billion in prices current for 1910–14; these structures accordingly represented slightly over 15 percent of the total. For the last two years in his table, 1948 and 1949, the estimates average $25.9 billion for farm structures and $55 billion for agricultural land, thus these structures had risen to 32 percent of the total. In Theodore W. Schultz, *The Economic Organization of Agriculture* (McGraw Hill, New York, 1953), p. 137, I had ventured estimates that put farm buildings relative to all farm real estate at 18 percent in 1910 and at 33 percent in 1950.

12 Simon Kuznets' estimates of net national product averaged $31 billion per year for 1910–14. Since his estimates for 1955–57 are not at hand we have taken the US Department of Commerce estimates of $379 billion and adjusted them down by 23 percent to make them approximately comparable with Kuznets' earlier figures.

13 There are all manner of difficulties in gauging the pure rental rates of farmland. When one uses changes in the value of the stock of such land, one is up against changes in the relevant discount rates. For instance, 1910–14 and 1956 were similar in that they were periods when the prices of farmland were rising and expectations may have been influenced by the belief that the rise then under way had not spent itself and that capital gains were still to be realized from owning farmland. The two periods were dissimilar in that the market rates of interest were substantially higher in the 1910–14 period than they were in 1956. This decline in interest rates, other things equal, would have reduced substantially the relative decline of those two of our measures based on the stock of farm real estate. Any measure of the quantity of farmland bristles with difficulties; acres are a very poor approximation. When one uses the return to real estate capital, one is relying on a residual in the way the net income to farmland is imputed. We have put the value of farm structures at 15 percent of the total value of farm real estate in 1910–14 and at 37 percent in 1956; but it is hard to believe that farm structures, thus estimated, represent all of the new net capital formations that have been embedded in farmland, especially during the last 15 years.

14 For a more extended review of these estimates and others, see Theodore W. Schultz, "Reflections on Agricultural Production, Output and Supply," *Journal of Farm Economics*, 38 (Aug. 1956).

15 In Francis S. Chase and Harold A. Anderson (eds), *The High School in a New Era* (University of Chicago Press, Chicago, Ill., 1958). The italicized words *below* and *above* have been added.

16 Morton Zeman, "Quantitative Analysis of White and Non-White Income Differentials in the United States," unpublished PhD dissertation (University of Chicago, 1955), table 25.

17 Zvi Griliches, "Hybrid Corn: An Exploration in Economics of Technological Change," *Econometrica*, 25 (Oct. 1957), 501–22; and "Research Costs and Social Returns: Hybrid Corn and Related Innovations," *Journal of Political*

Economy, 46 (Oct. 1958), 419–31.

18 Zvi Griliches, "The Demand for Fertilizer: An Economic Interpretation of a Technical Change," *Journal of Farm Economics*, 40 (Aug. 1958).

19 The substance of this paper appears above in Part II, No. 1, "The Declining Economic Importance of Agricultural Land."

Part III

Augmenting Resources by Organized Research

Part III

Augmenting Resources by Organized Research

1

Value of Research and Endogenous Agricultural Technology*

The totem pole of economists has on it few agricultural symbols. The fundamentals of economics, including stability and welfare, do not require agriculture. It is convenient to think of agriculture in low income countries as a parking lot for poor people. In high income countries the political clout of farmers increases as their numbers dwindle, a paradox and a puzzle.

The fact that agriculture was my first specialization in economics would be a weak excuse for me to turn to it on this occasion. There are, however, good reasons for doing so.

A diagram of the demand and supply of an agricultural commodity still gives instructors much delight. The land rent concept of Ricardo is being maintained despite its fatal limitations. The belief that a landed aristocracy resists economic progress is true history, and it is also the case when a government has control of all land.

A few alert economists in their youth ventured into the agricultural labyrinth as did Zvi Griliches, Marc Nerlove, and Vernon Ruttan with notable success. Economic puzzles and untapped data beckoned them. Their pick and shovel were theory and measurement. Henry Schultz in his monumental study was a pioneer. On the food demand part the list is long: Girshick, Haavelmo, Stone, Houthakker, Waugh, Tobin, Burk, Theil, and others. Concerning supply, data are still waiting for a theory that can cope with increasing returns.

* This paper was presented at the Latin American Econometrics Society meeting, August 2–5, 1988, San Jose, Costa Rica. It was published as "Value of Research, Endogenous Technology and Economic Progress: The Case of Agriculture," in J.R. Vargas and F. Delgado, *Progreso Tecnico y Estructura Economica*, Proceedings of VIII Meetings of Latin America Econometric Society, San Jose, 1990.

1   Practical Policy Issues

Before entering upon our in-house esoteric views about technical changes and advances in knowledge, I prefer to start with some practical policy issues pertaining to the International Agricultural Research Centers. Latin America has a large stake in the research contributions of these Centers. My hope is that these policy issues will provide some information about the basic problems that are on my agenda.

I shall consider four such issues.

1.1   *Over-organization is an Ever Present Danger in Organized Agricultural Research*

The success of the International Agricultural Research Centers is not in doubt. It is the allocation of the available funds to the Centers and to the agricultural scientists who do the actual research that matters greatly. In my view there are efficiency losses. Those who control the purse strings cannot know what the involved agricultural scientist knows. Nor can they comprehend the vast heterogeneity of agriculture.

This issue also burdens agricultural research in the United States. A 1982 report on *Science for Agriculture* is in essence a plea for more centralized control of this research in the United States. The fatal flaw of that report is its failure to comprehend the specific nature of research that is oriented to the requirements of agriculture. Agricultural production is soil specific, crop and plant variety specific, animal production specific, market specific and inescapably location specific. Because of all these specific characteristics, agriculture is by its very nature exceedingly heterogeneous. Even within most states agriculture is far from homogeneous and so is the required research. To assume that a government agency in Washington, blessed with a highly competent administrator who has at his service the best peer review, the best computer technology, and a highly competent staff could determine the optimum agricultural research that is required in the United States is wishful thinking. Priorities and control of agricultural research all vested in Washington would be a disaster akin to the agricultural failure of Gosplan.

When an agricultural scientist is required to spend a lot of his valuable research time justifying his research, it is a signal that there is too much organization. Beware of organization that impairs the research creativity of the individual scientist.

1.2   Lack of Funds for Salaries

This unsolved problem is specific to that large part of the world where wages, salaries and per capita incomes are low.

Competent specialized agricultural scientists are a critical and essential input in this research. They are scarce. The demand for this class of specialized skills has increased greatly. At salaries that prevail in most low income countries, qualified individuals are not to be had. The reason is clear. For an individual to become a competent agricultural scientist entails a large investment in a specialized form of human capital. Where the salaries for such skills are low, the supply that is required to do successful research will not be forthcoming. Within the confines of International Agricultural Research Centers this salary issue is solvable by location. But the problem has not been solved in most of the national agricultural experiment stations and agricultural research laboratories throughout the low income parts of the world.

I would be selling economics short if I did not point out that *research entrepreneurship* is also a critical factor in the performance of organized agricultural research.

1.3   *Failure To Reckon the Consumer Surplus Derived from Research*

We should keep on asking "Who benefits from agricultural research?" Private firms do research for profits. It is becoming increasingly evident, as agricultural modernization proceeds throughout the world, that a very large share of agricultural research is being done by public agencies.

Appeals to farmers for public financial support are being thwarted by unsolved surplus problems in North America and Western Europe. Moreover, the concerned governments are finding surpluses ever more costly. In most low income countries, farmers have relatively little political influence whether it be for or against public funds for agricultural research.

There are several important unsettled empirical issues: Under what conditions and for how long a period do farmers benefit from particular research contributions? Some farmers acquire a short term "producer surplus" while other farmers producing the same product suffer a producer loss; the issue is how come? How long does it take competition to transfer and transform the benefits from agricultural research into consumer surpluses?

For a Kellogg Foundation Conference on *A Look to the Future*, held three decades ago, I presented evidence that appropriations by states revealed strong urban support for agricultural research. Land grant institutions with large amounts of funds to support agricultural research of high quality are to be found in particular urban states.

The urban and labor political influence is also evident in the US federal *Food and Agriculture* appropriation process which includes federal funds for agricultural research. Here, too, there is evidence that funds for agricultural research are not viewed by urban people as harmful. On the contrary, they appear to perceive that they benefit.

The marked decline in the costs if producing wheat and corn is well documented. Agricultural research accounts for much of it. So too has the cost of many other agricultural commodities declined, despite the strong secular increases in the value of human time devoted to farming in high income countries.

The reduction in the cost of food is an important factor accounting for the decline in the part of the consumers' income that is spent on food. Since poor families benefit relatively more from the decline in costs of food than families who are not so poor, there is an income effect; namely, what occurs is some reduction in the inequality in the distribution of real income.

It is high time that we see clearly the economic importance of the consumer surplus that results from successful agricultural research. The fact that agriculture is a declining sector of an economy does not imply that future consumer surpluses will not be forthcoming.

The case for public financial support for agricultural research should be strongly linked to the achievable consumer surplus.

1.4   *Will Agricultural Research Grind to a Halt during the next 20–25 years for Lack of Advances in the Sciences?*

In the event of an extended period during which no advances in the sciences were realized, investment in agricultural scientists and in the other inputs that are used in producing useful agricultural knowledge would manifest strong diminishing returns.

The theoretical elaborations of economic models win high marks for subtlety, refinement, elegance, and for their analytical properties, but they do not tell us what is likely to happen in the sciences during the rest of this century. Judgements on what is happening and what is likely, taking a long view, involve issues and reasoned arguments that call for long conversations. My argument would be that the rate of increase in the advances in the sciences has not as yet peaked. As feedstock for agricultural research, there will be more than enough to warrant much more agricultural research.

All things considered, the implication of my arguments is that the long view of the economic value of agricultural research is such that it calls for a continuation of large increases in agricultural research to serve agricultural modernization and, in so doing, *create consumer surpluses.*

2   Economics of Agricultural Research

Growth theory has lost its analytical charm. In explaining growth it has been found wanting. Its treatment of technological advances as an exogenous variable takes most of the economics out of growth. At Chicago, by the early 1950s, we were puzzled to see that the increases in agricultural outputs were more and more over time exceeding the increases in inputs. This became for us a basic unsolved economic problem. One approach was to find the source of each observable technological advance and determine its cost and returns with the view of transforming it into an endogenous variable. Using this approach, Zvi Griliches made a classic contribution in his "Hybrid Corn: An Exploration in the Economics of Technological Change."[1] Another approach that has been rewarding is to capture the increases in skills and useful knowledge as components of human capital.

Compared to the long history of agriculture, that of organized agricultural research is short. The high rate of growth of agricultural research during recent decades tells us a good deal about the perceived value of this research. We are told that the population of the world has doubled since 1950, it having passed the five billion statistic. World food production has more than doubled since 1950, unevenly among nation-states to be sure. A clue to the demand for this research is in the more than sevenfold increase in real expenditures worldwide on agricultural research since 1950.

Malthusian population experts, vintage 1950, who were wedded to Ricardian land for food, were loud in their proclamations that there would soon be a world food crisis. In fact a remarkable increase in agricultural food production has been achieved by many low income countries. This achievement would not have been possible had there been no agricultural research.

3   Bare Bones of this Research

Public supported agricultural research has become institutionalized. It is done in experiment stations, in research laboratories and at centers that have acquired an international dimension. It requires specialized scientists. It also requires research entrepreneurs. These abilities are scarce and they account for most of the costs. The fact that agricultural research is institutionalized does not make it immune to changes that occur in the economic domain in which the research is situated. Research costs and the resulting research returns, covering recent decades, have received a good deal of analytical attention by economists.

However, the economics of agricultural research was still in its infancy as recently as 1950. Much has been learned since then. The costs of organized agricultural research, staffed with qualified scientists, are well documented in the case of public expenditures. But all too little is known about the international labor markets with particular reference to the factors that determine the salaries that are paid to highly competent scientists. Also lacking is a body of useful information pertaining to international markets for modern scientific equipment. The nature and the significance of the imbalances between basic and applied research are for the most part still unknown although there is much talk about such imbalances. The economic value of the research output is more difficult to ascertain than the public expenditures on it. How much to invest in this activity is a basic question.

4   An Investment Approach

Agriculture is too mundane to even entertain the thought that it is done to promote national prestige. It is done to enhance the production possibilities of agriculture. Treating it as an investment requires a long view, especially so since valuable research results are rarely to be had like picking fruit in the wild. Hybrid corn is one of the great research success stories. It took over twenty years of public research expenditures to develop a high yielding variety of hybrid corn that was deemed to be ready to be used by farmers. The pay-off began after 1933. The social rate of return has been and continues to be very high, many times as high as the prevailing "normal" rates of return.

To grasp the nature and economics of the research process, a short view will not do. Confined to a short view, one becomes beholden to a highly inelastic supply of agricultural products, whereas a long retrospect assessment reveals that the supply has been made more elastic over time. Then, too, Ricardian agricultural land loses its economic stranglehold as research discovers new ways of augmenting the capacity of land, ways that are in effect substitutes for land. The result is that the supply of such land does not remain fixed in quantity, in quality, or by location. One sees that the productivity of land is in large measure man-made.

5   Changes in Demand

What drives the demand for agricultural research? For that which is done by profit-making firms, it is profitability. But profits from this specific activity are not reported. What we know is that such research expenditures by industries that produce farm inputs to supply modernized agriculture are large. For the US for 1979 we have an estimate from Vernon Ruttan that it was between $814 and $909 million of expenditures on firm input research and, in addition, $270 million were expended on farm machinery and equipment including that for farm produce transport. The total purchases by US farmers of fertilizer and other plant nutrients, pesticides, various other chemical and biological agents, fuels, petroleum products, equipment and machinery, and other intermediate produce expenses totalled $71 billion in 1979, of which $19 billion were manufactured inputs.

An important new study by Wallace E. Huffman and Robert E. Evenson, which is close to completion, "The Development of US Agricultural Research and Education: An Economic Perspective."[2] presents estimates of private agricultural research expenditures that are fully twice as large as Ruttan's. But it appears that the part of the Huffman-Evenson estimate that contributes to agricultural production is about the same as the Ruttan estimate.

The economic argument for public sector agricultural research rests on a strong body of evidence which shows that social benefits from this activity are large, that the value of these benefits indicates a high rate of return on the resources committed to this activity, and that the public sector research agency should not be in the business of capturing whatever benefits for itself. Specifically, public research institutions should not seek to capture the resulting consumer surpluses.

As already noted, agriculture is a declining sector of an economy; that fact does not imply that future consumer surpluses from successful agricultural research will not be forthcoming.

6   Changes in Supply

Agricultural research is a specialized activity that produces forms of useful knowledge. Successful agricultural research increases the stock of such knowledge. To the extent to which this stock is enhanced, the supply increases.

The economics of producing this knowledge takes us into the domain of human capital. It takes human capital to produce human capital. Over time human capital has become increasingly more specialized. We need to reckon the implications of the fact that scientists are highly specialized human capital and that it takes scientists to produce scientists. Moreover, specialization abounds. There are two critical limitational factors. They are (1) the supply of competent specialized agricultural scientists – plant breeders have held the spotlight during the recent past, and (2) the advances in the sciences.

The availability of land for experimental plots is a very minor factor. Additional experiment stations and research laboratories can be had in a few years provided there are funds to pay for construction. The required modern scientific equipment is somewhat harder to come by. Clearly the critical input consists of competent specialized agricultural scientists. They are scarce. At salaries that prevail in most low income countries, all too few are to be had.

While there are no quick fixes, all of the inputs that are required to increase the supply can be augmented. We need to keep in mind that research results that prove to be valuable may take a couple of decades to achieve, as was the case with hybrid corn.

A potential limitational factor is in what happens in advances in the sciences. In the event of an extended period during which no advances in the sciences were realized, investment in agricultural scientists and in the other inputs that are used in producing useful agricultural research would manifest strong diminishing returns.

To repeat my earlier argument which is the long view, the economic value of agricultural research is such that it calls for a continuation of large increases in agricultural research to serve agricultural modernization and, in doing so, create consumer surpluses.

7   Endogenous Increases in Productivity

The origins of increases in economic productivity are basic in identifying the sources of growth. They originate either from outside or from inside the economy. Schumpeter used this dichotomy effectively in his theory of economic development. It is applicable to various other sources of economic changes in addition to the contributions of innovators.

In searching for the origins of the components of economic productivity one finds that virtually all of these components are man-made and that they originate from inside the economy. Neither the sun, the earth, the winds nor El Niño is in the business of increasing our economic productivity.

It stands repeating. Currently existing growth theory does not give us an economic explanation of the primary real sources of the increases in economic productivity. Technological advances are treated as if they originated from outside the economy. Increases in human capital, including entrepreneurial ability of economic agents, are treated in the same manner. The implied flaw of the analytics of existing growth theory is fatal when it comes to economic explanations of increases in productivity.

The high yielding wheat that India introduced in the mid-sixties was created by highly competent specialized plant breeders at CIMMYT (International Maize and Wheat Improvement Center) in Mexico. India's wheat production skyrocketed from 11 to 46 million tons by 1984. While we await a theory of economic productivity to rationalize this extraordinary event, we should try to explain, in the case of the Punjab, why the rates of return to land, fertilizer, equipment, labor, and to the entrepreneurship of farmers all exceed normal rates for a period of years?

The spark that ignited the Green Revolution in wheat in India had its origin in CIMMYT. It entailed years of costly research. Clearly, CIMMYT's high-yielding wheat originated from inside of the international economy. It was man-made and so were each of the complementary inputs that were required to produce the high wheat yields in India.

The economics of the dramatic increases in corn yields in the United States is well known to economists who know agriculture. Zvi Griliches' pioneer studies[3] traced the annual expenditures on hybrid corn research back to 1910. The rates of return on these research expenditures proved to be far higher than normal rates of return.

Ponder the economic meaning of the following evidence. The first application of hybrid corn began in the early 1930s. For the purpose at hand, 1933 is pre-hybrid corn. In 1933, the acreage planted to corn in the United States was 109.8 million. By 1987 only 76.7 million acres were in corn, or 33 million acres less than in 1933. Believe it or not, on 33 million fewer acres the 1987 production was well over three times that of 1933-8.25 and 2.40 billion bushels respectively.

The economic story of hybrid corn including all of the complementary inputs, the value of the output from the cropland released from corn, the reductions in the costs of feed to producing livestock products, and the resulting consumer surpluses, occur inside the economy. They are basic economic stuff in explaining increases in economic productivity.

Here we have strong clues as to why farmland rents decline as a fraction of national income and the economic underpinning of landlords declines socially and politically.

8   Summing Up

Try not to become fascinated by steady-state economics.

Hold fast to the belief that economics can explain increases in economic productivity.

Heed the evidence for clues on what to look for.

Observe that economic growth events and economic disequilibria are born twins.

The economics of restoring equilibrium is still in its infancy. The ability to deal with disequilibria is a part of it. So are the recent studies of the effects of schooling, health, age, and experience of farmers in their responses to new profitable opportunities.

The search for increasing returns got lost in the growth theory hubbub! Increasing returns insights of Allyn Young and also of Marshall and Smith are being rediscovered. Trade theory has become richer and so have other specialized parts of economics.

Schumpeter's innovator is one of the human agents who increases economic productivity. What this innovator does is from inside the economy. But does he create a disequilibrium or does he see that a disequilibrium exists and then proceed to profit from restoring equilibrium?

Investment in human capital matters greatly. The internal private effects of human capital are well documented. The external social effects of human capital, following Robert Lucas, are especially important in understanding the process of growth. The density of human capital hypothesis has rich implications.

The economics of private and public investment in Research and Development is robust. Its findings are being under-utilized in explaining the economics of increases in production, income and welfare.

I have featured investment in agricultural research. World-wide it has grown like Topsy. High rates of return on this set of investments have propelled its expansion. There is some over-organization; salaries of highly-qualified agricultural scientists are too low in low income countries; the case for funding agricultural research should be based on its contributions to consumer surpluses. A long view supports continuing increases in *agricultural research*.

Notes and References

1 Zvi Griliches, "Hybrid Corn: An Exploration in the Economics of Techno-logical Change," *Econometrica*, 25(4) (Oct. 1957), 501–22.
2 Wallace E. Huffman and Robert E. Evenson, "The Development of US Agricultural Research and Education: An Economic Perspective."
3 Griliches, "Hybrid Corn: An Exploration." See also his "Research Costs and Social Returns: Hybrid Corn and Related Innovations," *Journal of Political Economy* (Oct. 1958), 419–31; "Hybrid Corn and the Economics of Innova-tion," *Science* (July 29, 1960), 275–80.

2

Politics and Economics of Research *

We pay homage to Alfred Nobel, who made Stockholm the Mecca for scientists. The annual pilgrimage is now made mainly by Americans. It was not so at the beginning. Before the first World War, among the prize-winning physicists, chemists, and those in physiology and medicine, only three out of 51 were from the United States; during the two decades beginning in 1944 half, and more recently, from 1975 to 1979, virtually two thirds, came from the United States. Now it is being said that science in the United States has reached its peak and that its productivity may decline. It could be that Western Europe and Japan are coming up.

The notion that science may have peaked intrigues me. Is there some sort of a long cycle, or is it that our "big sciences" are showing diminishing returns? Such a cycle and declining returns have a familiar economic ring. But science and economics are not supposed to mix because economics is too close to the foibles of man. And in politics no one is beholden to peer reviews. I am acutely aware of the risk I take in dealing with my topic. There is much truth in Frank Knight's famous "law of talk", "The more intelligent people are, the more certain they are to disagree on matters of social principle and policy, and the more acute will be the disagreement." I also know that economists do not do what needs to be done to make friends. Scientists do not take kindly to the idea of costs and benefits. Governments are ever wary of being friendly with academic economists. The only real friends that economists have are impersonal, adverse events: inflation, unemployment, and hard times.

Since I shall criticize American institutions and public policies, I need to quell your anxiety. In my thinking, whether the advances in science are made for their own sake or for their ultimate usefulness, these two achievements are joint products. You always get both wool and mutton

* First published as "The Productivity of Research: The Politics and Economics of Research," in *Minerva*, xviii, No. 3 (Winter 1980), 644–51.

in producing sheep. Although one part may be emphasized, they are nevertheless joint. My approach in evaluating scientific research rests on two basic propositions. The first is that advances in knowledge augment the productive capacity of the economy and improve the welfare of people. Science obviously contributes to our stock of knowledge. Edward Shils dealt thoughtfully with these issues in his essay, "Faith, Utility, and the Legitimacy of Science".[1] The second is that most of the contributions of science have the attributes of a public good, which means that there is not a sufficient incentive for business enterprises to invest in the research of that part of science which generates public goods over time. Proceeding on these two propositions, we face two different issues, namely, the problem of ascertaining the value of the public goods which we obtain from the advances in science and the organizational problem of the public sector that provides most of the funds for science research. I shall argue that it is probably true that the value of the contributions of science exceeds in general the normal rates of return on investments. Academic scientists acquire more personal satisfactions from their work than do the scientists in government and in business research establishments, and for that reason they accept a somewhat lower salary. I shall also argue that the organization of the public sector in its financing of scientific research is beset with many distortions and that they have been increasing over time.

In addition to these two propositions, there are several side issues on which we should ponder. In the United States, large national research laboratories, accelerators, telescopes, oceanographic ships, instrumentation for control and precision and for computation entail large investments in plant and equipment. We have here many large, lumpy investments, which are, so it appears, indivisible. Is it possible to tailor modern scientific research to fit what small countries can do? Compared with that of any other non-communist country, the size of the scientific research establishment of the United States corresponds to that of General Motors in its domain. In expenditures and number of scientists, the Soviet Union and the United States are both very large. But there is a difference: the Soviet Union is more inefficient than the United States.

1 Research in Countries with Low Income

My concern here pertains to the lack of scientific research in most of the world's countries with low income. My assessment can be stated briefly.

Very few countries with low income have the scientific talent and funds to launch and maintain scientific research. In 1972 there were 129 such countries, each with a population of less than 50 million; 49 of them had less than a million people.[2] They are both poor and small. The prospects are also dim that most of the petroleum exporters, rich as they are currently, will soon become capable of developing effective institutions for scientific research. Among the large countries with low income Brazil, India and Mexico are exceptions. Agricultural research aside, at least four-fifths of the world's countries are not about to do any appreciable amount of basic scientific research. They simply cannot afford to do it. General Motors would be a monstrosity in Sri Lanka, or in Tanzania or in Guatemala. How divisible is modern scientific research?

We have become enamoured of large research institutes and large programs. They are difficult to administer and they are subject to what is known in economics as diminishing returns to scale. Some of them are "wholesalers" of funds for research which are allocated under regulations to guarantee accountability; these regulations are burdens on small enterprises. Creativity in research, however, is predominantly the hallmark of individual scientists whose research enterprises are small. It is my contention that many research establishments have become too large; they are relatively inefficient compared to small enterprises which best serve individual scientists. The National Institutes of Health in the United States are exceedingly large. In federal budget obligations they received a third of all federal funds for basic research in 1979. There are also large research programs in other parts of the sciences supported mainly by the National Science Foundation. I realize that the scientists who have acquired a vested interest in the National Institutes of Health or in the National Science Foundation are not inclined to protest and thereby place their acquired vested interest in jeopardy. But what is lost sight of in this over-organization of research is that small basic research enterprises are mainly in universities. Although it is difficult to get at the reasons which have favoured federal support for these large research establishments, the shift over time concentrating the federal funds in them has been a consequence of governmental decisions and in this important sense it has been the result of the politics of research.

The proposed budget for 1981 makes the United States Department of Defense the fastest growing "buyer" of basic research – up by 12 percent in real dollars.[3] Becoming more dependent on funds supplied by the Department of Defense does not imply happy days for academic scientists. Surely more federal funds allocated in this manner will not reduce the distortions in the support of basic research.

The promulgation of social reforms by the federal government within universities in the United States, with the government holding research funds as hostage in enforcing these reforms, is more than a side issue. I am mindful that all of the American Nobel laureates in science in 1979 are academics. Who determines what scientific research is to be done and who allocates the research funds to get it done are in my view major issues inherent in the politics of research.

2   Economics and Science

Science is a part of our stock of knowledge and scientific research adds to that stock. As knowledge, science influences our cultural and social behaviour. Some of it, usually with a considerable lag, alters our technology. Scientists privately also derive satisfaction from their creative work. As knowledge, science is a special form of capital which is strictly man-made. It is not a natural resource, nor is its acquisition and maintenance free. The scientific part of knowledge takes one of two forms. It becomes embodied in material forms – in scientific literature and, for instance, in computers or in hybrid corn. The rest of it is embodied in human beings, and it consists of human capital.

The process of adding to the scientific part of knowledge entails investment by using scarce resources to acquire future returns and satisfactions. It is an investment in a special form of capital. Scientific research is a dynamic process and it is subject to risk and uncertainty, as every scientist knows from his endeavors in probing the unknown or that which is only partially known. The result to be had from pursuing a scientific hypothesis is never wholly predictable; if it were it would not be research.

Advances in knowledge are important in augmenting our productive resources and improving the standard of living. Here I can cite agricultural research. By the early 1930s, plant geneticists had created hybrid corn after 23 years of research.[4] Many other contributions of research pertaining to corn followed in its wake. Complementary factors were added. By 1979 the acreage devoted to corn was 33 million acres less than it was in the early 1930s; total production of corn, however, was three times as large. In addition to the yield-effect, a remarkable substitute for cropland had been developed. Alfred Marshall put it succinctly when in 1890 he advanced the proposition that "knowledge is the most powerful engine of production."

I do not want to imply that all increases in the stock of knowledge are a consequence of the advances in scientific research. Private entrepreneurs and individuals on their own are inventive. Education is pervasive on this score and so are improvements in health, because a longer life-span adds years to the usefulness of the knowledge that students acquire in their youth. It is noteworthy that in many countries with low income the extension of the life-span adds years to the usefulness of the knowledge that students acquire in their youth. It is also noteworthy that in many countries with low income the life-span has increased more than 50 percent since the Second World War.

But when full allowance is made for the contributions from these various sources of knowledge, advances in science have become a major source of additional knowledge. For me it is appalling that the measurement of the value of these advances in science is so grossly neglected. I contend that scientists are largely to blame. They appear to believe that its value is self-evident, which it is not. Anyone who is not a scientist who attempts to determine the value of science is deemed to be an intruder. Economists are viewed as intruders and they are suspect. The belief is that they would surely debase science. While it is true that it is a difficult analytical task to determine the value of science, scientists are seldom timid in their own domain on this score and they are often proud of being impractical. But they shy away from the economics of research.

The economics of agricultural research has long been high on the agenda at the University of Chicago.[5] Extensions of theory and the acquisition of data require much effort. The first studies concentrated on the United States and then on Mexico, and then former students have taken up agricultural research in India and for particular crops in the Argentine and Brazil. The American studies, which began with corn and poultry, were extended to encompass all agricultural research. The findings are strong on the critical economic issue: namely, that the rates of return, taking into account the failures along with the successes, have exceeded the normal rates of return to investment in the economy.

The anti-science movement is not interested in reliable measurements of the value of science, but it tends to politicize science. Despite the lack of firm evidence on this value, from my long involvement in the economics of agricultural research and of the importance of basic research in this connection, I am inclined to believe that the economic and social returns to our total investment in scientific research may be relatively high. But I have some serious doubts about the efficiency of parts of the total range of scientific activity. We are spending, for instance, all too much on cancer research and in doing so do not spend enough on other worthwhile opportunities in basic research. There must be specific classes of research where diminishing returns indicate that it is no longer worthwhile. It will not do to continue to be silent on this issue. All too many parts of science are over-organized, which adds ever more to the time that scientists must spend on meeting the regulations imposed on scientific research.

Who pays for basic research? Taking basic research to be what gets classified as such, about which I am uneasy, the American taxpayer pays most of the bill. For 1968, which is the most recent year for which figures are complete,[6] 69.3 percent of the total expenditure on basic research was paid by the federal government, 14.8 percent by industry, 9.9 percent by universities, and 6 percent by various other non-profit-making institutions. Who actually did this research? The answer is that universities and their affiliates did 59.1 percent of it, federal agencies 16.1 percent, industry 16.1 percent and other non-profit-making institutions 8.7 percent. Since money matters, the federal government has most of the influence. It presumably has complete power over the 16.1 percent. Of this research which is done by federal agencies. For the basic research that is done by industry, industry puts up three dollars for every dollar allocated to it by government. For that done by the various non-profit-making institutions other than universities, the government provides a 60 percent share. The universities, which do virtually three fifths of the basic research, are in the weakest bargaining position. Their financial contribution consists of only one dollar of their "own" against four dollars of federal funds. In this sense they control a minor share of their basic research enterprises. Herein lies the rub.

3   Politics and Science

That there is a public interest in basic research is not in doubt. Nor is there any room for doubt that scientists have a private, professional interest in this research. It is also clear that the critical link is in the relationship between government and academic scientists, i.e., the universities. But all this does not tell us who should pay for basic science and under what conditions. The economics of who should pay is fairly simple for the part that is done by industry on its own account for profit. For the rest we are in the domain of social benefits, which must be paid for by private patrons who are willing to support this public interest and by public funds. What is treated all too lightly, however, is that decisions have to be made on what research and how much of each kind is most worthwhile doing, relative to its costs. It is not sufficient, in my view, to leave all aspects of these decisions to Congress and to the executive branch of the federal government. The need is great for public information on the value of research in negotiating with the electorate for the autonomy of our universities.

The United States federal government's support for research is not organized to support academic research directly. The Department of Energy is flooded with funds for applied or basic research. The proposed large increase in the budget for 1981 for basic research to be administered by the Department of Defense is an indirect way of supporting academic research. Nor is the large indirect support of this research through the National Aeronautics and Space Administration much better. A third of the total federal funds for basic research is funnelled through the National Institutes of Health.

I am much concerned about the distortions of research that are introduced by the influence of patrons, both federal and private, and the resulting decline in traditional academic research where immediate utility is not obvious. Of the federal basic research budget that supports research in the social sciences, about 60 percent was conducted in universities in 1973 but by 1978 it had decreased to 47 percent. The adverse cumulative effect on academic economists is dramatic.[7]

There is some comfort in knowing that our distortions of research are not what they must be in the Soviet Union. Nolting and Feshback compare the Soviet Union and the United States.[8] The number of scientists with advanced degrees in the physical and life sciences is slightly higher in the Soviet Union; in physics and astronomy they are about the same. The United States has more in chemistry and in biology. The Soviet Union has more in agriculture.[9] Except for agriculture, I leave it to you to venture a judgement on how much more inefficient the Soviet Union is compared to the United States.

Soviet scientists in agriculture who have advanced degrees, according to Nolting and Feshback, exceed those in American agriculture by at least 70 percent. Boyce and Evenson show a larger difference. Agricultural scientific publications "screened for quality" by three international abstracting journals show that the average annual publications by Soviet scientists for the period 1969–73 was 2,690; for the United States the comparable number was 4,700.[10] In 1929 I spent some time at the then well-known wheat research experiment station at Rostow on the Don. At that time, which was before the collectivisation of agriculture, that experimental station was doing work comparable in quality to that in the United States. In 1960, when I was a guest of the Soviet Academy of Sciences the quality of agricultural research was very poor. Except in the case of sunflowers, I know of no agricultural productivity advances in the Soviet Union that have come from Soviet research. Agricultural research is seriously impaired by Soviet biological doctrine.

4   Conclusions

Soviet doctrine and centralized control are not the pillars for supporting scientific research. The government of the United States also has a large measure of monopolistic control over basic research. It is wishful thinking to believe that it will fade away. Professor John T. Wilson began his analysis of the situation in the United States with the title "Grand Designs: Grand Illusions" and finds that "whether one is inclined to view the relationships between the federal government and higher education . . . as something which is currently just short of disastrous . . .", these relationships have been greatly impaired from what they were during the 1950s and 1960s.[11] His perception and criticism are grounded in his experiences as an administrator of the National Science Foundation and as the recent past president of the University of Chicago.

Mr Gerard Piel's address to the American Philosophical Society a year ago is both cogent and succinct.

> If the autonomy of American universities is to be secured on public support, the necessary protections cannot be decreed by the executive branch of the Federal government. Nor can Congress legislate the guarantee. The autonomy of our universities must be negotiatied with the electorate. People must be asked to render their support of the university with full understanding of its mission . . . Some significant percentage of the regular voters must be ready to entertain such a proposal, for thirty million college graduates are at large in the population.[12]

The electorate is understandably confused about the value of science. Scientists, except for those in agricultural research, have done all too little to inform the electorate about science and to seek their support. As a part of this effort, scientists must face the many sources of confusion that are identified by Dr. Philip Handler, the retiring president of the National Academy of Sciences, in his recent address, "The Future of American Science".[13] Scientists must expose "the anti-scientific and anti-rationalistic" movements, the "faddist approaches to nutrition", and the "unfounded allegations of environmental hazards". Scientists must "unfrock the charlatan" in order to establish the credibility of science with the electorate. They must also "contain the feckless debates concerning the magnitude of the risk of proliferation" from breeders. They must challenge the foolish arguments for a "risk-free society"; if they do not, "we succumb to a national failure of nerve". A telling part of Dr. Handler's remarks is, "a decade ago it may have been desirable to flag public attention to potential hazards . . . But that can also set us off in the wrong direction. For example, by doing so, public attention has been fastened on the perhaps five percent and certainly no more than 10 percent of all cancer that is caused by the sum of radiation, man-made chemicals and environmental pollutants, taken together. And it has done so at the expense of resources and talent that might more usefully have been utilized" in more important scientific endeavours.

My plea is that we dispel this confusion and find ways of negotiating with the electorate for financial support which is allocated directly to scientists with a minimum of regulations concerning accountability.

The autonomy of our universities is currently being impaired. Academic scientists are too beholden to government. The harsh truth is we have been moving bit by bit closer to the Soviet model. Unless this tendency is reversed, in due time fewer American scientists will be making the annual pilgrimage to the Swedish Academy of Sciences to be awarded a Nobel prize.

Notes and References

1   Edward Shils, "Faith, Utility and the Legitimacy of Science," in *Science and Its Public: The Changing Relationship* (Daedalus, Summer 1974), 1–15.
2   Based on *World Bank Atlas: Per Capita Product and Growth Rates* (Washington DC, 1974).
3   Eliot Marshall, "Defense," Science, CCVII, 4431 (Feb. 8 1980), 619–20.
4   Zvi Griliches, "Research Costs and Social Returns: Hybrid Corn and Related Innovations," *Journal of Political Economy*, 66(5) (Oct. 1958), 419–31. Professor Griliches has for some years been devoting a considerable part of his research to the economics of research and development in the United States.
5   Theodore W. Schultz, "The Economics of Research and Agricultural Productivity," Occasional Paper (International Agricultural Development Service, New York, 1979).
6   *National Patterns of R and D Resources*, NSF–78–313 (National Science Foundation, Washington DC, 1953–78/9), p. 4.
7   See above, Part III, No. 3, "Distortions of Economic Research," See also Richard C. Atkinson, editorial comment, "Federal Support in the Social Sciences," *Science*, CCVII, 4433 (Feb. 22 1980), 829.
8   L.E. Nolting and M. Feshback, "R and D Employment in the USSR," *Science*, CCVII, 4430 (Feb. 1 1980), 493–503.
9   Ibid., table 12, p. 502.
10 James K. Boyce and Robert E. Evenson, *Agricultural Research and Extension Programs* (Agricultural Development Council, New York, 1975).
11 John T. Wilson, "Higher Education and the Washington Scene: 1980," unpublished paper (University of Chicago, Oct. 1979).
12 Gerard Piel, "On Promoting Useful Knowledge," *Proceedings of the American Philosophical Society*, 123 (Dec. 28 1979), 337–40.
13 Philip Handler, "The Future of American Science" (Illinois Institute of Technology, Chicago, Ill., Jan. 29, 1980).

3

Distortions of Economic Research*

There are social scientists who are sure that economists debase social and cultural values in their monolithic concentration on economic values, neglect methodology, disregard social behavior that is deemed to be inconsistent with the rationality assumptions of economic theory, and have a penchant to be imperialistic. Scientists also are uneasy about the economists" treatment of the choices of human agents in the context of scarcity. The National Academy of Sciences looks with favor on economists who reveal some mathematical elegance, but is uncomfortable about economic criticism of the work that the NAS does on request for the US Government. Governments are most uneasy unless economists are beholden to them and provide support for their economic policies. The intellectual fashion at present is research on current economic policy regardless of how politicized and transitory the issues are.

The distortions in economic research, which I shall feature, are not a consequence of the reservations that other social scientists have about economic research. The distortions on my list have come about mainly because of the economic policy biases of some foundations and of most governmental agencies in allocating funds for economic research and because of the accommodations of a goodly number of academic economists to these biases in order to obtain research funds.

Economists have prospered from a long boom for their services. The demand for economic research has increased at a rapid pace largely as a consequence of the research activities of new institutions. These institutions are in the ascendancy in competing for research funds, and in this

* First published in William H. Kruskal (ed.), *The Social Sciences: Their Nature and Uses* (University of Chicago Press, Chicago, Ill., 1982). © 1982 by The University of Chicago. I am indebted to Zvi Griliches, D. Gale Johnson, William H. Kruskal, and T. Paul Schultz for their helpful suggestions and critical comments. A somewhat reduced version was published in *Minerva* 17, no. 3 (1979):460–68. Reprinted with permission.

competition the comparative advantage of university research is declining. Foundations have contributed somewhat to this new pattern in economic research; however, the increases in federal research funds are vastly more important in financing this development. One of the salient attributes of booms is that they tend to produce distortions, and on this score economic research has not been spared. From an academic viewpoint, disconcerting changes in the demand for economic research are clearly evident, and they favor strongly new types of institutes that serve the policy interests of governmental agencies. I am concerned about the adverse effects of this development on the research and the educational functions of academic economists.

Patrons of university activities are not renowned for their neutrality when it comes to economic research. Politicized economic research has become the order of the day. It is evident in the "targeted research" and the "mission oriented research" objectives enshrined in most projects that are funded by governmental agencies and also in some foundation grants. Nor are private patrons innocent in this respect.

My purpose is to question society's institutions that allocate funds to universities for economic research. It entails an examination of the distortions in the educational and research functions which are in substantial measure consequences of society's institutions. It also calls for a critique of the functions of university economists.

1   Institutions Involved in Economic Research

I do not want to imply that all economic research prior to two or three decades ago was being done by universities. Large business firms, including banks and trade associations, have been employing economists for many decades to do research deemed to be useful to them. Organized labor and national farm organizations have done likewise, especially beginning with the New Deal era. There are also bureau of long standing, staffed with competent economists, in the federal departments of agriculture, commerce, labor, and the treasury that have been and continue to be engaged in the measurement of economic components and in producing economic statistics. Among the early not-for-profit pioneers, two are noteworthy. The National Bureau of Economic Research, guided at the outset by the distinguished economist Wesley-Mitchell, did yeoman work. The NBER sought the assistance and criticism of university economists. It engaged in measurement and in producing data that required facilities and staff that no university could afford. The remarkable research of Simon Kuznets and his associates for the NBER developed the concepts and the measurements that are required in national income accounting. Now, however, the research of the NBER is largely devoted to policy issues, and it has become substantially dependent on public funds. The Brookings Institution, a long-established research organization, has been much favored by foundation grants and also by public funds. During its early years under the leadership of Harold Moulton, and at times since then, a good deal of the economic research of Brookings has been closely identified with that of particular current policy objectives.

The other research entities that have been less well known are the following: (1) the National Planning Association, which dates back to the New Deal period, has been over the years strongly policy oriented. (2) Following World War II, the Committee for Economic Development, in protest to the dominant views of business organizations, contributed substantially in clarifying some of the then policy issues. (3) Each of the long-established twelve Federal Reserve Banks has a research department headed by a vice-president. The economic staff in the systems headquarters in Washington is large. Most of the research of the Federal Reserve system, however, is confined to in-house purposes, and all too few of their studies are published in professional journals. For a few years while C.O. Hardy was at Kansas City Bank there was an exception, and more recently the St. Louis Federal Reserve Bank has also been an exception.

During the past twenty-five years the proliferation of institutes engaged in economic research has been extraordinary. They have emerged, as already noted, in response to the availability of the large increases in funds for specific economic policy research. A drastic shift has occurred in the allocation of research funds in favor of those that specialize in the appropriate research that is not encumbered by being too closely connected with a university. Some on-campus institutes that are not hampered by the academic duties of departments of economics have been favored. In large measure this shift has come about because most university departments of economics are deemed to be too rigid, because they resist interdisciplinary and team research projects, and because they are too committed to on-going traditional PhD research, to theoretical studies, and to esoteric empirical work. Moreover, universities in large measure are viewed as being either unable or unwilling to shape up and do the type of policy research that is wanted.

Following World War II nonprofit research institutes have become a robust growth industry. We now have all manner of institutes with much specialization. The list is indeed long: over three hundred in economics research.[1] There are institutes that specialize in economic development, econometric models, international trade, taxation, enterprise, education, urban development, energy, manpower, consumer affairs, environmental reforms, legal issues, health, population, and in poverty. Nor are the research funds for these purposes small; for example, the federal government is allocating approximately $90 million a year to support poverty research.[2] Since the growth of this industry has occurred predominantly outside of the confines of the universities, the implication is that university economic research has not satisfied this specialized demand for economic research.

Clearly some private patrons of economic research foundations, and virtually all governmental agencies have decided that universities lack the capacity or the desire to do the research that they demand. This decision having been made, one option that has been pursued by some foundations is to undertake and manage as an in-house activity the research they want. It is a way of establishing new policy areas that then serve to determine the type of grant proposals that will be considered. In a variant of this option, the Carnegie Foundation established the Carnegie Commission on Higher Education and allocated some millions of dollars to this endeavor. The Ford Foundation's first in-house report on energy, *A Time to Choose* (1974), is an example of harmful economic policy advocacy befitting a populist approach in coping with the energy problems. The third Ford Foundation (1979) in-house report, *Energy: The Next Twenty Years*, prepared under the direction of Hans H. Landsberg, makes a good deal of economic sense. The funding of new research institutes is the option that has been pursued on a grand scale. A few of them are doing first-rate research, producing analytical studies of high quality. A notable example is the performance over the past twenty-five years of Resources for the Future, a relatively small institute that concentrates on studies pertaining to natural resources and, although natural resources are a highly sensitive political area, has not become dependent on government project funds. RFF has successfully resisted a foundation effort to bring about a "forced marriage" with another much larger institution that has the proper policy qualifications.

The Office of Naval Analysis and Air Force Project Rand supported significant work in mathematical and theoretical economics during the 1950s and 1960s. Doctoral and postdoctoral research in human capital was broadly supported by the National Institute of Mental Health during the 1970s, when it was abruptly terminated because it was then deemed to be not sufficiently applied, given the legal mandate of NIMH. Earlier, research in agriculture economics at the University of Chicago and Harvard University, supported by US Department of Agriculture funds, was also terminated abruptly, in this case because of the whims of the chairman of a congressional appropriation committee. The majority of Congress tends to be opposed to having governmental agencies allocate research funds to economists who are presumed to be critical of particular public programs.

Up to this point I have featured the dynamics of the recent proliferation of economic research. No doubt a good deal of this research is useful in serving the specific purposes of the patrons who provide the funds. As a by-product, some of the new institutes contribute occasionally to the advancement of economics. But the success of these new institutes does not resolve the question of whether or not academic economic thought and research is useful in determining the merits and limitations of economic policies. I shall deal with that question later. The primary thrust of my argument thus far is that the professional personnel who manage the governmental agencies that allocate research funds under the restrictions imposed by Congress are constrained and thus not free, leaving aside the issue of the required competence, to determine the type of university support that would serve the proper function of academic economists. Although the National Science Foundation may be viewed as an exception, all too few NSF grants support criticism of the state of economic analysis. Despite the political opposition to economics, NSF has supported the research of Nelson and Winter criticizing the profit-maximizing analysis of the behavior of firms, Fogel's attack on society's institutions, and Lucas's criticism of existing macro-orthodoxy. The distortions about which we should be concerned also entail the accommodations that are made by universities to obtain research funds from foundations, from government, and from the new breed of institutes when they offer to subcontract some of their on-going research.

In questioning society's institutions, there have been tensions between what economists do and what the dominant institutions of society want them to do that antedate by centuries the current period. Differences on basic economic issues were as pervasive then as the tensions associated with the recent developments on which I have dwelt.

2   Questioning Society's Institutions

Economists have long been critics of society's institutions. Historically economists have criticized the economic doctrines of the church, the state, the property ownership class (landlords), and the mercantile doctrine, among others. Although the state of this uneasiness between these institutionalized doctrines and economic thought has a long history, the nature of the difficulties has changed over time. The scholarly studies of

Jacob Viner feature the economic doctrines of the early Christian fathers, the Scholastics, the secularizing tendencies in Catholic social thought, and of Protestantism and the rise of capitalism.[3] The doctrines of the church pertaining to usury, to the sterility of money capital, and the just price are examined in the context of the then prevailing scholarship. There is also the critical essay by Viner, "The Role of Providence in the Social Order."[4] While the tensions between religious and economic thought have declined, some differences persist on particular social and economic issues inherent in the doctrines pertaining to the relationships between church and state.

The remarkable decline in rent from land relative to the earnings of labor and other sources of income in high-income countries has very much reduced the social and political influence of landlords, and the tensions between them and economic thought have diminished as a consequence. Meanwhile, however, some of the economic entitlements that business firms, organized labor, organized agricultural, and organized environmental groups demand, strain the relationship between them and economics.

We are in an era in which the tensions between the university and the state have become increasingly acute. These difficulties are not restricted to private universities nor are they specific to the United States. They are worldwide, although they differ greatly among the more than 150 nation-states. In most nations the intellectual independence of the university is seriously constrained, especially so in the case of social and economic thought and research. What these nation-states want makes this relationship fragile and subjects it to much uncertainty for universities. It is true, even in the United States, that the more heavily the university is dependent on the patronage of government the less is the freedom of inquiry in the social sciences.

Throughout much of the world, what academic economists do is decidedly beholden to governments. It is obviously so in the Soviet Union, China, and in the other countries that have centralized the control of their economy. Meanwhile many low-income countries have opted for a partially controlled economy and for external subsidies to equalize the differences in per capita income between them and the rich countries. It is presumed that academic economists can, once they are required to do so, rationalize these objectives. Tensions have also increased during recent decades on issues pertaining to economic policy in Western Europe and North America, where democratic governments have long prevailed.

I believe it is fair to say that within the university economics is more vulnerable to off-campus intrusions than university research in the natural sciences. The vulnerability of biological research to governmental regulation, however, has become serious, but even at that economics is decidedly more exposed to subversion. I hasten to acknowledge that recent antiscience movements are changing the relationship between science and the public perception of the sciences, and in this process these movements have to some extent politicized the allocation of public funds for science research. Edward Shils has dealt thoughtfully with this issue in his essay, "Faith, Utility and the Legitimacy of Science."[5]

3   A Modest Critique of Academic Economics

Despite inflation and the university's financial stringency, academic economists have not fared badly in large part because of the non-university market for the services of economists. By this market test it would be all too easy to conclude that economists are highly productive of something that the university or society want. But in fact the utility that either the university or society derives from what academic economists do is not obvious. While economists are not reluctant to ascertain the value derived from the use of scarce resources by people in any other activity, they are shy when it comes to reckoning the utility of their own work. It is my contention that most academic economists are complacent about their freedom of inquiry, about safeguarding their university functions, and about the conditions under which research funds are made available to them by institutions other than the university. This complacency about the special and specific usefulness of inquiry that is free of outside intrusion is exemplified in their failure to challenge publicly private patrons, foundations, and governmental agencies on their allocation of funds for economic research. But to do this competently requires firm knowledge of the utility of economic thought and research appropriate to the functions of the university. It also requires courage, because it entails the risk of alienating the patrons and causing them to reduce further their support of university research. This risk is neatly avoided by the art of accommodation, by quietly and gracefully submitting proposals for research grants that seem to fit the demands of the patrons.

Suffice it to say that economics deals with a mundane part of human activities. It is useful to the extent that it is practical. Its utility is not in its beauty, which it lacks, nor in the elegance of its mathematics. The fundamentals of economics are useful in both private and public affairs and especially so in determining the economic consequences of public policies, which is the essence of the domain of political economy.

According to my critique, the distinction between the concepts of applied and basic research is not meaningful in determining the function of academic economics. The now fashionable concepts of targeted and mission-oriented research are as a rule subterfuges for intrusion. Peer review of economic research proposals by individuals who are selected by the granting agency, notably so in the case of some governmental agencies, is a convenient device for obtaining sufficient differences in evaluations to give the administrator of the agency a free hand in deciding whether or not to approve the proposal. Turning to the positive function of academic economists, its forte is in comprehensive analysis and criticism of private economic behavior and of public policies. Comprehensiveness in this context does not restrict academic economics to improvements of the internal consistency of economic logic and thereby making it more rigorous, nor does it limit economics to advances in quantitative analytical tools and improvements in empirical analysis, although these endeavors are exceedingly important. To be comprehensive, academic economists cannot divorce themselves from the social attributes of society and from the insights of the humanities and of history. Hayek[6] could say with good grace, "Nobody can be a great economist who is only an economist," and he added "that an economist who is only an economist is likely to become a nuisance if not a positive danger." It is my contention that this "Dilemma of Specialization" remains unresolved.

One of the primary functions of at least a subset of economists, whose freedom of inquiry is protected by their university, is to devote their talent to comprehensive social and economic criticism. Scholarly criticism of economic doctrines and society's institutions by economists is at a low ebb – criticism, for example, of the quality of the work of Jacob Viner, Frank Knight, and Harry Johnson, and also of Thorstein Veblen, Henry Simon, and Friedrich A. Hayek, all of whom were members of the faculty of the University of Chicago. It is noteworthy that the studies and publications of only one of this group were supported by foundations, governmental agencies, or by private patrons. I find it highly unlikely that university economists of their caliber and with their scholarly interest could today obtain funds from off-campus sources. But what is also distressing is that the search for talent is for a different set of economic qualifications, and as a consequence there is a lack of incentives for the on-coming generation of economists to acquire the competence that is required to pursue scholarly criticism of economic doctrines and of society's institutions. It is my contention that one of the primary functions of at least a subset of economists, whose freedom of inquiry is protected by their university, is to devote their talent to comprehensive social and economic criticism.

The criticism that is lacking is fairly obvious. There are all too few competent critical studies of the economic doctrines of the host of United Nations' organizations, despite the fact that most of them are debasing economics. Whereas the early economic doctrines of the Church were supported, as Viner has shown, by considerable scholarship, the economic doctrines that prevail within the United Nations are not burdened by scholarship. It is to the lasting credit of Harry Johnson that he did challenge these doctrines.[7] Peter Bauer of the London School of Economics is another exception in his dissent on economic development doctrines.[8] The pronounced drift toward soft economics by some of the foundations goes unchallenged by economists. This adverse drift is in large measure a consequence of a "live and let live" policy which requires accommodation to demands of the prevailing international organizations and to the current politicized demands within the United States.

In analyzing choices and scarcities, economists tend to hold fast to the preferences of individuals and families, including the perferences that are served by household activities. Some of society's institutions, however, distort these preferences. There is a pervasive intellectual and popular commitment to the belief that the failures of the market are the primary source of what is wrong with the economy. Each interest group has its own agenda of such market failures. To overcome them, an increasing number of organized groups seek protection and redress by means of public programs and institutions created by government. Business groups have a long history of serving their special interest by this means. Organized labor and organized commodity groups have been doing this on behalf of their special interests for decades. This pluralistic process is currently confounded by the politics of health, of the aged, of poverty, of income transfers, of energy, of environmental politics, and others. The resulting modifications of the political economy in general do not correct actual market failures but tend to bring about other forms of economic failures. My concern on this point is that, in part by design but mainly unwittingly, some of the specialized research in departments of economics supports this special interest fragmentation of the economy by means of governmental intervention. Surely, it is not the function of academic economists to contribute to such fragmentation of the political economy. This type of distortion of economic research is in some measure induced by the conditions attached to research funds that are available to academic economists.

Economic research in most universities is less than optimum for several additional reasons. PhD research in general is not well organized. There is a lack of opportunities for graduate students to make progress reports on their research at regularly scheduled meetings organized to provided useful criticism by other graduate students and faculty. Members of the faculty who are in charge of supervising PhD research are frequently involved in off-campus consulting to private business and government agencies. Such consulting can divert their intellectual endeavors from research that is appropriate to the functions of the universities.[9] Although the administration and faculty of universities proclaim that research is one of their major and vital functions, the bureaucratic financial organization of the university provides little direct support for economic research. This financial issue is more acute in economics than in the sciences. Economics does not require laboratories and expensive physical facilities. All an empirical economist needs is a research assistant, perhaps a programmer, access to a suitable computer, and funds to acquire data. The effects of this unsolved university problem on the incentives of academic economists are beset with distortions.

4   Concluding Remarks

The charters of our not-for-profit foundations do not require that they support primarily all manner of short-range, politicized economic policy research. Foundations have on occasion provided funds for comprehensive, long-range, policy research. The Rockefeller Foundation, for example, has generously funded the agricultural economics workshop at the University of Chicago continuously since the early 1940s. At an earlier period the Rockefeller Foundation on its own initiative offered the Ames group of economists a generous grant without any restrictions on the range of policy issues that would be investigated. I would be less than grateful if I did not acknowledge the six recent years of support I received from the Ford Foundation for research and writing of my own choosing. There are of course other examples of this type of support by foundations. The secular drift, however, as I have argued, has been to support the wide array of new institutes that specialize on current, short-range, economic policy issues.

Government agencies, however, do not have the freedom that foundations have when it comes to providing funds for comprehensive economic policy research. These agencies are constrained by congressional mandates that determine the research purposes to which federal funds can be put. The National Science Foundation has more degrees of freedom than other government agencies, but it too is hampered by some particular short-range tests of useful research imposed by Congress. It must be said that Congress has wantonly politicized the policy research of the vast number of administrative units of government that have been established to promulgate the declared policies mandated by Congress. The politics of research is bad for economic research. Whereas the funds authorized by Congress for research are large, in allocating these funds virtually every administrative agency of government is restricted to research that will support its particular policy mandate. It is not within the domain of the agency to finance competent economic criticism of the agency's activities or of the adverse effects of economic policy fragmentation.

Federal research funds have not always been allocated in this perverse manner. The Purnell Act is a clear case of federal funding of university research that has had continuity and stability, sufficiently so to make tenure appointments. It is now fifty years ago that the Purnell Act authorized an annual appropriation of $60,000 (read $250,000 in 1979 prices) for each of the land grant universities to be used for rural social science research.[10] Agricultural economics is the primary recipient of these federal funds. These funds provide continuing core support for faculty and PhD research. This research is not beholden to the federal government, although it has not always been free of political intrusions on the part of the states.

The core of my argument is that one of the primary functions of academic economists is to question society's institutions. Economists are all too complacent about their freedom of inquiry. They are not sufficiently vigilant in safeguarding their function as educators. They should give a high priority to scholarly criticism of economic doctrines and of society's institutions. The distortions of economic research will not fade away by accommodating patrons of research funds.

Notes and References

1 Archie M. Palmer (ed.), *Research Centers Directory*, 6th ed. (Gale Research Co., Detroit, 1979), lists 304 nonprofit research organizations in the United States and Canada engaged in economic research. Many of them have some sort of affiliation with a university.

2 National Research Council, National Academy of Sciences, *Evaluating Federal Support of Poverty Research* (G.K. Hall & Co., Boston, Mass. (cloth), Schenkman Publishing Co., Cambridge, Mass., 1979 (paper)).

3 Jacob Viner, *Religious Thought and Economic Society*, four chapters of an unfinished work edited by Jacques Melitz and Donald Winch (Duke University Press, Durham, NC, 1978).

4 Jacob Viner, *The Role of Providence in the Social Order: An Essay in Intellectual History* (American Philosophical Society, Philadelphia, Pa., 1972 (cloth), Princeton University Press, Princeton, NJ, 1976 (paper)).

5 Edward Shils, "Faith, Utility, and the Legitimacy of Science," in *Science and*

Its Public: The Changing Relationship (*Daedalus*, summer 1974).

6   F.A. Hayek, "The Dilemma of Specialization," in Leonard Dupee White (ed.), *The State of the Social Sciences* (University of Chicago Press, Chicago, Ill., 1956).

7   Harry G. Johnson, *On Economics and Society* (University of Chicago Press, Chicago, Ill., 1975).

8   P.T. Bauer, *Dissent on Development*, Studies and Debates in Development Economics (Harvard University Press, Cambridge, Mass., 1972).

9   While I am uneasy about some aspects of this consulting, the evidence reported by Carl V. Patton and James D. Marver suggests that from 1969 to 1975 there has not been any increase in academic consulting. The evidence also indicates, controlling for type of institution and rank of faculty, that paid consultants do somewhat more research, more graduate instruction, publish more, and more of them serve as chairmen of departments than do those faculty who are not paid consultants. See their "Paid Consulting by American Academics," *Educational Record*, 60 (Spring 1979), 175–84; and an earlier paper by them, "The Correlates of Consulation: American Academics in the 'Real World' ", *Higher Education* (Aug. 1976), 319–35.

10 Theodore W. Schultz, with the assistance of Lawrence W. Witt, *Training and Recruiting of Personnel in the Rural Social Studies* (American Council on Education, Washington DC, 1941).

4

*Economic Policy Research for Agriculture**

1   Central Issues

Each of the central issues may be stated as a question, as is my wont.

1   How will you select competent economists and induce them to enter upon this research enterprise? You have in Canada a number of highly qualified economists for this task. In this you are exceedingly fortunate. But you must select them and this will not be easy, and you must win their services and this will be even more difficult.

2   How will you organize this research enterprise in order to keep important, real problems on the research agenda without controlling the research or impairing its intellectual integrity? Canada obviously faces real economic problems requiring the best intellectual efforts that one or more teams of economists can bring to bear. How will you make sure that these problems will receive the attention of your research economists? Can you do this and not dictate the results? Most countries in the world haven't learned how to do this and even in western countries where there are long traditions favorable to freedom in research there are many not so subtle pressures to contend with. I shall point out later that our record in the United States has been quite mixed on this score, and that you may be breaking new and important ground here in Canada in your approach to economic policy research.

3   You will want above all good work which will stand the test of the highest intellectual standards. How will you organize this research enterprise to make reasonably sure that your economists will be subject

*This paper was presented at the National Conference on Farm Policy Research, Winnipeg, Manitoba, April 24, 1961, and published in *Canadian Journal of Agricultural Economics*, ix, No. 2, 97–106.

to constant, competent criticism by qualified peers, without becoming another university? This question hides a number of uncharted icebergs.

4   You need a research enterprise that will have continuity, stability, and the capacity to learn from its mistakes. Here the underlying question comprehends the others. How will the real problems, the scientific quality of the research, and the efficiency of economists be determined in making promotions, salaries, and other rewards that go to provide effective incentives?

2   Lessons from US Experiences

I don't have the answers to these questions, but there is some experience that is relevant, to which I now turn. Let me do this in three parts, regarding: (1) non-university-connected research enterprises; (2) university-connected research enterprises; and (3) where public funds go directly into agricultural economics research.

2.1   *Non-university-connected research enterprises.*

Here I want you to visualize a group of competent economists who are doing research and who are addressing themselves to major economic problems in an organization that is only loosely connected with university-based economists. Under this arrangement the difficulties are that the research may get too close to policy and enter upon advocacy or the research may err in the opposite direction and avoid policy questions altogether. Research enterprises of this type, as I see them, face a special difficulty in developing and administering high standards for their work.

There are some lessons in the experiences of two of our well known national organizations – the Brookings Institution and the National Bureau of Economic Research. Both have, over the years, tried to keep their economic studies under critical review. But how can organizations of this type obtain hard criticism from their peers in economics? The Brookings studies in economics floundered badly for some years prior to the appointment of Dr. Robert Calkins as Director. Some of its major studies, prior to his appointment, had become too enmeshed with policy. There was in some of them much advocacy. The capacity to bring high economic standards to bear was for a time lost. Fortunately, Dr. Calkins corrected this shortcoming. It remains to be seen whether he and those who follow can hold the high standard he has set. It will be exceedingly difficult to do so, given the loose connections that the organization has with university-based economists.

The National Bureau of Economic Research, on the other hand, did not operate close to policy. If it has "erred", it has been in the opposite direction. Economic variables that can be identified and measured have predominated the research of the NBER. The research effort has been subject to considerable university criticism through some "joint" appointments. The research results have been high in quality. But they have not been close enough to major questions of public policy in my judgment. It is true that the studies of the NBER have been the building stones of many policy studies made by other economists. Nor is it amiss to note that Arthur F. Burns took leave from the NBER to serve as Chairman of the President's Economic Council and gave an extraordinarily good account of himself in dealing with national economic policy.

My observations of the way the economic division of RAND has functioned are limited to seeing their studies and to some insights in an advisory capacity. RAND has done research on real policy problems in its area of specialization and it has maintained high standards. RAND has been successful, also, in recruiting first-rate economists. So far much of this success of the economic division of RAND must be attributed to the genius of Dr. Charles Hitch who has now left to serve in Washington.

The Committee for Economic Development (CED) is an instructive model. Although one might not give it a high score as a research enterprise per se, it has had a good record in the area of national economic policy, especially on monetary and fiscal issues. It has drawn heavily on university economists and on their intellectual capital. Although the CED has a narrow base, composed as it is of businessmen, it has learned how to learn from economics and it has demonstrated a substantial capacity to be objective on most questions of economic policy upon which the CED has entered.

I could review here the long experience of the National Planning Association, and the more recent emphasis on policy research by Resources For the Future. But since the lesson to which I wish to direct your attention is mainly suggested in the experiences of the Brookings Institution and the NBER, I shall not extend these remarks. Let me, however, force this lesson to its extreme, thus going beyond the experience cited. A research enterprise of this general type faces the ever-present danger of being drawn too close to policy and thereby losing its objectivity and its competence to do research that meets high technical and scientific standards. In the opposite direction, it is in danger of staying too far from basic issues of policy and of settling for routine statistical work without reaching for inferences and interpretations that are relevant to major policy choices.

2.2   *University-connected Research Enterprises*

Here the main difficulties are three in number: teaching tends to predominate, specialized research groups within a university become isolated intellectually, and so-called formal or theoretical questions receive altogether too much attention relative to empirical studies in economics.

Why does teaching dominate. The reasons are several. There is the strong hand of tradition; a faculty is employed to teach; economists come with books and with graphs and formula that can be drawn on blackboards; and no labor forces are required. University funds are for instruction and many who administer these funds often fail to see the connection between research and instruction. It is no wonder that most departments of economics in our private universities and colleges are not effectively organized to do research.

With respect to funds, the land-grant colleges and universities have had substantial resources to support social science research, especially for agricultural economics. The federal government, through the Purnell Act, began to make grants to each state for this purpose at an early date. At Iowa even in the early 1930s, about one-third of the regular departmental budget was specifically allocated to support research. Most of the ablest economists were on a one-half time research and one-half teaching arrangement, or half research and half extension appointments.

In recent years, private universities have given more attention to economic research. In no small part, faculty members have been motivated in this direction to free themselves from an excessive amount of classroom teaching. Prestige has also played a part.

Clearly, at the advanced level, research is an essential part of graduate instruction; nevertheless, formal classes and traditional seminars predominate with all too little of the basic instruction being done through research "workshops". In this respect, the natural and biological sciences have achieved a better organization of their research than has economics.

It has been fashionable to establish in and about departments of economics new groups to undertake specialized research and to call them *Centers, Institutes,* or *Committees.* Many of these have prospered because they have appealed to creative impulses within foundations. The argument for doing this has been that real problems as a rule cut across departmental lines. It is also a way of maneuvering around the traditional preoccupation of established university economists. Do not be disquieted, however, the gilded phrase now is "policy oriented research"! The difficulty in this approach is that these specialized groups as a rule become isolated intellectually within the university and when this happens they are not subject to the technical and scientific standards set by the core of economics. They are vulnerable as well to the same dangers that have already been discussed.

In an earlier period some specialized groups were established in universities to undertake particular empirical studies or, if you please, not to work forever on theory and tools for economic analysis. The Stanford Food Institute was one such group. It has produced many useful studies. These studies have not, however, made a major impact either on the core of economics or on thinking about economic policy, although members of the faculty have frequently spoken on policy issues. In my judgment the connection between those in economics and those in the Institute has been too tenuous to have achieved an optimum result in these respects.

The Center for International Studies at Massachusetts Institute of Technology has achieved a rather good score. Joint appointments have undoubtedly played a part, and so has the leadership of Professor Max Millikan. I cite their record because it stands as an exception, for it has subjected its work to high professional standards where economics has been relevant. Undoubtedly there is much to be learned from the way this Center has functioned that may be helpful to universities wishing to launch specialized research enterprises of this type.

For six years now there has been a major University-to-University contract between the Department of Economics of the University of Chicago and its counterpart at the Catholic University of Santiago, Chile. From the outset, this enterprise, which is predominantly research and graduate instruction, has been an integral part of the department in the sense that all major decisions with regard to faculty appointments and broad outlines of work to be undertaken have come before the faculty of the departments as would similar decisions related to the normal instruction and research activities of the department. The results have been gratifying and this outcome in no small part has been a consequence of the fact that the Chile enterprise has been fully integrated into the department. It is, I feel confident, a model that has much merit in indicating how to organize an activity of this kind within a university.

University-based economists overemphasize formal and theoretical work. It might have been better to have stated this difficulty the other way around; that is, too little empirical or real research is undertaken. It is not a question of either one or the other, but of an optimum combination. Again and again real research raises new theoretical issues and, conversely, advances in econometric and statistical techniques open new doors for real research. The underemphasis of empirical studies in economics in most universities is mainly, I am sure, a consequence of the wholly inadequate financial resources available to do such research; and where there are some resources for this purpose, there is the essentially unsatisfactory organization of university departments to enter upon empirical studies.

2.3 *Public funds supporting agricultural economics research*

Here I shall concentrate on experiences within the land-grant colleges and universities and on what has been done from time to time to the "Bureau of Agricultural Economics" in the USDA. The basic difficulties are: (1) public influences that impair intellectual integrity; (2) provincialism; and (3) instability in government and its adverse effects upon the Bureau of Agricultural Economics (BAE).

I strongly recommend taking Charles M. Hardin's fine study, *Freedom in Agricultural Education*,[1] to heart. Let me mention only two of the many "political incidences" that have arisen which Hardin has examined with care. One of these arose in Kentucky with respect to low nicotine tobacco research. This incident wasn't about economics at all. It involved the biologists, the plant people, who were trying to produce a tobacco plant that would yield leaves low in nicotine. Suddenly they found themselves in a violent political controversy, with the legislature trying to pass bills to stop this research at the University of Kentucky. Fortunately the bills didn't pass, but it took courage on the part of the academic people and even the governor to avert all of this happening.

Another small event, which I vaguely remember, Professor Hardin refers to as the "Iowa Oleomargarine Incident". Reading his treatment of what happened, I was much surprised to see how all this appeared through his objective eyes, detached, writing from the vantage point of Harvard, and from there seeing us as little creatures struggling with formal and informal political forces. I would have used quite different adjectives to describe these particular forces. Yet that incident is relevant to what I am trying to establish with regard to integrity in research.

Professor Hardin, at one point, says, "No ivory tower exists for agricultural workers . . . on the public payroll. For them, academic freedom is not a moat but a shield and buckler which they themselves must largely fashion and keep in repair. As with the ancient Spartans, their walls are in their own wills and abilities to resist and, indeed, to turn resistance into attack."

I also stressed provincialism. What I mean is that agricultural economics in state colleges or universities concentrate on problems of their particular state. The larger and much more important national policy questions are not on their research agenda. To illustrate, take the talented faculty of the Giannini Foundation of the University of California. The empire called California has been their oyster; few of them have undertaken truly national studies, a notable exception being M.R. Benedict. Let me illustrate more precisely what I mean. US agriculture has been affected very adversely during the last three years by the failure of the monetary and fiscal policy which caused the weak recovery that occurred during 1959 and early 1960. Excessive unemployment closed off industrial jobs for farm people who were trying to transfer out of agriculture. Agriculture was adversely affected by these monetary and fiscal policy decisions and yet, to the best of my knowledge, no one in agricultural economics, or in economics for that matter, in our land-grant institutions has concentrated his analytical work on this area of economic policy despite its importance to the economic welfare of farm people.

A word is in order here about the two large Kellogg grants, one to Iowa and the other to North Carolina. In both states, the agricultural economists are breaking important new ground. I have no doubt that it will be money well spent. Nevertheless, they are mainly "regional" research enterprises. The one at Iowa State University is already far enough along so one can make a tentative judgment. Good as the work is, it is not *national* but primarily "corn belt" in scope; whereas the real economic policy questions that matter most in the welfare of farm people are not regional or even agricultural, but rather monetary, fiscal, international trade, and importantly, industrial jobs for people who want to leave agriculture.

In Washington, DC, economic research in the USDA has had its ups and downs reflecting a serious instability in our federal government measured in terms of its capacity to support first rate research and not insist that economists who are employed be simply a corps of "Yes" men. Professor Hardin has documented a part of this sad history in his study of the BAE under fire, in the *Journal of Farm Economics*, August, 1946. In 1953, the old BAE was completely fragmented by the then Secretary of Agriculture.[2] Now another Secretary of Agriculture is putting the pieces together again. It is going to take considerable time, however, before an effective new research organization can be built. The price of all this governmental instability in the way it impairs economic research in the USDA is high indeed.

3   Requirements for Research Enterprises

Lastly, I come to the several major requirements for first rate research enterprises. In the main, I can only state these conditions for there will not be time to elaborate on each of them. While I shall draw on the US experiences already cited, I shall not stop there because other considerations must also be taken into account.

1 *Size.*   It is all too easy to make such a research enterprise all too large. As the lower limit it should consist of at least five economists and each should give at least half of his time to research. In the United States, research staffs are often too large. A number of our major departments of agricultural economics would be much better off if they were smaller and the several competent men were not so burdened with colleagues. Complementarity is important. If I had to develop a staff like this I would prefer three agricultural economists and two general economists. I wouldn't want them all to be in agricultural economics because many of the economic issues that impinge on agriculture are not of agriculture.

2 *Number of research centers.*   At least two research enterprises should be established at the outset. One is not enough. You can't afford to put your eggs all in one basket. There is much at stake in this requirement. I learned this lesson from the natural scientists and if it is applicable to their endeavors, it is much more relevant to economics. Dr. James Conant, some years ago, argued most persuasively that if the particular group were to undertake a major project to determine how "best" to teach mathematics, it would not do to proceed on the assumption that there was a "best" way. Dr. Conant simply said, "Do not accept a grant until plans and funds permit you to undertake at least two and preferably three programs to determine how 'best' to teach mathematics. There are a dozen good ways; there is no perfect way."

3 *Dangers inherent in part-timism.*   The economists should be on full time bases in their commitment to this research and the related university teaching. This means they should not engage in outside work to garner consulting fees. Inflation and the lag in salaries have fostered the reaching for outside earnings on the part of some university-based economists. The main task, the research, suffers; the costs of such outside distractions are high. This requirement, however, implies a level of

salaries such that the economist is not compelled to seek outside earnings to keep going. Given the price level and the "market value" of competent economists, these salaries presently would fall between $15,000 and $20,000 (Canadian) dollars.

4 *University-connected.* As already implied, each of these research enterprises should be university-connected because this is the best way of placing the economists under qualified technical and scientific criticism which is indispensable in maintaining research work of a high standard. The source of the funds cannot provide this particular criticism. Those who provide or administer these funds are not qualified for this task. If presidents, deans, administrators or others charged with responsibility of administering funds were to set themselves up as competent to provide this type of criticism, the whole research enterprise can only come to naught, because suppliers of the funds will impair its intellectual integrity.

5 *A Board.* Another requirement is a board to relate these research enterprises to the community. Such a board, or council, should have the responsibility of determining in principle the research agenda so that important real economic problems, where agriculture and policy join, will receive major consideration. (Note again that this board is not to enter upon analytical questions involving causality, economic logic, theory, models, identification, measurement and statistical inference.) This board should "administer" mainly by acting as a buffer between those who provide the funds and the research enterprise. In meeting this particular requirement, you can learn much from our (US) mistakes and you also can teach us how to employ substantial public funds for economic research and not impair the intellectual integrity of the research.

6 *An Institution.* Finally, both the board and the research enterprise should be so organized that they have continuity and a real capacity to learn from their mistakes.

4   Concluding Remarks

You are about to embark on a new venture. As pioneers you will face risks and there will be those who will be suspicious of your motives. So did those who had the vision that became the land-grant colleges and universities. These institutions are now celebrating their centennial and there is much indeed in their achievements to be proud about. But it should not be forgotten, as the historian Professor E.D. Ross has pointed out, that the Morrill Act was not enacted in response to demands of farm people. On the contrary, farm people generally were indifferent and not a few were suspicious of the great idea that knowledge and education were essential to bring dignity to farm people which strongly motivated Mr Morrill and his colleagues.

I hope indeed that you will launch this venture and proceed to pioneer in economic policy research. I wish you every success.

Notes and References

1 Charles M. Hardin, *Freedom in Agricultural Education* (University of Chicago Press, Chicago, Ill., 1955).
2 See *Journal of Farm Economics*, Feb. 1954.

5

Entrepreneurship in Organized Research*

Entrepreneurship is a pervasive economic activity. Not even ivory tower professors or institutionalized priests can escape the disequilibria that entails entrepreneurship.

At various points over the life cycle, every person is an entrepreneur. No one is spared in making adjustments in the allocation of one's own time to changing circumstances. Thus, in this all-inclusive sense we are all entrepreneurs. Since our own time is a scarce resource along with other scarce resources that are involved, entrepreneurship qualifies as an economic activity. It is, however, far from easy to ascertain the factors that determine the supply of entrepreneurs and the demand for their services.

To set the stage it may be helpful to consider the pervasiveness of the process of resource allocation that occurs in response to economic disequilibria. No matter what part of the economy is being investigated, we observe that people are reallocating their resources in response to changes in economic conditions. This reallocative process is not restricted to farmers and businessmen. People who supply labor services for hire or who are self-employed are reallocating their services in response to changes in the value of the work they do. So are housewives in devoting their time in combination with purchased goods and services in household production. Students likewise are reallocating their own time and the educational services they purchase as they respond to changes in expected earnings along with changes in the value of the personal satisfactions they expect to derive from their education. Within our universities, academic entrepreneurship is much more important than we realize. Show me a university that allocates its resources in a purely routine manner over any extended period and I will show you that that university is on a declining path. Presidents, deans, and directors of research are obviously academic entrepreneurs. So are heads

* Kaldor Memorial Lecture, Iowa State University, October 15, 1979.

of departments. Nor do I exclude teachers and those who do research. The stock of knowledge and the opportunities in research are not fixed once and for all. Routine teachers are a liability. Routine research workers contradict the meaning of research. If nevertheless there are such, they are failures. Not least is the fact that consumption opportunities are also changing, and inasmuch as pure consumption also entails time, here too people are reallocating their own time in response to changing opportunities.

My argument is that over our respective life cycles all of us, given our dynamic economy, are entrepreneurs. Whether a person is bad or good in performing this function is quite another matter.

It will not suffice, however, to deal only with the observable allocative responses. There is the question: What determines the ability of human beings to perceive that which needs to be done? We now have a substantial body of evidence which shows that education tends to enhance this particular ability. Among the pioneering studies of this effect of education are those by Finis Welch. It is noteworthy that Margaret Reid while she was at Iowa State published *Economics of Household Production* long before this approach began to flourish in academic research.[1] The education of labor in this context including its effects on migration has received a good deal of research attention. I have devoted a major survey to "The Value of the Ability to Deal with Disequilibria."[2]

There is also the question: What are the sources and the attributes of the economic disequilibria that determine the demand for entrepreneurs? Theory to deal with this issue has been much neglected. There are some studies, but they are not especially useful for reasons that I shall comment on later. The critical and unsettled question pertains to the attributes of the information on which entrepreneurs are dependent.

In extending economic theory to analyze the function of entrepreneurs, all too little attention has been given to either the supply of or the demand for the services of entrepreneurs. We are inventive and sophisticated in applying supply and demand analytical techniques to labor, reproducible capital goods and natural resources, but not to entrepreneurs. The economic value of their activities is concealed by the concern about *pure* profits and *pure* losses that are not and cannot be anticipated. It is clear from the literature in economics that the risk-uncertainty dichotomy has great intellectual appeal, but its usefulness is limited.

A small group of economists using Austrian theoretical approaches are analyzing entrepreneurship anew. I refer here mainly to Israel M. Kirzner's *Competition and Entrepreneurship*,[3] and to three recent unpublished papers by Kirzner, O'Driscoll and Rizzo presented at the

American Economic Association (AEA) meetings of August 1978. Using a labor theory of value, my investment in these papers is large. It entailed re-reading Knight, including his perceptive 23 page preface to the London School of Economics reissue of *Risk, Uncertainty and Profit*, dated August 1933.[4] My most rewarding endeavor has been in trying to extend and use the various expectation approaches in analyzing the behavior of students when the expected earnings from education change, and of farmers coping with technological changes and with inflation. My investment in these issues made me unduly critical. Surely entrepreneurship is not confined solely to collecting unanticipated windfalls and bearing unanticipated losses.

Although these papers share the assessment that there is no room for the entrepreneur in standard equilibrium theory, the economic logic of received theory is for them so compelling that no room for the entrepreneur is forthcoming. Unanticipated profits and losses are not sufficient for this purpose. To establish a useful place in theory for the entrepreneur, what entrepreneurs do must have some economic value. Collecting windfalls and bearing unanticipated losses are only a part of the story. If entrepreneurship has an economic value, it must perform a useful function and the supply of entrepreneurs must be constrained by scarcity, which implies that there is both a supply of entrepreneurial capacities and a demand for entrepreneurial services. My argument is that until it is established that entrepreneurship has an economic value that is in fact "earned," entrepreneurs have no room in economics.

The trouble is that economists are unduly indentured to *one* of the implications of Knightian uncertainty. This particular implication of "genuine (Knightian) uncertainty" dominates. If this were the sole valid implication, our much vaunted profit system merely distributes in some unspecified manner the windfalls and losses that come as surprises. In an economy in which changes and disequilibria go hand in hand, I find Kirzner's conclusion counterproductive. He closes his paper with the assertion that entrepreneurs are not a useful resource. What they do, according to Kirzner, has no ascertainable economic value. Thus, the conclusion is that entreprenuers, in an economy where disequilibria are the order of the day, are nevertheless not a valuable resource. Let me cite Kirzner on this issue: "... entrepreneurship is not to be treated as a resource ... The market never recognizes entrepreneurial ability in the sense of an available useful resource."

What went wrong in arriving at this conclusion? It arises out of Kirzner's concept of the unique vision that he attributes to entrepreneurs and Kirzner's concept of pure profit. Whether there are returns that are not pure profits is not made explicit. Accordingly, the returns that accrue to those who bring about the equilibrating process do not surface. I hasten to add that Kirzner's paper and the conclusion that I have cited do not do justice to his *Competition and Entrepreneurship*. I find his book a perceptive analysis of the state of economic theory with respect to the entrepreneur, but in it he also ends up not seeing the rewards that accrue to those who bring about the equilibrating process.

Knight's seminal treatise is not confined to the pure profits and pure losses that are a consequence of surprises. Much of it is devoted to the behavior of entrepreneurs in a dynamic economy. Knight deals at length with the risk-uncertainty problem inherent in nature, in technological changes and in the instability of prices. Knight later came to see that advances in knowledge are the most pervasive and important part of economic progress.[5] His treatise is rich with insights on the limitations of information and of expectations as change and progress occur under actual conditions. Knight is indeed much concerned with the contributions of entrepreneurs to the equilibrating process. He devotes a long chapter (chapter V) to the theory of change and progress with uncertainty absent and he returns (chapter XI) to this *"unchanging property of changing,"* noting that it would require a completely knowable world which is in his view a pure artifact of our minds, a refuge to whcih we flee. But there is a critical, unsettled issue. It pertains to Knight's "distinction between *risk*, as events subject to a known or knowable probability distribution, and *uncertainty*, as referring to events for which it was not possible to specify numerical probabilities" (Milton Friedman's *Price Theory*, p. 282).[6] The L.J. Savage view of personal probability denies any valid distinction along these lines.

In my thinking what is required are extensions of theory from which we can derive implications with respect to the supply of and demand for entrepreneurship in order to determine its economic value. I attempted to do this in my 1975 *Journal of Economic Literature* survey.[7] How much can be accomplished along this line by pursuing, extending and applying the conceptual theory of rational expectations is as yet to be determined. Surely, aspects of adaptive expectations could be made an integral part of rational expectations. There are, however, difficult unsolved problems in determining the actual sources of information that shape and alter over time the rational expectations of entrepreneurs. Disequilibria, whether they are of recent vintage or are being anticipated, are transitory events. They differ by type and they differ over time. No doubt the expectations of students are attuned to the value of education in our unstable economy. The expectations of farmers are in turn attuned to tech-nological changes and to inflation. But whence are these expectations derived? In what manner are they perceived and acted upon? As yet answers to these questions are not at hand.

All research in the sciences, including agricultural research, is a venturesome business. It entails the allocation of scarce resources. It requires organization and someone must decide what research is most worthwhile to undertake given the resource constraints and the state of knowledge. It is not a routine activity like working on an automobile assembly line, or planting corn, or baking a well-known cake. Research is a dynamic process and in a true sense it is a venture in doing that which has not been done before in an endeavor to add to the stock of knowledge. The individuals who make these research decisions are, in my book, research entrepreneurs. Who are they? To what extent are they qualified? Is agricultural research in the United States over-organized? I shall argue that it is indeed over-organized.

In retrospect there have been a number of outstanding agricultural research entrepreneurs. My list includes the distinguished biologists E.C. Stakeman and Herbert K. Hayes over the years as members on the faculty at the University of Minnesota; George Harrar's success in developing the agricultural research enterprise of the Rockefeller Foundation and the Mexican government in Mexico which has gradually evolved into CIMMYT stands in my view as a remarkable entrepreneurial achievement; likewise the success of Ralph Cummings during the years that he was in India place him high in this context. Turning to economics, the distinguished Wesley Mitchell and his role in developing the National Bureau of Economic Research; and the careers of John D. Black and, over the last two decades, Sir John Crawford surely qualify. An academic research entrepreneur of the highest order, to whom I have a very large debt during the years that I was at Iowa State, is R.E. Buchanan.

In closing, I draw briefly on my recent paper, "What Are We Doing to Research Entrepreneurship?"[8] A few remarks are required to restate the function of entrepreneurship as I turn to its application to research.

The dynamic attributes of research are pervasive both in the domain of economic growth and in the conduct of actual research. Over the long run new and better knowledge is one of the mainsprings of economic growth. Were it not for advances in knowledge, the economy would arrive at a stationary state and all economic activities would become essentially routine in nature. Over time new knowledge has augmented the productive capacity of land, and it has led to the development of new forms of physical capital and of new human skills. *A fundamental dynamic agent of long term economic growth is the research sector of the economy.*

The essence of research is in the fact that it is a venture into the unknown or into what is only partially known. Whereas funds, organization and competent scientists are necessary, they are not sufficient. An important factor in producing knowledge is the human ability that I have defined as research entrepreneurship. It is an ability that is scarce; it is hard to identify this talent; it is rewarded haphazardly in the not-for-profit research sector; and it is increasingly misused and impaired by the over-organization of our research enterprises. What is happening in agricultural research is on this score no exception.

Who are these research entrepreneurs? In business enterprises that are profit oriented, the chief executive officers perform an entrepreneurial function. Whereas administrators who are in charge of a research organization may be entrepreneurs, much of the actual entrepreneurship is a function of the assessment by scientists of the scientific frontiers of knowledge. Their professional competence is required to determine the research hypotheses that may be most worthwhile pursuing.

In the quest for appropriations and research grants, all too little attention is given to that scarce talent which is the source of research entrepreneurship. The convenient assumption is that a highly organized research institution firmly controlled by an administrator will perform this important function. But in fact, a large organization that is tightly controlled tends to be the death of creative research regardless of whether it be the National Science Foundation, a government agency, a large private foundation, or a large research oriented university. No national research director in Washington can know the array of research options that the state of scientific knowledge and its frontier afford. Nor can the managers of foundation funds know what needs to be known to perform this function. Having served as a member of a research advisory committee to a highly competent experiment station director for some years and having observed the vast array of research talent supported by funds that we as a committee had a hand in allocating, I am convinced that most working scientists are research entrepreneurs. But it is exceedingly difficult to devise institutions to utilize this special talent efficiently. Organization is necessary. It too requires entrepreneurs. Agricultural research has benefited from its experiment stations, specialized university laboratories, and from the recently developed international agricultural research centers. But there is the ever-present danger of over-organization, of directing research from the top, of requiring working scientists to devote ever more time to preparing reports to "justify" the work they are doing, and to treat research as if it were some routine activity.

In a modernizing economy, entrepreneurs perform a necessary function of considerable economic value. It is a bit disconcerting that the entrepreneur should be a stranger in standard equilibrium theory. No wonder that the determinants of the supply of and demand for entrepreneurs have been neglected.

Conclusions

1   The history of the development and achievements of US organized agricultural research and extension activities is a good vaccine for not becoming infected by the gloom and pessimism of doomsday, limits of growth, and the annual crop of new crises.

2   No one in Washington or elsewhere in the United States actually knows the environmental specifications that will, over future decades, equate our values with the use we make of our resources. Stay flexible, skeptical, and affirmatively critical.[9]

3   The person who understands research needs to know the state of scientific knowledge, its frontier and the hypotheses it affords. It is the competent working scientists who know most of these options and who are research entrepreneurs so essential to creative research.

4   Inasmuch as the production of knowledge is costly, allocative decisions must be made. Whether or not we have a taste for the market, the price signals provided by the market are an essential part of the information that should not be neglected in allocating funds to research and also in allocating our own time to the research enterprise we pursue.[10]

Notes and References

1   Margaret G. Reid, *Economics of Household Production* (John Wiley & Sons, New York, 1934).
2   See above, Part I, No. 3, "The Value of the Ability to Deal with Disequilibria."
3   Israel M. Kirzner, *Competition and Entrepreneurship* (University of Chicago Press, Chicago, Ill., 1973).
4   Frank H. Knight, *Risk, Uncertainty, and Profit* (London School of Economics and Political Science, Reprint No. 16, 1933).
5   Frank H. Knight, "Diminishing Returns from Investment," *Journal of Political Economy*, 52 (Mar. 1944), 26–47.
6   Milton Friedman, *Price Theory* (Aldine Publishing Co., Chicago, Ill., 1976).
7   See above, Part I, No. 3.

8   Theodore W. Schultz, "What Are We Doing to Research Entrepreneur-ship?," in Wm. F. Hueg Jr and Craig A. Gannon (eds), *Transforming Knowledge into Food in a Worldwide Context* (Miller Publishing Company, 1978), pp. 96–105.

9   See the editorial by Charles J. Hitch, "Unfreezing the Future," *Science* (Mar. 4 1977).

10 See Theodore W. Schultz, "The Economics of Research and Agricultural Productivity," *International Development Service* (IADS Occasional Paper, New York, Nov. 1979).

Part IV
Origins of Modern Agriculture

Part IV
Origins of Modern Agriculture

1

Modernizing Traditional Agriculture*

Whatever the reason, it is much easier for a poor country to acquire a modern steel mill than a modern agriculture. When it wants a steel mill, whether for production or for prestige, it can turn to Europeans, Russians, or Americans with assurance that it will get what it wants. But to whom can a poor country turn with confidence when it wants a modern agriculture, knowing that what it gets will be successful? To the Soviet Union? Surely this would be carrying ideology too far. Of course, the place to turn is to one of the countries in which a modern agriculture is making a large contribution. Thus we qualify. We have a modern agriculture. But our product has not performed well abroad. What are the reasons?

Why are we, as builders of agriculture, not skilled in undertaking this task abroad? We are renowned for our land-grant agricultural colleges, experiment stations, and extension services and for the US Department of Agriculture. We place a high value on the industries that supply agricultural inputs and that process and distribute farm products, on the network of communications that serves farm people, and on the abilities of farmers, although we often overlook the importance of the schooling of farm people. Yet seemingly we do not know how to institutionalize this type of public-private approach abroad.

It cannot be said that we have not been trying to help poor countries modernize their agriculture, for we have committed large sums and much talent to this task. Our government for several decades has been engaged in technical assistance to agriculture. Our leading foundations have been pioneers. Our agricultural colleges have undertaken counterpart work

* First published as "Economic Growth from Traditional Agriculture," in A.H. Moseman (ed.), *Agricultural Sciences for the Developing Nations* (American Association for the Advancement of Science, Washington DC, 1964), pp. 185–205. Copyright 1964 by AAAS. Reprinted with permission of the publisher.

abroad. We are involved in country planning to achieve, among other things, increases in agricultural production. We are also involved in land reform, the establishment of rural credit institutions, community development programs, and other types of agricultural extension services, technical assistance to agriculture, university contracts, and an array of specialized training programs. But despite all these programs, these approaches have so far not achieved results that come even close to expectations. There is understandably a growing doubt both among ourselves and among leaders in countries abroad whether we are efficient in these matters. What accounts for this apparent lack of success?

One difficulty in answering this question is that there are too many explanations. There are those who believe it stems out of our failure to understand the real basis of the success of US agriculture. It could be that we have as yet not identified the institutional components that matter most. It could also be true that we have had wholly unwarranted expectations as to what can be accomplished in any short period of time. The way we reckon costs and returns may be inadequate and therefore the test of our efficiency may be defective. But regardless of the source of the difficulty, some programs are undoubtedly better than others. Meanwhile the present danger is that since we and the governments concerned are unable to rate these programs correctly, even the best of them may lose support or even be discontinued altogether. It is therefore imperative that we take stock. What then accounts for this lack of success?

To find answers to this question I shall proceed as follows:

First, state the economic basis of traditional agriculture;
Second, show where private profit activities require complementary public activities;
Third, establish the reasons for the lack of success of most programs to modernize agriculture in poor countries;
Fourth, present the essential components of an efficient approach.

1   Economic Basis of Traditional Agriculture

The core of my book, Transforming Traditional Agriculture,[1] is an analysis of the economic basis of the sources of growth from agriculture. I shall therefore only summarize the logic and the empirical results with respect to two crucial economic properties.

First, it will come as a surprise to find that farmers in poor countries are in general not inefficient in using (allocating) the agricultural factors of production that they have at their disposal. Yet the reason once understood is simple. These farmers are as a rule subject to particular economic restraints that are typical of traditional agriculture; specifically, they are subject to a set of preferences for acquiring and holding wealth, and to a state of the arts, both of which have remained virtually constant for generations. As a consequence they have long since attained a type of stationary equilibrium. Thus the popular assumption that a different (better?) allocation of the existing poor collection of agricultural factors in these communities would substantially increase agricultural production is inconsistent both with economic logic as applied to the behavior of farmers in such an equilibrium and with the available empirical evidence. Strange as it may seem, it is true that on the basis of a strict allocative test, these farmers are more efficient than farmers in most of modern agriculture, because the latter are in a state of disequilibrium, a consequence of their "rapid progress."

Second, when it comes to investment to increase agricultural production, farmers who are bound by traditional agriculture have in general exhausted all profitable opportunities to invest in the agricultural factors at their disposal. This means that the marginal rate of return to investment in agricultural factors of the type which farmers have long been using is low, so low that there is little or no incentive to save and invest. Therefore economic growth from traditional agriculture is very expensive. It means, in practical terms, that adding a few more wells and ditches for irrigation, several more draft animals and implements, and other forms of reproducible capital of the type farmers have been using for generations will increase agricultural production very little, so little in fact that it yields an unattractive rate of return.

These two economic properties are basic in understanding the behavior of farmers in traditional agriculture. As I build on them, let me refer to the first property as *efficient allocation* and to the second as *unrewarding investment opportunities*. What they imply for economic growth from agriculture in many poor countries is both real and relevant. Programs aimed solely at improving the economic efficiency of farmers are doomed to fail. Let me repeat: paradoxical as it may seem, farmers in traditional agriculture are generally more efficient by strict economic standards than farmers in the technically advanced countries in using the particular collection of land, labor, and material reproducible capital that they each have at their disposal. Likewise, programs designed solely to induce farmers in traditional agriculture to increase their investment in precisely the same type of agricultural factors they have been using for generations will fail for lack of acceptance, simply because the pay-off is too low.

What then are the rewarding sources of economic growth from the type of agriculture under consideration? Is it more land? In old, long-settled communities with no open frontiers, additional land suitable for cultivation is hard to come by. Some, yes; for even in India it appears that a part of the recent increases in agricultural production has come from this source. But it is not likely to be nearly so important a source during the next ten years. In some parts of Latin America, notably in Brazil, new roads are opening new land for settlement. In general, however, increases in agricultural production will have to come from the vast areas of land already under cultivation, especially so in the long-settled poor countries.

Additional irrigation is on approximately the same economic footing as land. India, for example, already has three times as much land under irrigation as Japan, measured on a per capita basis. Yet India has invested large sums during recent years in still more irrigation. Had India invested enough of these sums to develop a low-cost efficient fertilizer industry, the pay-off undoubtedly would have been much higher in terms of profitable increases in agricultural production. But in Mexico, which is clearly an exception in this respect, irrigation facilities have been an important source of economic growth from agriculture. Additional draft animals, implements, and related tools and facilities of the type now being used in poor countries, as already noted, are unpromising sources of increasing returns.

It will be helpful at this point to distinguish between agricultural inputs that originate within agriculture and those that are supplied from outside of agriculture. With few exceptions, all the inputs that farmers in poor countries can produce for themselves are low pay-off sources. On the other hand, virtually all agricultural inputs that hold real promise come from outside of agriculture. This is obvious for commercial fertilizer, machinery, tractors, insecticides, and the development of genetically superior plants and animals. Though less obvious, it is also true for schooling and other means to improve the skills of farm people.

The high-pay-off sources are predominantly *improvements in the quality of agricultural inputs*; these inputs can be acquired by farmers only from nonfarm firms and from agencies engaged in agricultural research, extension work, and schooling. It is therefore necessary to develop ways and means of improving the quality not only of the material reproducible inputs, but also of human agents engaged in farming. Thus far, in our attempts to assist poor countries in modernizing their agriculture, we have been vague and uncertain with regard to these sources of economic growth, and where we have happened to concentrate on the correct objective, we have with few exceptions failed to do things in the right order and in ways that would institutionalize the process.

The people who build steel mills may have the easier task, but clearly they also have demonstrated that they have a better concept of what needs to be done than we have had for modernizing agriculture.

2   Where Economic Incentives are Weak

Two factors hold the key to economic modernization in farming. They are, first, improving the quality of agriculture inputs, and, second, supplying them at a price that will make it worth while for farmers to acquire them and to learn how to use them efficiently. But firms for profit unassisted by research, schooling, and extension work are too weak to turn this key. What this means is that a pure market approach is not sufficient. Although there is a good deal of tilting at ideological windmills in the area of economic policy, there is fortunately little of it in the case of agricultural research, extension work, and schooling for farm children by Americans who have had their apprenticeship in institutions that serve US agriculture. The reasons why the economic incentives of firms for profit in the nonfarm sectors are frequently weak when it comes to supplying inputs to modernize agriculture will be presented shortly.

There are two preliminary issues with respect to economic incentives which I must consider in order to forestall being misunderstood. By weak incentives I do not mean that farmers in poor countries are not responsive to prices. The doctrine that farmers in poor countries either are indifferent or respond perversely to changes in prices, including the terms on which credit is available, is patently false and harmful.

Not enough attention has been given to product and factor prices in our efforts to assist countries in modernizing their agriculture. Where product prices are suppressed or where they thwart farmers, no program however well conceived and administered can succeed. It should be obvious that where the price of fertilizer is too high relative to the price of the farm product, no extension program can be devised that will induce farmers to use more fertilizer. Farmers will not and of course should not apply additional fertilizer under these circumstances. In Japan, where farmers apply many times as much fertilizer per acre as do farmers in India, the price of fertilizer is vastly lower in relation to the price of farm products. It takes less than half as many pounds of wheat in Japan to buy a pound of nitrogenous fertilizer as it does in India (see tables IV.1.1 and IV.1.2). In the case of rice, the differences in prices are even larger. Rice farmers in India pay between three and four times as much for fertilizer as do farmers in Japan in terms of the price that they receive for rice, while the farmers in Thailand pay more than five times

Table IV.1.1 Fertilizer and Farm Product Prices: Comparisons by commodities and countries, 1960–1961 (*Source:* FAO, *Production Yearbook, 1961*, Vol. 15)

Country	Price paid by farmers for fertilizer, 1960–1961[a] ($US per 100 kg)			Price received by farmers for products, 1960 ($US per 100 kg)	Ratio of fertilizer price to product price		
	Nitrogenous	Phosphate	Potash		(1/4)	(2/4)	(3/4)
	(1)	(2)	(3)	(4)	(5)	(6)	(7)
				Wheat[b]			
India	37.00[c]	26.20[c]		6.75[d]	5.48	3.88	
Japan	24.70	21.90	9.20	10.40	2.38	2.11	0.88
France	30.00	21.50	8.30	8.10	3.70	2.65	1.02
US[e]	26.90	19.70	9.40	6.40	4.20	3.08	1.47
				Rice[f]			
India	37.00	26.20	9.20	7.80[g]	4.74	3.36	0.48
Japan	24.70	21.90		19.30	1.28	1.13	
US[e]	26.90	19.70	9.40	10.10	2.66	1.95	0.93
				Corn[h]			
India	37.00	26.20		5.30	6.98	4.94	
US[e]	26.90	19.70	9.40	4.10	6.56	4.80	2.29
				Sugar cane[i]			
India	37.00	26.20		9.10	4.07	2.88	
US[e]	26.90	19.70	9.40	9.50	2.83	2.07	0.99

[a] Table 174, FAO source. Prices paid by farmers for bagged fertilizer on a plant nutrient basis.
[b] Producer price, 1960. Table 126, FAO source.
[c] 1959–1960.
[d] 78.5 percent of the wholesale price in table 126, FAO source. For adjustment, see *Indian J. Agr. Econ.*, 17, 81–84, Jan.–Mar. 1962.
[e] Average of bagged and bulk.
[f] Producer paddy price, 1960. Table 133, FAO source.
[g] 83 percent of the wholesale price of coarse rice shown in table 133, FAO source. See *Indian J. Agr. Econ.*, 17, table 1, p. 48, and Appendix 1, pp. 51–52, Jan.–Mar. 1962, for adjustment, based on 1957–1958, Bolpur market seasonal distribution.
[h] Producer price, 1960. Table 130, FAO source, India wholesale price adjusted to a 75 percent basis.
[i] From Table 134 of FAO source.

Table IV.1.2 Fertilizer and rice prices in eight countries, 1960–1961 (*Source*: FAO, *Production Yearbook, 1961*, Vol. 15, Tables 133 and 174)

Country	Prices paid by farmers for nitrogenous fertilizer ($US per kg)	Prices received by farmers for rice* ($US per kag)	Ratio (1/2)	Index based on Japan (128 = 100)
	(1)	(2)	(3)	(4)
Japan	24.70	19.30	1.28	100
Italy	21.00	9.30	2.26	177
US	26.90	10.10	2.66	208
Ceylon	36.80	12.10	3.04	238
India	37.00	7.80	4.74	370
Thailand	27.90	4.30	6.49	507
UAR	40.30	5.20	7.75	605
Burma	28.60	3.00	9.53	745

* The figure for Japan includes packaged rice. The figure for Thailand is the wholesale price in Bangkok.

as much. Little wonder then that farmers in India[2] and Thailand find fertilizer unprofitable.

There are also the probable adverse effects of Public Law 480[3] exports, not only upon world prices, but, more important in relation to the task at hand, upon farm product prices in some of the poor countries receiving large quantities of P.L. 480 products from the United States. Although the total quantity of resources available to the receiving country is increased, the P.L. 480 imports are likely to depress particular farm product prices within the receiving country below what they otherwise would have been, and to this extent the economic incentives to farmers to increase agricultural products are impaired. We are indeed remiss if we fail to detect and help correct the underpricing of farm products and the overpricing of agricultural inputs so widespread in poor countries.

The other preliminary issue pertains to the economic incentives influencing farmers who are bound by traditional agriculture, even though there were no overt policies causing the types of underpricing and overpricing referred to above. The economic basis for the observable allocative efficiency and for the unrewarding investment opportunities has already been presented. The implication is that farmers situated in such a penny economy use the existing poor collection of agricultural resources so that every penny counts; measured in economic terms, marginal costs and returns are equated exceedingly fine. These farmers accordingly have exhausted for all practical purposes the gains to be had from economic efficiency. They also have exhausted the gains to be had from additional investment in agricultural factors of production of the type that have long been at their disposal. The state of arts available to them has been pursued to its outer limit in equating with a penny fineness marginal preferences to save and marginal rates of return to investment.

Returning now to the key issue, why is it that firms for profit unassisted by nonprofit agencies that concentrate on agricultural research, extension work, and schooling are not capable of modernizing agriculture efficiently? The answer is really quite simple. The benefits from these activities accrue in substantial part to individuals and firms other than those who produce them. This means that if firms for profit were to undertake them, they would be saddled with all the costs but they would not be able to capture all the returns. Therefore, they would enter upon agricultural research, schooling, and extension work only up to the point where that part of the marginal returns which accrued to them would cover their marginal costs. Since there are substantial additional (social) returns which firms for profit cannot capture, it is a mistake to expect such firms to pursue these activities to their social optimum. Clearly, then, the basic economic reason why firms for profit cannot attain a social optimum in this respect is simply a consequence of the fact that it is impossible for them to capture all the benefits that flow from these particular activities.

3 The Lack of Success and the Reasons for It

I began with a judgment that as builders of agriculture we have not done well in poor countries. But have our agricultural programs abroad really been as unsuccessful as I have implied? I would be the first to concede that the available evidence is not good enough for strong inferences. Relevant data are hard to come by. It is unfortunately true that no one has had the foresight to see the experimental nature of these programs, and thus no one has kept the necessary records that would provide a basis for drawing inferences from these experiments.

As of 1960 there was some evidence to back my judgment. It is implicit in the weak association between increases in agricultural production in foreign countries and what we have been doing for agriculture in those countries. With one or two exceptions, the most impressive increases in agricultural production since the war have occurred in countries where we have had no programs. Japan and Israel have been among the most successful. So have Austria and Greece in the western European

Table IV.1.3 Country and regional increases in agricultural production, total and per capita, 1935–1939 to 1962 (Based on Supplements to *The World Agricultural Situation, 1963*, USDA, 1963; *Indices of Agricultural Production for the 20 Latin American Countries*, FAS, USDA, Oct. 1959)

Country	Total		Per capita	
	1935–1939	*1962*	*1935–1939*	*1962*
			(Cols. (1) and (2) divided by a	
	(1952–1953 to		*1953 = 100*	
	1954–1955 = 100)		*population index)*	
	(1)	(2)	(3)	(4)
Japan[a]	83	159	102	146
Taiwan	89	144	144	107
Philippines	73	143	104	108
India	83	130	102	107
Pakistan	103	121	126	100
(South Asia and Far East)	88	133	110	111
Mexico	47	157[b]	70	126[b]
Brazil	73	150[b]	106	116[b]
Colombia	64	124[b]	91	99[b]
Chile	73	118[b]	99	91[b]
Peru	61	117[b]	82	98[b]
(Latin America)	72	129[c]	103	101[c]
Israel	70	212[c]	115	155[c]
Turkey	66	122[c]	90	95[c]
(West Asia)	69	129[c]	97	101[c]
	Prewar		Prewar	
Austria	94	137[c]	97	135[c]
Greece	85	135[c]	103	125[c]
(Western Europe)	81	121[c]	92	113[c]

[a] Italics indicate key countries in terms of success.
[b] 1961–1962.
[c] 1962–1963.

complex (see table IV.1.3). The US aid missions to Greece undoubtedly contributed somewhat to the recent upsurge in agriculture there. Then there is Mexico, which has been establishing a remarkable record of economic growth from agriculture; in all probability there has been a real connection between the agricultural research with which The Rockefeller

Foundation has been identified and some of the Mexican increases in agricultural production. The Philippines and Taiwan are often cited as countries which have done well and where we have had a substantial hand. Total agricultural production has indeed risen more there than in most countries. Turning to India and Pakistan, where our commitments of both public and private funds and of talent have been large, the agricultural sector has had a poor record.

A few years ago I and some colleagues investigated the effects of technical assistance programs under way in Latin America upon the economy of these countries.[4] Our technical assistance program began early in Latin America. From 1943 to 1955 the United States contributed $44 million to agriculture and natural resource programs in Latin America, and the annual rate of US expenditures for this purpose rose to $9 million. The production effects of these programs during the years from 1943 to 1954 should have become evident during the period since then. Though it is true that agricultural production in Latin America as a whole has continued to increase, the increase has been at a rate no higher than that of population. On a per capita basis, between 1953 and 1961–1962 nine of these countries lost ground; in two of them we had no programs (Argentina and Uruguay), and among the other seven were Chile, Colombia, Costa Rica, Paraguay, and Peru, in each of which we had large agricultural technical assistance programs. Among the eleven countries that gained somewhat on a per capita basis, one had received no US technical assistance for agriculture (Venezuela), and in two of the others agricultural production has risen very little by this measure (Haiti and Dominican Republic). This evidence, so it seems to me, suggests a weak association between our programs to modernize agriculture and the increases in agricultural production that have been realized.

Why is the record no better than this? The answer depends upon one's concept of the task. There is a profusion of concepts. Each is based on a particular view and a bit of experience, for we are above all practical, relying heavily upon pragmatic wisdom, and our wisdom is based on a wide array of experiences. But such wisdom is often swamped by extraneous considerations for lack of a general theory to guide decisions and to evaluate what we have done.

A part of the difficulty stems from a confusion between means and end. Yet it should be obvious that the basic objective is not a set of new agricultural institutions per se; these modernizing institutions are warranted only where they become a source of economic growth from agriculture. Nor is it sufficient by this test to show that agricultural production has increased as a consequence of these institutions; it is also necessary to show that in terms of costs and returns it is a relatively cheap source of economic growth – more precisely, that it is at least no more expensive than the next best alternative source open to the country.

Many farmers in poor countries are under the economic restraints of traditional agriculture. Wherever agricultural extension programs have been launched, based on the assumption that these farmers are necessarily inefficient in using (allocating) the agricultural factors at their disposal, it is highly probable that the programs have not contributed and cannot contribute to economic modernization.

There are also agricultural extension and rural credit programs which are based on the belief that farmers in poor countries are not saving and investing enough of their income in agriculture and that they are using less than an optimum amount of credit. What has been overlooked in launching these programs is the fact that there are no rewarding investment opportunities open to farmers within the economic confines of traditional agriculture. Therefore it is not possible by means of such programs to win increasing returns from this type of agriculture.

It is all too fashionable to malign farmers in poor countries. What is often said is that they have a penchant for idleness, that they are neither industrious nor thrifty, and that they lack entrepreneurship. They are said to be deficient with respect to such essential economic virtues because of some flaws in their culture. To be sure, there are cultural limitations; for example, with regard to restraints upon schooling. But these limitations are seldom relevant in connection with the economic attributes mentioned above. Let us cease and desist from maligning farmers in poor countries with respect to these particular economic attributes. Many agricultural extension programs abroad with which we are identified are attempting to induce farmers to adopt and use one or more new agricultural inputs that simply are not productive enough to make it worth while for farmers to introduce them and use them. In the case of such new agricultural inputs, including techniques and practices, farmers are not innately averse to improving their lot, but they are reacting correctly because of the small or zero or even minus rewards that can be realized from such inputs. Therefore, there can be little or no gains from such programs.

It is highly probable that in the vast majority of situations where farmers in poor countries are not responding to our agricultural approaches in assisting those countries, no really profitable or rewarding new agricultural inputs have been *developed* and *produced* and *supplied* to farmers cheaply enough to make it worth their while to adopt them and learn how to use them efficiently. This lack of profitable new agricultural inputs is the crux of the matter. Where such inputs have become available to farmers, for example in Mexico, farmers have responded andone observes substantial economic growth from the agricultural sector.

The lack of success under consideration is therefore probably not a consequence of the long list of conventional reasons that clutter the literature on this issue. By this I mean that it is probably not because the US workers in agricultural extension abroad are inadequately trained in soils, crops, animal husbandry, and farm management. It is not because they do not stay abroad long enough, nor because their activities are badly organized and insufficiently integrated into the culture of the farm community. Although rural credit facilities may be meager, they are not necessarily a primary factor until new highly productive agricultural inputs become available; it is then that credit begins to count. Farms may be exceedingly small, but this too does not account for the lack of success. Nor is it, as some would like to believe, because farmers in these countries are prone to idleness, are not industrious and thrifty, and lack entrepreneurship. The plain fact of the matter is that these programs are unsuccessful primarily because no profitable, rewarding new agricultural inputs have been available to farmers which they could adopt and use.

4 An Efficient Approach

What then is the time and place for extension, research, schools, and firms for profit? Is there a natural order? In what respects are they competitive or complementary? Reflections on these issues will help us see the requirements for an efficient approach. Simply pressing for more agricultural production regardless of costs is no solution. Costs must be reckoned against returns which become streams of income. Thus, additional income is the economic aim, and the critical question is, at what price? Accordingly, the economic test is in the price of the sources of such income streams, whether from farming or from any other activity. A high price, which is characteristic of traditional agriculture, discourages investment to expand production. It follows that one of the requirements for modernizing agriculture is a supply of low-priced sources. In modern agriculture the suppliers of these sources are a mixed group consisting of firms that operate for profit and of public and private nonprofit agencies. The demanders of these sources in the first instance are farmers who are dependent upon information and learning about these sources. An efficient approach, therefore, is one that organizes (combines) these firms, farms, and agencies, functioning as suppliers and demanders of new sources of income from agriculture, so that they achieve an optimum rate of increase in income.

A concept of economic advance which underlies this analysis indicates that the programs to modernize agriculture successfully must be built on the following foundation:

New agricultural inputs that have a relatively high pay-off are required.

A supply of these inputs must be available to farmers.

As farmers accept them they must learn how to use them efficiently.

With regard to the first part of the foundation, the implication is that any program to modernize agriculture must begin with agricultural inputs (sometimes referred to loosely as practices and techniques) that are unmistakably rewarding. Such inputs consist predominantly of particular quality components which become an integral part of material inputs and of human agents. These quality components are embedded in tools, machines, chemicals, soil structures, and the genetic attributes of plants and animals. They also enter through an array of new skills acquired by farm people. That such rewarding inputs are an essential part of the foundation seems obvious. Yet there is little room for doubt that most of the lack of success of our efforts on behalf of agriculture abroad can be traced back to a failure to provide this part of the foundation.

High-pay-off agricultural inputs with rare exceptions have not been discovered and developed by our best farmers. The early corn yield tests, based on searching for superior seed corn on Iowa farms over twelve years from 1904 to 1915 and testing these seeds on 75,000 field plots, as summarized by Martin L. Mosher,[5] tell us how slow and difficult it was to improve corn yields by this approach even with exceptionally competent and inspired workers and leadership. Corn yields in Iowa, which had averaged 32.4 bushels an acre from 1896 to 1905, averaged only 33 bushels during 1913, 1914, and 1915.

Nor has our own agricultural research establishment had a long history of providing a stream of new, high-pay-off agricultural inputs. Though it has been doing so since about the mid 1920s, we have been blind to the fact that for decades before that, it produced a trickle of such advances. Increases in agricultural production between 1900 and 1925 can be entirely accounted for by increases in conventional agricultural inputs. The rate of increase in agricultural output was small, about 0.9 percent per year, while conventional agriculture inputs rose 1.0 percent per year.[6] Thus, we might well have been on our guard and not have taken it for granted that the agricultural experiment stations in India, or in the various countries of Latin America, or elsewhere in poor countries had already discovered and developed a supply of high-pay-off agricultural inputs waiting to be adopted by farmers. Although there may be some exceptions, in general these agricultural experiment stations as of 1960 had not yet produced large successes; in this respect they are at a stage that is comparable to our own between 1900 and 1925.

How little or how much can be accomplished by transferring particular agricultural inputs that are highly productive and rewarding in the United States, is undoubtedly something we had to learn largely from experience. The tuition has been high, but we now know that as a rule such direct transfers are not a rewarding source of agricultural inputs for poor countries.

There is, however, a fourth source, namely new agricultural research. But why should it be any more fruitful than the old agricultural research already considered? The reason is fairly obvious. There have been important recent advances in scientific knowledge, consisting of theories and principles that have been tested and found useful. Not that they will suffice in coping with all phases of tropical agriculture; nevertheless, they represent a major scientific asset waiting to be mobilized. But such new agricultural research has been neglected in what has been done for agriculture abroad.

By 1964, although the US government had been actively engaged in technical assistance in agriculture throughout Latin America for two decades, not a single first-class agricultural research center has been developed as a consequence of these activities. Mexico had done well, but not because of any technical assistance from the US Government. The funds and talent provided by The Rockefeller Foundation, however, played a part in the Mexican advance. Japan had done exceedingly well on her own. But throughout South Asia, where we have both public and private commitments to assist agriculture, with few exceptions new agricultural research had been neglected. The new research to develop superior wheat, corn, and grain sorghum varieties in India and the recently established International Rice Research Institute in the Philippines were among the exceptions.

There are three unresolved issues with respect to such agricultural research centers in poor countries: (1) the number, (2) the scientific personnel, and (3) the optimum size. No doubt there are some small countries that cannot afford even one first-rate center. But what about countries as vast and diverse as Brazil and India?[7] Here, again, our own experiences are most telling. It would have been absurd to opt for only one such center in the United States and to locate it at Washington, DC. It is fully as absurd to conceive of Pusa at New Delhi as the agricultural research center for all of India. As to the second issue, clearly there is no substitute for scientific competence. The AID-university contracts in general have not succeeded on this score. On the other hand, the International Rice Research Institute in the Philippines has acquired a highly competent staff, as has the agricultural research establishment in Mexico. On the matter of the optimum size of such centers, all too little is known. No one to my knowledge has examined the complementarity among scientists with a view to resolving this issue. A lone scientist is absurd; a small core may be far less than optimum. Our own experiences seem to support two inferences: first, research scientists should be an integral part of a college or university, and, second, a number of competent persons no larger than that in most of our state agricultural experiment stations is inadequate. It may well be true that by this test less than ten of the agricultural research centers in the United States are of optimum size.

Turning now to the second part of the foundation, that is, a supply of the high-pay-off agricultural inputs that farmers can acquire: Once such inputs have been discovered, developed, and tested, who will produce and supply them to farmers? The multiplication and distribution of new seeds is an example. In general this is not the kind of activity that experiment stations and extension services can carry on efficiently. Nor can a ministry of agriculture, or cooperatives that do not operate for profit, perform this task efficiently. Ways and means, therefore, must be found to transfer these activities to firms that operate for profit. Needless to say, many of the governments in poor countries either distrust such private profit-making firms, or seek to build little empires for themselves within the public domain, and they therefore prefer not to transfer these essential supply functions to firms that are subject to the discipline of the market.

The third part of the foundation consists of information for and learning by farmers. In a strict sense, it can be undertaken only after the other two parts have been built. Thus there is a kind of natural order, a basic sequence in what is done to modernize agriculture. But we have repeatedly made the mistake of undertaking this last part before the other two were in place. In Peru, for example, already by the early fifties, the fountainhead of a fine agricultural extension service had been developed, but unfortunately it ran dry because the supply of rewarding agricultural inputs was inadequate. In the early 1960s, this was also the situation in India. Our state agricultural extension services during the early years appear to have had little worth-while information for farmers. The many efforts that we made during World War I to expand agricultural production and the lack of success of these efforts support this inference. Agricultural production in the United States during 1917–1919 came to only a scant 1 percnet more than that during 1912–1914.[8] Where the aim is economic growth from agriculture, there is no escaping the fact that unless there is a supply of rewarding inputs that farmers can acquire, an agricultural extension service is an empty institutional gesture.

But the right time for extension work is only one of the facets of information and learning. The costs to farmers are another facet. These costs depend among other things on the complexity of the new production process facing farmers. In considering costs, there is a basic proposition with respect to the rate at which farmers will accept a new agricultural input. It is here proposed as a hypothesis: *The rate of acceptance depends predominantly on the profitability of the new input.* Unquestionably, the greater the complexity of the new process, the larger the costs. Suppose there is a new highly profitable variety which requires only a few simple changes in traditional farm practices. In this case the costs of acquiring information and of learning by farmers are small, and it follows that an elaborate extension program would be superfluous. One observes that some new inputs are so profitable that as they become available farmers swamp the suppliers with their demand for them. Though such inputs, like striking a gushing oil well, are not frequent, there is much to be said for finding and developing precisely this class of input in launching agricultural programs abroad. Drawing on our own experience, hybrid corn was such a discovery, and, as a consequence, farmers in the heart of the corn belt where hybrid corn proved to be most rewarding adopted the hybrid seed rapidly in spite of the very low corn prices that prevailed during the early and middle thirties.

As the process of modernizing agriculture proceeds, however, farming becomes increasingly more complex. Many new inputs become profitable only after a multiplicity of changes in practices which require much information and learning on the part of farmers.

Still another facet of this type of information and learning is the complementarity between the activities of firms for profit, chiefly the suppliers of new inputs, and nonmarket agencies such as the extension service and schools. This facet is often overlooked in our activities abroad, despite our success in this respect in the United States. Since I have dealt with this complementarity elsewhere, I shall not enter upon it here.[9]

There is one more facet of information and learning that I can only mention in closing, although it may well be the most important of them all. Taking the long view, it is essential to see that the acquisition of new skills by farm people is also one of the primary new profitable inputs. Though I have concentrated on new material inputs, and though they are necessary, the fruit from the advance in knowledge that is useful in economic endeavors is to an even larger extent dependent upon new skills. The necessity for learning the skills that are required for modernizing agriculture brings us to the issue of investing in farm people.

How to do this most efficiently is a matter about which we know all too little as yet. Crash programs are warranted under some circumstances. So are demonstrations designed to instruct farmers. There is also a place for some on-the-job training. But investment in schooling is in all probability the most economical way when one takes a ten- to twenty-year view of the process. What this means is that the rate of return to the costs of schooling, especially at the primary level, is probably exceedingly high, higher than the return to the investment in any of the alternative ways of acquiring these new skills.

Anthony M. Tang's study of inputs and the output of Japanese agriculture[10] permits me to close with an exceedingly encouraging estimate of the rate of return to investment in agricultural research, extension, and schooling. This estimate is for the period from 1880 to 1938. During the first five years of this period fully 98 percent of the total outlays for these purposes was for schooling. At the end of the period, that is, in the last five years, agricultural research and extension represented about 9 percent of the total outlays. The social rate of return to all this schooling, research, and extension was a handsome 35 percent per year. Where could one do better than this in achieving economic growth?

No doubt some day soon in our role as builders of agriculture we shall learn how to develop a modern agriculture in poor countries and become as successful at it as the builders of steel mills, even though ours is a much more difficult task.

Notes and References

1 Theodore W. Schultz, *Transforming Traditional Agriculture* (Yale University Press, New Haven, Conn., 1964).
2 In India the price of sugar cane and apparently also of potatoes relative to the price of fertilizer has been attractive to farmers, to judge from their recent production behavior.
3 Public Law 480 of July 10, 1954 allocated US funds to finance foreign aid using "surpluses" of agricultural products.
4 See *Technical Cooperation in Latin America* (National Planning Association, Washington DC, 1950). These studies were sponsored by the NPA. Several books were published based on these studies, and are listed in the report cited.
5 Martin L. Mosher, *Early Iowa Corn Yield Tests and Related Programs* (Iowa State University Press, Ames, Iowa, 1962).
6 Vernon W. Ruttan, "Technological change and resource utilization in American agriculture," *Proceedings of the Indiana Academy of Sciences 1961*, 71 (1961), 353–60. Between 1925 and 1950, agricultural output rose

at a rate of 1.5 percent per year while conventional inputs rose at a rate of only 0.4 percent per year.

7   We do well to remember that the United States, too, was relatively poor at the time when we established the land-grant colleges. The Morrill Act came in 1862, when US real per capita gross national product was about one-seventh of what it is in 1964; and the Hatch Act, providing federal funds for agricultural research, came in 1887, when we were at one-fourth of the present per capita GNP level.

8   See Neal Potter and Francis T. Christy Jr, *Trends in Natural Resource Commodities* (Johns Hopkins Press, Baltimore, Md, 1962), table EO-1, p. 81.

9   Schultz, *Transforming Traditional Agriculture*, chapters 10 and 11.

10 Anthony M. Tang, "Research and Education in Japanese Agricultural Development, 1880–1938," *Economic Studies Quarterly*, 13(1963), table 2 and p. 97.

2

Economics, Agriculture, and the Political Economy*

The increase in the economic value of agricultural products since 1972 raises several important questions. Are the high world prices of these primary products here for the long pull or are they transitory prices? The answer, as I see it, depends in large measure on what governments do to agriculture. What then are the agricultural cost implications of the acts of governments? In this context, the issue of value and price can be put as follows: Are the underlying costs such that world agriculture could produce, over the next decade and longer, a supply of products that would be adequate to equate the demand at substantially lower relative world prices than the prices that prevailed during 1974 and 1975? I shall argue that the technical and investment opportunities to increase agricultural production are such that the answer to this key questions is in the affirmative. But this is not to say that these opportunities will be realized. It is not a prediction that governments will act appropriately.

I take it to be obvious that what governments do to agriculture differs greatly from country to country. It is also obvious that the economic performance of the agricultural sector differs markedly among countries. What is not obvious, however, is that much of the difference in the economic performance of the agricultural sector is a consequence of what governments do to agriculture. Most agricultural economists see this issue as too controversial and too unsettled for analysis. Some will say that it entails special values, welfare objectives and maintenance of political authority and that these are matters that go beyond positive economics. It is my contention, however, that economics can deal with major parts of this issue, and that economists can evaluate the economic effects of what governments do to agriculture.

* First Elmhirst Memorial Lecture, published in Theodore Dams (ed.), *Decision-Making and Agriculture* (Alden Press, Oxford, 1977), pp. 15–24. Reprinted by permission of the International Association of Agricultural Economists and the University of Nebraska Press.

To suggest what I have in mind, consider the marked differences in the responses of agriculture throughout the world beginning in 1973 to the sharp rise in the economic value of agricultural products. The actual incentives that would warrant an expansion in production by farmers varied widely from country to country. A large part of the differences in these incentives is the result of actions taken by governments. Accordingly, the 1973–1975 period is akin to an "ideal" experiment to measure the influence that governments had on incentives and to determine the effects that these differences in incentives had on the production responses of farmers. I shall be returning to this "experiment" presently.

Using Viner's definition, agricultural economics is what agricultural economists do. Much of what they do is done well. The use of theory in empirical work has been justly praised by Wassily Leontief in his American Economic Association presidential address. He criticized the drift in economics toward theoretical assumptions with insufficient concern about observable facts. He noted, however, that "an exceptional example of a healthy balance between theoretical and empirical analyses and of the readiness of professional economists to cooperate with experts in neighboring disciplines is offered by Agricultural Economics".[1] Professor Leontief's assessment, however, is only part of the story. It is true that we who are agricultural economists know a good deal about soils, agronomy, crops and livestock, and we stay abreast of the contributions of agricultural scientists. We are not naive and simple-minded about the role of farmers as workers, capitalists, and entrepreneurs. We are skilled in using modern quantitative techniques, and occasionally there is one among us who contributes to their advances. Our studies of the management and production of farms are guided by the theory of the firm, and our macro models are designed to deal with agriculture as an integral part of the general economy. But what Leontief fails to see is the increasing opposition to economics in social and political thought, the debasement of economics by governments, and the unwillingness or inability of economists to challenge this adverse drift. That "healthy balance between theoretical and empirical analyses', attributed to agricultural economics, does not suffice to make this challenge.

This opposition to economics is not confined to either the low or the high income countries. Nor is it restricted to a particular type of government. It is not limited to agriculture, for clearly other parts of the economy are not spared. Most of the high priests of national and international politics, whether they speak for the first, second or third world, are at heart contemptuous of economics. But despite differences in political organization, in cartels, in marketing boards, in commodity agreements and in internal pricing of factors and products, *there is no free lunch*. The hard realities of the costs of producing goods and services are not abolished by either national or international politics. Herein lies not only the hope but the necessity of economics.

The easy road is to accommodate opposition. But the utility of economics is reduced by making it ever more permissive. Although corporations, labor unions, farmer organizations and consumer advocates perform useful functions, they are not innocent economic agents for they do conspire to exact benefits for themselves at the expense of others. To disassemble economics for the purpose of serving the special interest of these organizations is to sell economics short. While it is also true that governments are necessary, to make economics subservient to them regardless of what they do to the economy is to take the heart out of the utility of economics. What all this implies for us in agriculture is that it will not suffice for agricultural economists to take the particular economic goals of governments as given. For economists to proceed in this manner means that economics becomes hostage to government. When this occurs, and it can be readily observed, the result is that economists become "yes-men" in the halls of political economy.

I believe that the core of economics is sufficiently robust to evaluate the cost and welfare effects of various political-economic institutions. One need not become stranded on value judgments. No doubt I am now vulnerable; I obviously need a cloak of credibility. It is at hand from the pen of my colleague, Harry G. Johnson.

> One of the penalties or privileges of advancing age and professional maturation in an academic career in the social sciences is that one is forced to think in terms of progressively broadening frames of institutional and cultural reference. The young economist . . . comes out of the graduate student mill with a narrow range of specialized skills and the stamp of his teachers' ideas heavy upon him. He makes his way initially by applying his skills . . . in an institutional and social context taken as an immutable part of his environment. Only as he acquires self-confidence, on the one hand, and abrasive experience of the larger . . . world, on the other, can he afford again to accord himself the liberty to question society's institutions . . .[2]

Needless to say, agricultural economists are not renowned for their critical evaluations of the economic effects of various political institutions on agriculture. At a more general level, the positive implications of value and price become weaker as economists become more permissive. To reach the Promised Land, never introduce value-judgments into your analysis, always screen your assumptions with great care to make absolutely sure that they are not contaminated!

There are two academic styles for dealing with economic assumptions and value judgments. From the twenties to the fifties it was the style to question the assumptions of theoretical analysis and dispute the value-judgments asserted to be implicit in the theory. It has been called, quite properly, "negative economics".[3] Since then the emphasis has shifted to whether or not the implications of the economic theory, given its assumptions, are validated by observable economic behavior. This approach has become known as "positive economics".

It is not difficult to question the simplistic assumptions of the early English economists. Nevertheless, particular implications of their theory are valid empirically, for example, that the removal of the tariff on imported wheat increases the real income of the working class. Marx accepted this implication of the tariff on wheat and called this tariff a "bread tax". Despite the criticism levelled against the assumptions on which Marx's theory rests, one of the implications of his theory is that technical advances in agriculture over time reduces the income share of landlords. The economic history of high income countries strongly supports this implication. There are, however, other parts of classical theory and of Marxian theory that fail to meet the test of positive economics.

The analytical task that I deem to be possible and necessary need not be confined to current developments. Economic history is replete with political-economic experiments from which we can draw information. To gain an historical perspective, I shall begin with an account of the interactions between social thought and the institutional order to show the rise and decline of particular political-economic institutions and the apparent reasons for the instability of these institutions. I shall then consider some of the more important economic effects of various political-economic institutions on agriculture currently and in the recent past.

1   Interaction between Social Thought and the Political Economy

I shall appeal to three assumptions, namely, that social thought consists of various social, political and economic ideas, that the dominant social thought shapes the institutionalized order of society (country), and that the malfunctioning of established institutions in turn alters social thought. The ideas that are embodied in social thought are of two historical types: those that rationalize and contribute to the codification of the prevailing order, and those that arise in protest to the established order which become embodied in social thought and then become strong enough to induce a real alteration in political-economic institutions.[4]

The mercantile economy that prevailed for at least a century, for example in England, prior to 1776 was buttressed by the established Church and the Law. It was also rationalized by the economic "literature" of that period which provided support for governmental restrictions on trade, on internal prices and wages and on migration – *restrictions which have once again acquired a modern ring.* The advocates of mercantilism had a theory which implied that keeping wages low increases the national product. It is this implication that provided support for the utility-of-poverty doctrine.

In retrospect, the utility-of-poverty doctrine of that period is startling not because it is no longer pursued by many countries but because it was so openly supported at that time. The doctrine held sway for a century in English history during which the poverty of the lower classes was declared to be desirable. Between 1660 and 1776, the mercantilism of England produced an intricate system of foreign and domestic policies, and it sought to rationalize the utility of poverty. Edgar S. Furniss[5] in his prize-winning Hart, Schaffner and Marx essay devotes a long chapter to "The Doctrine of the Utility of Poverty." The beliefs of illustrious individuals of that period should increase our ability to doubt the social thought of any period. Thomas Mun's view was that "penury and want do make a people wise and industrious." Arthur Young asserted that "every one but an idiot knows that the lower classes must be kept poor or they will never be industrious." John Law argued that "laborers were to blame for recurring high prices because of their insufferable habits of idleness contracted when food was cheap." William Petty joined in this chorus. There should be taxes on consumption and out-migration should be curtailed. Charity was thought to be the nursery of idleness. A larger population would keep the laborers poor, and immigration should be encouraged. George Berkeley, Bishop of Cloyne, proposed to reward parents of large families and to tax families with no children in support of the doctrine of the utility of poverty.[6]

One of the contributions of the classical economists was to show that, contrary to claims of mercantile economists, low wages imposed by governments reduce the national product. I view their analysis bearing on this issue as an excellent example of positive economics.

The ideas that are associated with liberalism emerged in large part as a protest to the adverse social and economic effects of mercantilism. The basic ideas of liberalism gradually developed into a strong internally consistent body of social thought, and over time liberal political and social institutions replaced mercantile institutions. 1776 has become a convenient birth year of liberal thought. What is often referred to as the bible of economics, namely the *Wealth of Nations*, carries this date. The argument of Adam Smith rests on the proposition that people, in responding to their own diverse self interests in their economic activities in an open competitive economy which is not fettered by private and public monopolies and which is supported by a political order in which the functions of government are greatly restricted, will maximize the social product. The economics of Smith became an integral part of the core of liberal social thought which, over the decades that followed, profoundly altered the institutionalized functions of many governments.

In Adam Smith's economy there is no room for the doctrine of the utility-of-poverty. The utility that matters is revealed by what people do in serving their own self interests. Smith's argument for an open competitive market implies free trade and a free labor market paying wages that are not fixed or restricted by government. It also implies that people are free to migrate from farms to towns and to leave the country if they choose to do so. Migration boomed in response to changes in institutions and to the economic opportunities associated with economic growth and the related growth in population which in turn also induced migration. Even in Russia of that era, we have August von Haxthausen's account[7] covering his 1843 tour into Russia of the liberal approach of that government in the opportunities that it accorded the Mennonites and Hutterites.

But the actual performance of the institutionalized liberal political economy in turn gave rise to protests which featured what was seen as a critical flaw of the liberal economic system, namely that it favored private property rights, and in doing so it gave rise to capitalism and to industrialization with insufficient protection of the rights of labor. The ideas advanced to correct this flaw are embodied in a body of social thought that calls for a political-economic order in which the functions of government are much enlarged, even more so than they were under mercantilism. As social thought it is viewed as socialism; as a political-economic system it ranges from centrally planned economic development to a system of command economics. The ideas that emerged from these protests prior to those of Karl Marx called for various forms of socialism. The contributions of Marx, however, came to dominate the political and economic foundations that are required for socialism. The response to Marxian ideas has altered greatly the institutions of many nation states, and as noted, the economic functions of the governments of these states are much enlarged.

An essential part of the argument in support of socialism is that an open competitive system is blind and that the self interests of people must be directed and controlled in order to achieve efficiency and equity in economic development. Prices, wages and migration are instruments to be used by government in achieving its goals.

There now are signs of a nascent neo-liberalism. Because of the dependency of socialism on a vast increase in the functions of the government, which in some countries consists of strong authoritarian nation states, and because of the now widely observed adverse effects that the governments of these states have on personal freedom, protests akin to those of two centuries ago are once again the order of the day.

The historical record of the last three centuries is not inconsistent with the view that social thought and institutions are far from stable. The pattern of instability has some of the earmarks of a cycle. When institutions function badly they produce the seed for their decline. In my thinking, this cycle of instability is an indication of the incompleteness (inadequacy) of the social thought that shapes institutions.

2   Agriculture and the Political Economy

Much of the economics of agriculture that really matters is in the differences of the political-economic institutions. When markets are segmented by governments, the advantages of the extension of the market are lost. When imports and exports are controlled, agricultural prices do strange things. When marketing boards have a monopoly, farmers and consumers are well advised to beware. When governments authorize the procurement of agricultural products from farmers, the agricultural economy is placed in receivership. When the ministers of agriculture treat agricultural scientists as clerks, the agricultural research enterprise becomes stagnant.

The economics of agriculture in this context has both short and long run implications. Those which are short run are most readily put to test when a major change occurs. The events of 1973–75 came unexpectedly, and suddenly they resulted in large changes. I shall appeal to this period in commenting on particular short run implications. For the long run, I shall consider various governmental effects on agricultural production during the last three decades.

As I noted at the outset, the 1973–75 period on world agriculture is an instructive "experiment" in prices. We all know that the shortfall in food and feed grains enhanced the economic value of these products, but what is over-looked is the fact that this increase in value was greatly distorted by various governments. A major set of countries suppressed the economic signals that were called for by the shortfall. Consumers in these countries were spared from adjusting their consumption to accommodate the shortfall, and thus, the burden of the required consumer adjustment was increased in the rest of the world. Similarly, in agricultural production throughout the European Economic Community, agricultural prices were held in check and farmers did not have the required economic incentives to increase their production. In sharp contrast, in Australia, Canada and the United States, the food and feed grain markets were open and competitive and farmers responded sharply to the higher prices. So did the farmers in Brazil in the case of soybeans. In general, on this issue, many of the low income countries have a better economic record than the European Economic Community.

Does the control of agricultural prices in one part of the world increase instability in the other part? Looking at the price effects of the 1973–75 change in the supply-demand balance in food and feed grains, the answer is in the affirmative. Theory and evidence tell a consistent story on this point, namely, when a government achieves internal price stability by controlling agricultural exports and imports, it increases the price instability in the rest of the world.

The open market instability of agricultural prices that occurred in the early seventies was much greater than that of the sixties although the shortfall in grain production caused by poor crops in the sixties departed farther from the trend level in world production than did the shortfall in the early seventies. The reason commonly cited for this difference in the behavior of prices between the two periods has been the grain storage policies of the United States, Canada and Australia. But a careful analysis of the price effects of these stocks indicates that a large part of the greater price instability of the seventies remains unexplained.

D. Gale Johnson (1975)[8] has advanced the hypothesis that this unexplained instability of agricultural prices in the 1970s is a consequence of the fact that "a much larger percentage of the world's grain production and consumption in the early 1970s than in the 1960s occurred in a framework of policies to achieve internal price stability through the controls of imports and/or exports." The evidence supports the Johnson hypothesis: fixed internal agricultural prices have become increasingly the rule in the Soviet Union, the European Economic Community and China; these countries account for about half the world's grain utilization in recent years. As a consequence, prices in about half of the world "do not serve the function of influencing either consumption or production when the world's demand–supply balance has changed." Accordingly, all of the adjustments must be made in the other half of the agricultural world. In the early 1970s "these adjustments fell primarily upon two groups of countries – major grain exporters and the low income developing countries that imported grain." Theory implies that the increase in price resulting from a given shortfall of grains would be approximately doubled in that half of the world where prices are not fixed compared to the rise in prices that would have occurred if the other half had not fixed their internal prices of agricultural products. This important implication of the theory does not depend on value judgments; it is a testable implication, and in terms of positive economics, the evidence supports the implication.

In developing agriculture for the long pull, what types of public control machinery are on the recommended list of agricultural economists? A pointless question no doubt, since we have not made it our business to analyze and publicy certify the economic performance of alternative control devices. For my part in the spirit of the Mikado, I've got a little list of economic offenders who never would be missed – who never would be missed.

I know of no country in which the productive capacity of agriculture has been in fact increased by large Public Law 480[9] grain transfers from the U.S. to the receiving country. PL 480 is on my little list because when it comes to building agriculture, PL 480 is a liability.

The procurement of agricultural products from producers by the anthority of the state is bad economics, and when it occurs it is a sure sign that the country which uses its police powers for this purpose is in deep agricultural trouble. Needless to say, command procurement is one of the major economic offenders on my list.

In marketing it is necessary to distinguish between cooperatives that are subject to competition and marketing boards that are vested with monopoly powers as agencies of the state. I find it odd that agricultural economists have so grossly neglected P.T. Bauer's excellent studies of West Africa's marketing boards. Marketing boards are always established for a noble purpose, e.g., to stabilize agricultural prices. But if the commodity is mainly exported, the board becomes a convenient device for raising revenue for the government; as the sole buyer it can pay a low price to farmers and sell abroad at a high price. It is a successful public device for pricing the best export crop to death! Then, too, some boards "employ" an inordinate number of people who are favored by the government – the well known practice of the "spoils system." A cogent and useful economic assessment of the various marketing boards in Kenya is at hand in *Agricultural Development in Kenya*.[10] I list state monopoly marketing boards as economic offenders.

While it is not difficult to detect the adverse effects of large PL 480 imports, of command procurement, and of state monopoly marketing boards on agricultural production, there are other and more important unsettled economic questions. Is it true that rents, interest and profits "never will be missed" once they have been eliminated? Why not substitute administered prices for competitive prices? When black markets prosper, what are the economic implications?

My own visits to the Soviet Union began in 1929 and I have extended them to observe agriculture in the other socialistic countries of Eastern Europe. Compared to most of the world, these are highly skilled, technically advanced and in general well-equipped countries. The puzzle is in the below par performance of agriculture. Despite the recent very large investments to increase agricultural production, it is evident that the cost of producing milk and meat is exceedingly high; the quantities that consumers are demanding are not forthcoming. Weather, climate and soils do not hold the key to this puzzle. Nor can the disappointing performance be attributed to a lack of competence in the management of agricultural production. In an analysis of the disappointing performance of Soviet agriculture since World War II, my colleague, D. Gale Johnson, finds that it is not primarily a consequence of the very large collective farms.[11]

The key to this puzzle is in the allocation of resources that are devoted to agricultural production. Economic inefficiency is the problem. Viewed as an allocative problem, it is not confined to the socialist countries. It is in fact pervasive throughout most of the low income countries, although the administrative devices that are used in allocating resources differ widely from country to country.

When the dominant social thought proscribes the use of rents, interest and profits and declares that market-oriented competition is blind, the accommodating political economy is severely handicapped in allocating resources for agricultural production. It may use all manner of devices – distributing fertilizer and other inputs by issuing quotas, controlling the migration of farm people from farm to farm and from farms to cities, segmenting the market for agricultural products within the country and allowing no movements between the different areas except as approved by the government, and even preventing farmers from buying and selling to each other.

The heart of the problem then becomes one of knowing what the real economic values are, values to be used in commanding production and consumption. In this context no matter who is making economic decisions, be they planners, managers of collective farms or small private farms, using the information that is thus provided leads to economic inefficiency. This is not to argue that the supply of valid, usable economic information is costless. It becomes very expensive under the above circumstances for the available supply in many countries has two attributes:

the quality of economic information is exceedingly low and, nevertheless, very costly. It should also be noted that improvements that are to be had from the work of the agricultural scientists in terms of better plants, animals, fertilizers and equipment – important as they are when they are used efficiently – in no way solve the problem of ascertaining the real economic value of agricultural products and factors. Nor is the solution to be had by simply using more advanced computer technology.

I return in closing to the question with which I began, what about future costs of agricultural products? In terms of technical possibilities and pure economic opportunities, the prospects for lower costs are good, but in terms of what is being done politically, the prospects are bad. Meanwhile, international food conferences produce a lot of weak reports, and social thought produces strong ideologies. But reports and ideologies do not produce food. Fortunately, plants and animals do not read reports nor do they discriminate against the ideology of any government. One thing is certain – what farm people will be able to do holds the key to our story. Would that agricultural economists would help them to write that story!

Notes and References

1 Wassily Leontief, "Theoretical Assumptions and Nonobserved Facts," *American Economic Review*, 69 (1971), 1–7.
2 This quote is from Harry G. Johnson, "Learning and Libraries: Academic Economics as A Profession: Its Bearing on the Organization and Retrieval of Economic Knowledge," *Minerva*, 13(4), 621–32.
3 Harry G. Johnson, *On Economics and Society* (University of Chicago Press, Chicago, Ill., 1975), p. ix.
4 In part drawn from Theodore W. Schultz, *The Economic Value of Human Time* (Economic Research Service, USDA, Washington DC, 1977).
5 Edgar S. Furniss, *The Position of Laborers in a System of Nationalism* (Houghton Mifflin, Boston, Mass., 1920), chapter 6.
6 See Theodore W. Schultz, "Public Approaches to Minimize Poverty," in Leo Fishman (ed.), *Poverty Amid Affluence* (Yale University Press, New Haven, Conn., 1960).
7 August von Haxthausen, *Studies on the Interior of Russia*, edited by S. Frederick Starr and translated by Eleanore L.M. Schmidt (University of Chicago Press, Chicago, Ill., 1972).
8 D. Gale Johnson, "World Agriculture, Commodity Policy, and Price Variability," *Proceedings of the American Journal of Agricultural Economics* (Dec. 1975).
9 See Part IV, No. 1, note 3.
10 Judith Heyer, J.K. Maitha, and W.M. Senga (eds), *Agricultural Development*

   in Kenya (Oxford University Press, Nairobi, Kenya, 1976): see especially
   chapter 10.
11 D. Gale Johnson, "Theory and Practice of Soviet Collective Agriculture,"
   unpublished paper 75:28 (Office of Agricultural Economics Research,
   University of Chicago, Dec. 1975).

3

Efficient Allocation of Brains in Modernizing World Agriculture *

When prices become shadows, the allocation of resources becomes a fine art. When human resources become brawn or brains, the choice of language is that of the poet. But when we speak of wages and salaries and of unskilled and skilled workers, shadows become economics. If the poet would listen, we might say to him that the market for brawn is weak and that for brains is strong; he could then follow the market as Alice did her imaginary rabbit.

Salaries are prices and they imply a market. For particular high skills the market is becoming international in scope. In response to salaries in this market, there are movements of persons among countries. Some human resources are thus allocated internationally. While these responses are viewed by some observers as bad – the pejorative is the "brain drain" – the economist should be on his guard in condemning this market for brains. Although it is obviously an imperfect market, that there is such a market, however rudimentary, is an institutional achievement. Our proper task, as I see it, is to try to get at the sources of the imperfections of this market. We might learn how to make it work better than it does presently in allocating persons with skills that contribute especially to economic growth. It is my thesis that instead of impairing and weakening this market we should strengthen it and make it more efficient.

The problem to which I turn is that of allocating efficiently the services of agricultural scientists and technicians among countries. Economists are excluded so that I can be unbiased, not because the skills

* First published in *Journal of Farm Economics*, 49, No. 5 (Dec. 1967), 1071–82. I am indebted to Lowell S. Hardin, Herbert G. Grubel, D. Gale Johnson, George S. Tolley, and Lawrence W. Witt for their critical and clarifying comments.

of economists are of no value in modernizing agriculture, or because there is no international market for their skills, or because they are distributed efficiently.

It is useful to think in terms of equality of returns as the test. I plan first to sketch alternative ways of equalizing the returns to this particular set of human resources; second, to consider two major conditions causing inefficient allocations that are not obvious; and last, to present possible solutions to the problem of equalizing the returns to these skills among countries.

A clarification of the conditions surrounding this problem will be necessary: (1) the distribution of inherited abilities within a population, including those necessary to acquire the competence under consideration, is approximately the same whether a country is rich or poor; (2) the natural endowment (land) of a country is given and the possibility of transferring any part of it is zero; (3) the stock of durable reproducible nonhuman capital including land improvements can be altered but only at some modest rate per year; and (4) agricultural inputs which farmers purchase on a year-to-year basis are supplied either from domestic production or from abroad and some modern agricultural inputs can be acquired in this way.

There are some additional conditions, however, which may seem less plausible; they might therefore be viewed as assumptions of convenience. They are as follows: (1) individuals here and abroad respond to earnings both in acquiring skills and in the jobs they take once they have acquired the necessary skills to qualify them as agricultural scientists and technicians, that is, they move among countries not only to acquire the necessary training but also to obtain jobs; (2) there is a fairly strong tendency towards equilibrium reckoned privately, especially so within countries; (3) there is a substantial _complementarity_ in production between new classes of high skills and modern physical inputs. Over the course of time, these new high skills and modern physical inputs are in general _substitutes_ for traditional agricultural inputs, that is, in traditional physical capital (including land) and unskilled human beings; and (4) there is a disequilibrium between the developed countries and the less developed countries in agricultural production which is in large measure a consequence of the differences in the supply of such high skills and of the complementary modern physical inputs.

But is this not simply a consequence of the "brain drain"? Fashion and confused thinking aside, the cogent answer is, no. The term "brain drain" is a "loaded phrase, involving implicit definitions of economic and social welfare," as Professor Harry G. Johnson has noted.[1] It is a phrase which bespeaks the goal of economic nationalism and not the welfare of individuals who migrate. Recent studies have done much to clarify these issues. But despite the clarification of the international movement of educated persons, notably by Johnson,[2] Herbert G. Grubel,[3] and Grubel and Anthony D. Scott,[4] there still are many muddled policy assertions on how to deal with the so-called "brain drain." Instead of "Yankee, go home," the refrain is "Don't go to Yankeeland." Economic nationalism then calls for all manner of restrictions on the outward movement of knowledgeable persons across the national boundary. Their freedom of choice and welfare are thus impaired. Despite our cultural values, there is a rash of proposals from our midst which debase the individual. These proposals are a return to forms of indentured service, to keep the individual from leaving or, in the case of one who goes abroad for advanced training, to make him return. Why not simply erect more Berlin Walls! A short-sighted approach is for governments to keep the salaries of highly skilled people low and then try to confirm it with an "adequate supply" by various social and political devices. The underlying philosophy of this approach is akin to the economic nationalism that prevailed in England from 1660 to 1775 in support of the Utility of Poverty doctrine for laborers.[5]

Another way of clarifying the problem before us is to distinguish between different states of our knowledge. We know that the supply of agricultural scientists and technicians is highly concentrated in the developed countries, and we know that it costs a lot to employ persons that have these skills. But we are less explicit with regard to the skills that are necessary in modernizing agriculture, namely skills that are a good investment in terms of rates of return. The capability of private firms for profit in equalizing the rates of return to this form of human capital either within or between countries, is another advantage. We know that the less-developed countries have been falling behind in producing and exporting agricultural products relative to the developed countries, and we fail to see that a substantial part of this change is a consequence of the advance in knowledge associated with the work of agricultural scientists and technicians and the difference in the rates at which it has become available to the less-developed countries relative to the developed countries.

1   Equalization Pathways

I now turn to the theory of international trade for guidance. Factor price equalization is possible theoretically through trade. But is this path pure fiction, "a supreme example of non-operational theorizing" built on "the arid factor-price equalization theorem" as Caves[6] would have us believe? Aridity also makes for good roads! There may be more equalization mileage on this road than Caves and others have allowed themselves to see.[7] Moreover, in the case of agricultural scientists and technicians, we also have their movement internationally in equalizing factor prices. Thus we have international trade in the products of such human capital, and also in the movement of this form of human capital among countries, and accordingly in some combination of the two as pathways in equalizing the rates of return to investment in this activity. The adage of the better mousetrap tells the same story. The world will beat a path to your door to buy it, or, if you will come, arrangements will be made for you to go abroad to make your mousetrap there. To determine the traffic on each of these pathways, we must appeal to empirical behavior.

The value added by agricultural scientists and technicians enters into trade as parts of agricultural inputs and of agricultural commodities. What they publish also enters into trade. In addition, there is the movement of such persons internationally. Let me comment briefly on these.

1   They produce professional papers. The more theoretical the journal, the more erudite the jargon, the more prestigious the citations! For the biologists, an *International Journal of Genetics* would be the hallmark of success. It is where the plant breeder concentrating, say, on wheat would prefer to display his intellectual ware. But cultivators producing wheat in the Punjab are not in that market. Nor are the extension workers and economic planners of India reading and profiting from such a journal. Even the plant breeder working on wheat may let this scientific journal collect dust. Nevertheless, the most valuable fundamental new knowledge is distributed internationally in journals *at no more cost* than the annual subscription rate. It would be all too easy to underrate the economic importance of this form of "trade" in new knowledge in any long-run setting. But even here "trade" is very uneven. I am sure one would find, for example, that individuals and institutions in Japan and the Soviet Union are subscribing to a large number of high- and lowbrow journals in this area, whereas those in Pakistan, India, and the Argentine are not subscribing to many of them.

2   There is trade in agricultural inputs that scientists and technicians discover and help to develop. These inputs consist of better varieties of seeds, strains of chickens, soil and feed additives, including medication, mechanical contrivances, and many more. While some of them are highly specialized and suited only to particular classes of farms, some are much less specialized in their applicability. The cost and returns of attaining a greater range in applicability is a matter of importance. The success in the

case of wheat in increasing the range of geographical adaptability is noteworthy, as Norman Borlaug of the Rockefeller Foundation and colleagues are demonstrating in their work in Mexico.

Public agencies can be traders. The Indian government's purchase of 200 tons of certified Sonora 64 wheat seed and 50 tons of Lerma Rojo 64 from Mexico in 1965 and another 18,000 tons of Lerma Rojo 64 in 1966 is an example of this. Yet the demand for this seed by farmers in India exceeded the supply, contrary to the frequently alleged indifference of Indian farmers to ways of improving their economic lot. The multiplication of this wheat within India has been rapid; "after the current year's harvest, seed supply of the short, fertilizer-responsive wheat varieties should no longer be a limiting factor".[8]

Business firms operating for profit are of course traders. They are suppliers of particular agricultural inputs internationally, that is, they are suppliers of modern equipment, insecticides, pesticides, other chemicals used in agricultural production, and, of major importance, fertilizer. It is as a rule unprofitable for them to produce for sale specialized modern agricultural inputs for which the market is very small.

3   We should not overlook the role of trade in agricultural commodities. It is of course very large. If the advance in knowledge from the work of agricultural scientists and technicians were applicable only to the agricultural production in the developed countries, that is, if none of it could be adapted and applied as agricultural inputs in the less-developed countries, the equalization of returns to such knowledge would depend upon adjustments in the trade of agricultural commodities. Under these conditions, an advance in such knowledge, other things equal, would tend to enhance the comparative advantage of the developed countries in this type of trade. There are economists who believe that a basic shift of this sort has occurred and that it is here to stay. But they are undoubtedly mistaken. They fail to distinguish between a transitory and a permanent shift. The advance in knowledge under consideration is not specific to the agricultural production of the developed countries; on the contrary, the basic scientific advance in knowledge is in large measure transferable and adaptable to the less-developed countries. Thus, transitory shifts aside, this new knowledge relevant to agricultural production need not impair over the long run the comparative advantage of the less-developed countries in agricultural commodity trade.

4   In addition to these channels of trade, persons who know how can go abroad to work. This movement of persons is also a way of equalizing factor returns internationally. Private firms in the less-developed countries can recruit and employ agricultural scientists and technicians

Table IV.3.1 Americans overseas in 1960, selected classes of persons

	Federal civilian employees	Other citizens	Source*
Persons 25 years and over	33,000	115,800	Table 2
Median years of school completed	16.1	13.6	Table 2
Occupation of employed			
Professional, technical, kindred	15,900	31,400	Table 3
Employed in agriculture			
Farmers and farm managers	2	476	Table 3
Farm laborers and foremen	1	205	Table 3
Foresty and fisheries	7	1,089	Table 3
Highest degree received by persons with major field of study in agriculture and foresty			
Bachelor	303	319	Tables 8 & 18
Master	117	73	Tables 8 & 18
Doctorate	73	38	Tables 8 & 18
In biological sciences			
Bachelor	192	306	Tables 8 & 18
Master	66	97	Tables 8 & 18
Doctorate	123	200	Tables 8 & 18

* *US Census of Population 1960, Americans Overseas*, PC (3) IC, Selected Area Reports.

from the developed countries. Public agencies can also induce some of them to move and work abroad. Then, too, agricultural scientists and technicians can be developed by training a core of indigenous persons, who can go abroad for the training should this be necessary, as Mexico has done with marked success during recent decades.

Where are the relevant shadow prices? Who pays whom for what? Even elementary data to determine the number of Americans who qualify as agricultural scientists and technicians and the salaries they receive are hard to come by. The 1960 US Census in its special report on *Americans Overseas* gives a few clues with respect to these numbers. From this report I infer that about 400 American agricultural scientists and technicians are working abroad and that somewhat less than half of them are federal civilian employees.[9] This is equal to about 2 percent of the number at work in the United States (in US agricultural experiment stations and in the USDA, 10,900 scientist man-years were utilized in the fiscal year 1965; an equal number were employed in industry on research related to agriculture).[10]

2 Inefficient Allocations

By way of review, the human resource under consideration consists of a small set of persons who have special skills. They are employed by business firms or are engaged in organized research working in experiment stations, laboratories, and institutes. In the United States, about as many are employed by private firms operating for profit as by nonprofit organizations. The market for these skills is active and strong, and no one would contend that agricultural scientists and technicians are indifferent to differences in salaries. The value added by their work is tradable when it becomes a part of the trade in agricultural commodities or trade in products which are used as agricultural inputs. In addition, there is the movement of such persons internationally. Under these circumstances, should we not expect to observe a strong tendency towards equilibrium within and among countries in the allocation of this set of human resources? If the test of this expectation is a dynamic process which comes close to maintaining an allocative equilibrium, it is not what we observe, for the allocation of these resources is far from efficient.

The reasons for a substantial part of this inefficiency are fairly obvious. Since World War II, most of the less-developed countries have been pursuing cheap food and import substitution policies with a view to hastening their own industrialization and favoring their urban consumers. Thus, farm product prices within many of these countries have been depressed relative to other prices and agricultural input prices have been relatively high. For want of efficiency prices, malallocations have grown like weeds. Furthermore, the record of the developed countries in the areas of aid, trade, and international monetary organization has also been bad for the profitability of agriculture and the economic growth from this sector in the less-developed countries.[11]

But efficiency in this realm is also thwarted by two not so obvious developments. One of these is the rate at which the advance in knowledge relevant to agricultural production occurs. The other is the limited extent to which firms for profit can afford to invest in the production of such knowledge.

Let us suppose that the tendency towards equilibrium is strong but that the advance in knowledge pertaining to agricultural production is not a once-and-for-all affair but a continuing long-run process. Given this condition, even a strong tendency towards equilibrium could not arrive at an equilibrium. Moreover, if the rate of advance in this knowledge were to rise, the disequilibrium might become greater with the passage of time. Several decades ago we entered upon an era during which the advance in knowledge that is economically relevant here has been rapid, and it has been advancing at an increasing rate. As a consequence, the disequilibrium that has already occurred during this era between the developed and the less-developed countries is very large. The latter countries are further behind than they were several decades ago in benefiting from the knowledge under consideration.

The second of these conditions is neatly concealed in most of our production economics, namely, that firms (farm and nonfarm) operating for profit are not sufficient for achieving an optimum allocation of resources in this activity. This condition is inherent in the nature of the products. Assume that agricultural scientists and technicians discover and develop over a period of time two different streams of products. The product of one of these streams is *specific* to the productivity of the firm, in the sense that only the firm can patent or otherwise appropriate the product to its benefit. Where the product from the work of agricultural scientists and technicians is specific, firms for profit will presumably equate marginal costs and marginal revenue in employing them. Less than half of the workers with these skills in the United States, are employed by firms for profit. The product of the other stream is *general* in the sense that its productivity is not specific to that of any firm. This product appears in the public domain. If a firm were to produce a product of this class, it would not be able to appropriate or capture all or even a significant part of the productivity that might come from it. Accordingly, where the product is general, as here defined, a firm would not equate marginal costs and marginal social returns. Therefore, since the products are in substantial part general, it follows that if all of the employment of agricultural scientists and technicians were wholly dependent upon private firms for profit, all too few resources would be allocated to their employment. Stated another way, if there were only private activity for profit, the expenditures of private firms would be less than optimum because many of the returns are not available to such firms but are widely diffused, with some going to other firms and some to consumers. Even though private firms were to have access to strong patent coverage, such coverage would not assure a socially efficient allocation of resources in employing agricultural scientists and technicians.[12]

What then is the picture when we turn to the real world? It can best be sketched by presenting the following propositions:

1   Where the product is *specific*, as set forth above, firms for profit perform in accordance with our theory, with the proviso that there is a much longer lag in the response to profit from this type of employment than from investing in traditional capital and in employing workers with traditional skills, because even in the case of specific products the profitability is frequently fogged by uncertainty, and it takes considerable time and experience to acquire information with respect to the payoff.

2   Where the product is *general*, the production activity is necessarily organized by public agencies, foundations, and universities. Here we enter the realm of social accounting and the relevant shadow prices are hard to come by, especially so for the value of the products and the social rates of return. The combination of this type of organization and the inadequate information is not conducive to economic efficiency.

3   Comparatively, the less-developed countries are much less efficient than the developed countries in the production and distribution of both of these two streams of products. With regard to the specific products, private firms in the less-developed countries are less informed and less experienced and thus their lag in response is longer still than in the developed countries. But the difference is even greater in producing and distributing the general products associated with the work of agricultural scientists and technicians.

4   Although the developed countries perform much better than the less-developed countries when it comes to the general products here under consideration, there is strong evidence which shows that their underinvestment in this activity is nevertheless large.

3   Possible Solutions

The problem, as stated at the outset, is that of allocating efficiently the wares and the services of agricultural scientists and technicians among countries. The unsettled question is, how can this be done best between the less-developed and the developed countries? International trade is one of the means, and the movement of persons with these skills among countries is another.

In an endeavor to bring the economic calculus to bear more effectively, the solution to this problem entails two major reforms: (1) shifting more of this activity to profit-oriented firms and reducing the lags in their response to profits from this source, and (2) developing a system of accounting to guide nonprofit organizations in allocating resources to this activity so that they can come closer to equating marginal costs and social marginal returns than is now the case.

1   The key to the first reform is in the distinction between the *specific* and the *general* products from this activity. It is my belief that there are many specific products in this realm which are concealed presently, and, furthermore, that it is possible to design agricultural research in its quest for new knowledge so as to increase the probability of discovering products that are specific. A real effort, therefore, should be made to specify and identify the anticipated products in accordance with this classification. We will discover as a result, I feel sure, that there are many unexhausted opportunities to enlarge the role of both domestic and foreign firms operating for profit and through them the part that international trade by them can play in equalizing the returns among countries from this activity.

2   There are clues which suggest that experiment station workers are in general not disposed to make the distinction between specific and general products. On the contrary, many of them are inclined to blur this distinction in order to hold on to projects even though the work has reached the stage of developing specific products. To the extent that this is true, the desired shift to firms for profit is delayed.

3   Since the size of the market for the product, once it is deemed to be specific, is an important factor determining the potential profitability and thus influencing firms to enter this market, the search for general products which are the foundation for the specific products should be designed so as to accommodate the largest possible market. This is not an empty proposition. Work oriented toward general products can search on the one hand for gains to be had from increasing geographical specialization, for example, hybrid corn that is best suited to a region, then refined to a type of farming area and ultimately to an even more homogeneous subarea consisting of parts of a county or two. But it can also be oriented to discover products that are less specialized with respect to area and other farming conditions, for example, new varieties of crops that are less photosensitive and that are capable of utilizing a wider range of applications of fertilizer.

4   The ways and means of reducing the lags on the part of firms in responding to profit opportunities in this area are too important and complex to be treated adequately here. Suffice it to say that the less-developed countries have a penchant for erecting barriers to trade (including inputs) and for devising rules and regulations to reduce the

profitability of foreign firms establishing plants in these countries, whether or not the product would contribute to the economic growth of their agriculture. But the factors underlying these lags in response are more pervasive than these barriers and devices; these factors are also at work in the developed countries, although much less so. They pertain to the cost of acquiring economic information to gauge the prospective profitability where new forms of risk and uncertainty cloud the economic horizons. The search for ways of reducing this set of costs should be high on the agenda of economists, with a strong assist from agricultural scientists and technicians.

5 Turning to the second reform, the requirements are (1) that non-profit organizations in this area specialize on general products, (2) that accounting systems be devised to determine the costs and social returns from this part of the activity, (3) that these nonprofit organizations treat this research as an investment activity and make decisions in accordance with the priorities set by the prospective relative social rates of return, and (4) that an international market for the high skills which this activity entails be built, not by erecting walls and impairing the freedom of persons to move from the less-developed to the developed countries, but by paying salaries and related rewards in the less-developed countries to these persons commensurate with the social marginal returns from their work.

6 But are these returns sufficient to pay the necessary salaries and related costs? There are some hard facts which support an affirmative answer. Before turning to them, a comment on the International Rice Research Institute, a joint enterprise of the Rockefeller and Ford foundations, may be helpful. It is an expensive enterprise in the sense that the salaries of the scientists are high and the housing and extra facilities for good schools for their children are costly. The competence of the scientists and the appropriateness of the organization and perhaps a bit of good luck have already produced enough to leave little room for doubt that it is a high-pay-off research venture.

The hard facts to which I alluded are from Griliches' studies[13] and the study by Peterson[14] on the high pay-off to agricultural research which is organized and supported by public funds in the United States. There is now also one such study for a less-developed country, namely Ardito-Barletta's study of agricultural research in Mexico.[15] From this agricultural research, covering the period from 1943 to 1963, Mexico has realized an annual rate of return of 290 percent. The salaries and work arrangements in Mexico were sufficient to have developed by 1963 a core of workers who were agricultural scientists and technicians, consisting of 156 Mexicans with MS degrees, 81 Mexicans with PhD degrees, and 700 related workers. In addition, there were 10 scientists who presumably were not Mexicans who were supported by the Rockefeller Foundation. Given the rate of return to this activity in Mexico and the fact that not all of the costs consist of salaries, had it been necessary to have paid salaries *three times* as high as those that were paid, it would still have produced for Mexico an annual rate of return of at least 100 percent.

The Mexican high-pay-off experience, I am convinced, could have been duplicated in many a less-developed country. The opportunities to make such investments in organized agricultural research are still there to be exploited. Salaries sufficiently high to reverse the so-called "brain drain" could be paid and these enterprises would still be very profitable for the countries concerned. Important as financial assistance from US public agencies and foundations may be in bringing these opportunities to a head, the unfinished business here is to transform the relevant shadow prices pertaining to this activity into real economic choices and demonstrate to these governments that it is one of the very best investments they can possibly make in obtaining economic growth from their agriculture.

Thus shadows become salaries and salaries an international market for brains. Then efficient allocation becomes possible, and our imaginary rabbit becomes a real rabbit.

Notes and References

1   Harry G. Johnson, "The Economics of Brain Drain: The Canadian Case," *Minerva*, 3 (Spring 1965), 299–311.
2   Ibid.: see also Johnson, "International Economics: Progress and Transfer of Technical Knowledge," *American Economic Review*, 56 (May 1966), 280–83.
3   Herbert G. Grubel, "The Brain Drain: A US Dilemma," *Science*, 154 (Dec. 16, 1966), 1420–24.
4   Herbert G. Grubel and Anthony D. Scott: "The Characteristics of Foreigners in the US Economic Profession," *American Economic Review*, 57 (Mar. 1967), 131–45; "The Cost of US College Exchange Student Programs," *Journal of Human Resources*, 1 (Nov. 1966), 81–98; "The Immigration of Scientists and Engineers to the United States, 1949–61," *Journal of Political Economy*, 74 (Aug. 1966), 363–78; and "The International flow of Human Capital," *American Economic Review*, 56 (May 1966), 268–74.
5   Edgar S. Furniss, *The Position of the Laborer in a System of Nationalism* (Houghton Mifflin, Boston, Mass., 1920), chapter 6, 17.

6   R.E. Caves, *Trade and Economic Structure* (Harvard University Press, Cambridge, Mass., 1960), p. 92.

7   I am indebted to Professor Anne O. Krueger for her unpublished paper, "Factor Endowments and Per Capita Income Differences Among Countries," (University of Minnesota, 1967).

8   Ralph W. Cummings, *Wheat Production Prospects in India* (The Rockefeller Foundation, New York, Feb. 8, 1967).

9   In table 1, I show particular Americans overseas in 1960. Federal civilian employees whose field of major study was in agriculture and forestry and in the biological sciences with a master's or doctoral degree totaled 379, and among "other citizens" abroad who qualified, there were 408. I assume that about half of this total of 787 were on jobs as agricultural scientists and technicians.

10 See *A National Program of Research for Agriculture* (Association of State Universities and Land-Grant Colleges and the US Department of Agriculture, Washington DC, Oct. 1966), table F-1

11 Harry G. Johnson, *Economic Policies Towards Less Developed Countries* (The Brookings Institution, Washington DC, 1967).

12 Theodore W. Schultz, *Transforming Traditional Agriculture* (Yale University Press, New Haven, Conn., 1964), chapter 10.

13 Zvi Griliches, "Research Costs and Social Returns: Hybrid Corn and Related Innovations," *Journal of Political Economy*, 66 (Oct. 1958), 419–31; and "Research Expenditures, Education, and the Aggregate Agricultural Production Function," *American Economic Review*, 54 (Dec. 1964), 961–74.

14 Willis Peterson, "Returns to Poultry Research in the United States," unpublished PhD dissertation (University of Chicago, 1966).

15 N. Ardito-Barletta, "Costs and Social Returns of Agricultural Research in Mexico," unpublished PhD dissertation (University of Chicago, 1967).

4

Economics of Agricultural Productivity in Low Income Countries *

Our economic thinking is constrained by our economic language. Since the 1950s, we have become beholden to the term, the Green Revolution. What is implied by this term is not a new event; inasmuch as such events had occurred frequently over time since agriculture was invented. Green Revolutions occurred long before the historians began to write about the Industrial Revolution. For our purpose, however, neither of these two so-called revolutions is useful in discovering and asking the important, right questions about the interacting agricultural and industrial processes that are integral parts of modern economic modernization.

The following questions should be high on our agenda. (1) Are governments and people privately investing enough in human capital? (2) Is enough being invested in the knowledge producing sector? (3) Does the organization of the economy provide optimum economic incentives? (4) Is the economic value of private entrepreneurship being fully realized? It is my contention that the answer to each of these questions is in varying degrees in the negative for most countries.

My approach to the issues inherent in these questions entails several basic concepts and assumptions.

1 I shall use an all-inclusive concept of capital. It encompasses all physical and all human capital. The stock of both parts of this capital is augmented by investment. It is well documented that the stock of human capital increases relative to that of physical capital as modernization proceeds. The functional distribution of income shows that the higher the

* This paper was presented as the First Chung-Hua Lecture to the Institute of Economics, Academia Sinica, Taiwan, and published in *Conference on Agricultural Development in China, Japan and Korea*, December 17–20, 1980, pp. 15–27.

income of a country the larger is the part of the income derived from wages, salaries, and self employment including that derived from entrepreneurial activity. In the United States about one-fifth of the National Income is derived from physical capital, i.e., from property and close to four-fifths from human capital, i.e., from wages, salaries, self employment and entrepreneurship.

2   Economic disequilibria are inevitable as a consequence of modernization as new forms of physical and human capital are acquired by means of investment. These new forms of capital alter the production processes and the equilibrium that had been attained. Such economic disequilibria cannot be avoided by policies, by laws and surely not by rhetoric.

3   In dealing efficiently with these disequilibria, the economic value of entrepreneurial ability is high as modernization proceeds. The economy would fall apart were it not for entrepreneurs. Furthermore, markets are essential in organizing the function of entrepreneurs.

4   Economic organizations and investments to increase the stock of knowledge are more important than additional conventional capital in achieving additional production and welfare. This assessment of organization and knowledge goes back to Alfred Marshall who in his *Principles of Economics*. Book IV, Chapter I, saw clearly that "knowledge is our most powerful engine of production" and that "organization aids knowledge."[1]

I now turn to the economics of agriculture. Rich people, who are mostly urban people, know the least about agriculture. They are, however, not inhibited when it comes to making pronouncements on agriculture. Our rich urban experts on food and agriculture produce a flood of dire predictions that no farmer takes seriously. There is an ancient biblical law which is that being rich makes it hard to get into heaven; the corresponding law in economics is: Being rich makes it hard to comprehend the economic behavior of poor people.[2]

The recent abundant supply of dire predictions rest on the view that there is a virtually fixed area of land suitable for growing crops, that the supply of energy for tilling the land is being depleted and that future increase in agricultural productivity to be had from agricultural research is diminishing; and thus, it will soon become impossible to produce enough food for the still growing human population. Most of these predictions are rhetoric based on very little hard analysis. There have been many pessimistic predictions on the supply of food during the past century which have turned out to be wrong. This fact, of course, does not prove that such current predictions are wrong. We should, however, look with care at the evidences pertaining to the dynamics of modern agriculture and its implications for the future food supply.[3] It is my contention that the productivity of agriculture has been increasing at an impressive rate in a goodly number of countries throughout the world and that the sources of these increases in productivity are far from being exhausted.[4] More specifically, the biological possibilities of plants, animals and soils are not about to be exhausted. We are not, during the next decade or two, entering into a period of diminishing returns provided investments are made to improve the schooling and health of farm people and to provide for agricultural research and the dissemination of the contributions of that research.

I have spent more than fifty years trying to understand the complexities of agriculture in various parts of the world. In 1929 I established a number of benchmarks in the Soviet Union. I have been back to check on changes that have occurred in agriculture at these places. My first endeavor to observe farms and farm people in Mexico was in 1930. I have gone back frequently since then.

I have been privileged to see agriculture first hand in most of the countries of the world. My thinking and studies have been influenced considerably by these observations. I have observed both failures and successes. I know that the performance of agriculture is uneven among countries and that governments learn much more slowly from their economic mistakes than farmers learn to take advantage of new worthwhile economic opportunities.

It is said that women invented agriculture. They did it out of necessity when men no longer provided enough food by hunting. Our major food crops were developed thousands of years ago. Now for better or worse, all of us – governments, banks, planners, engineers, economists and scientists – believe we know the secrets of agriculture. We tell the poor farmer what to do and how to do it and we frequently overlook the importance of the role of farm women.

I am neither pessimestic nor optimistic about agricultural prospects. In my thinking, as I have already suggested, they will not be determined by the physical properties of the earth; that is, not by space, by land suitable for crops, or by energy. A decisive factor will be the abilities of people, and on that score, the prospects are open-ended. It is not possible to anticipate what human beings will achieve over the decades ahead. It is noteworthy that Malthus could not have anticipated the substitution by parents of quality for quantity of children. Nor could Ricardo have anticipated the results of modern agricultural research that have become substitutes for land in agricultural production. It does not distract from the merits of Adam Smith's *Wealth of Nations* to observe that neither he nor anyone else at that time could have anticipated that there would be nations in which about four-fifths of the national income would be derived from earnings and only about one-fifth from property, as is the case in the United States where most of its wealth consists of acquired human abilities, its human capital.

Economic value of agricultural research is now widely acknowledged. Real progress is being made in financing and in increasing agricultural research that is oriented to the requirements of low income countries. Although organizational problems abound, given time the prospect is that these problems will be solved. Many low income countries during the past three decades have made substantial investments, both publicly and privately, in improving health, schooling and skills and, thereby, enhancing the acquired quality of the population.

There are reasons for being pessimistic about economic organization. At its worst it is very bad. It could be that the glamor of centralized control of economic affairs is losing its appeal and the dogma of market failures is also losing ground. Nevertheless, the economic role of markets is still very much impaired and government intervention in restricting markets continues to reduce the productivity of agriculture. All too few countries are committed to the enlargement and the strengthening of markets. Most international donor agencies have an anti-market bias. On these issues most private foundations are ambivalent except in their support of agricultural research.

The countries with strongest centralized economic control institutions, the Soviet Union and most of the eastern European countries, are likely to be slow in making room for viable markets for the agricultural sector. China may become an exception, but one must wait and see.

The instability of many governments in parts of Africa does not bode well for agricultural development. In Latin America, even the countries with fairly high per capita income – with a historical record of impressive economic progress and considerable investment in human capital – are experiencing political instability. Agriculture is not spared from the adverse effects of the instability.

Most of the people of the world are in Asia, and most of them earn their living in agriculture. The real test of agriculture prospects will depend on the economic success of these Asian countries. China aside because of major changes in economic policy now occurring, a goodly number of these Asian countries show real signs of doing what needs to be done to increase agricultural productivity.

With this background, I now will review recent developments affecting the potential economic productivity of agriculture. I will then consider the essential conditions for achieving the economic potential of agriculture production.

1　Overview of Developments

My list of favorable developments includes: (1) Less subsidization of industry at the expense of agriculture, (2) improvements in health, (3) gains in the comparative advantage of agriculture, (4) more and better schooling, and (5) advances in agricultural research. There is an unevenness in economic development within countries which gives rise to difficult agriculture problems in location economics. Agricultural production is adversely affected (a) by markets that are impaired by governments, (b) by distortions of public investments in physical and human capital, and (c) by private economic activities of farmers that are not optimum as a consequence of the distortions in agricultural incentives. Let me now consider these developments briefly.

1　The monolithic commitment to industrialization with little or no concern about agriculture and, in large measure at the expense of agriculture, has declined during recent years. Although cheap food policies still prevail in many low income countries, fewer countries neglect agriculture than during the 1950s and early 1960s. This is clearly a favorable development.

2　Improvements in health are enhancing the productivity of labor in agriculture. The best available measure of improvements in health is the increase in life-span. The life-span of people in many low income countries has increased upwards of 50 percent over the past three decades. This remarkable achievement surpasses the rate of increase in life-span in European countries when they were poor. It is noteworthy that the long-standing large difference in life-span between low and high income countries has been much reduced since the early 1950s. The implications of this achievement are decidably favorable for agricultural development.

3　More and better schooling, the acquisition of information about better production techniques, and learning from experience enhances the productivity of farm people. Each of these investments in human capital enhances the quality of human beings. The younger adults now have acquired a good deal more human capital in their person than their forebears had. Their labor is more productivity; many farmers in low income countries have become robust entrepreneurs.

4   Beginning in the late 1930s, the productivity of agriculture in some of the high income countries increased at a rapid rate. Crop yields and other measures of productivity outran those in low income countries. As this gap in productivity increased, the comparative advantage in agriculture shifted in favor of particular high income countries. This gap is now being reduced. As this occurs, the comparative advantage of agriculture shifts in favor of some low income countries.

For a crude measure of this change I turn to the production of wheat. It is clear that farmers in North India have increased their productivity of wheat relative to the recent gains in wheat yields in Canada and the United States. Comparable changes in favor of low income countries are also occurring in some other crops as well as in poultry and livestock although at a less rapid rate.

5   These shifts in comparative advantages are made possible largely by agricultural research that is being oriented to requirements of low income countries. The innovations and successes of the international agricultural research centers are a part of this story. More important, however, is the progress being made in financing and organizing national agricultural experiment stations and laboratories. While much needs to be done, the momentum is well-established. The implication is that the contributions of agricultural research are being equalized throughout the world.

6   But difficult problems occur as a consequence of the economic of development in general and of agriculture in particular. Development alters substantially and, as a rule, gradually over time, the locations within the country where people have the best opportunities to earn their living. High income countries have not escaped these problems. The agricultural part of these problems has in large measure been solved, for example, in Japan, in some of the Western European countries in Canada and in the United States. For the most part, these problems have been solved – not by government policies – but by the private migration of farm people out of agriculture or by farm families combining off-farm work with their farming activities.[5]

In agriculture this relocation problem arises because the economic possibilities to increase productivity occur unevenly because of the diversities in land, climatic conditions, markets and the acquired abilities of farm people. It also arises because the agriculture sector declines relative to that of the rest of the economy. A universal empirical truth is that the farm population declines relative to the non-farm population and it declines absolutely at the more advanced stages of economic growth.

When I entered on my first academic job a fourth of the US population were farm people; they are now only three percent of the total. Since then more than 30 million people have moved out of agriculture, which may well be the largest migration ever in so short a period.

Also, as the locational comparative advantage of agriculture changes within a country, some localities lose out relative to others; for instance, the proportion of farm people who have moved out of the Plains States has been much larger than from the corn belt. Correspondingly the economic opportunities available to the farm people in the Deccan of India have not stayed abreast of those in the Punjab.

2   Essential Conditions for Agricultural Development

I shall now consider the essential conditions for agricultural development. It is less difficult to build modern steel mills, as India has done, than it is to modernize agriculture. Many low income countries have a better record in textiles than in food crops. Hong Kong is much more successful in producing electronic components for world markets than Bangalesh is in producing rice for its own people. Engineers do better in designing dams to produce electricity than in designing large scale efficient irrigation projects. Most international donor agencies are strong on social reform but thay are weak when it comes to agricultural productivity.

Many government officals and planners find it exceedingly difficult to comprehend the essential conditions for a productive, prosperous, dynamic agriculture. It is a bit too simple and too convenient to believe that parcels of land, a few crude tools, and strong backs will do. The biology of agriculture is not simple. Nor can the physical and chemical requirements be learned by reading a couple of elementary books. All too few government officials are aware of actual economic prowess of farm people.

There are three economic fundamentals in agricultural production: (a) Farmers perform a function in allocating resources in the domain of the farm that government administrators cannot do, (b) agricultural research is a creative activity that cannot be directed and managed from the top, (c) any economic organization of agriculture that does not provide viable markets cannot optimize agricultural production and the returns to farm people for their work and entrepreneurial abilities.

Farm people are not robots. They are not dull and indifferent to economic opportunities to improve their lot. They are calculating economic agents who reckon marginal costs and return to a fine degree. Nor are agricultural scientists routine workers to be treated as high class clerks. Centralized control of farm activities and of agriculture research is bound to fail.

Over a wide range of issues economic theory and empirical evidence tell a consistent story about the requirements for agricultural development. Learning from the successes and failures of countries has contributed to advances in this branch of economics. Differences in the agricultural achievements among Asian countries is instructive. Japan has over-achieved in rice production. South Korea has done fairly well in rice. The Philippines shows promise in modernizing parts of her agriculture. The record of Taiwan is one of the best. In South Asia the economic success of West Malaysia in palm fruit is remarkable; in sharp contrast is the failure of Nigeria which had a head start. The economic policy of Nigeria has been a disaster for palm production.

In agricultural research India is far ahead of China. There is a serious lack of skilled agricultural scientists in China, whereas India now has a substantial core of competent scientists. Rare, indeed, is the country that has fully satisfied the economic requirements of agriculture; most governments distort the economic incentives of farm people. To point to a model economic policy, we find that it is approximated where there is no agricultural sector, for example, in the two city-states, Hong Kong and Singapore. It is a point to ponder.

Investment and the organization of economic activities are essential in the development of agriculture. Regardless of how competent human beings are in their economic affairs – be they farmers, engineers, administrators or government officials – inefficient organization results in malinvestments. By investment I mean all types of capital formation undertaken to increase future income and satisfactions. My concept of organization includes all public and private economic institutions. In the case of agriculture it includes the organizational connections between agriculture and the rest of the economy. As entrepreneurs famers are constrained not only by land, equipment, and other factors of production but also by information about worthwhile economic opportunities and by incentives which more often than not are distorted by the prevailing economic organization. It is evident that the potential productivity of agriculture is not being realized in many countries because of malinvestments which are the consequence of inefficient organization. I begin with investment.

3 Investment

The formation of capital that will yield the largest return among the available options is the objective of investment. Since there are many forms of capital, the first step is an all-inclusive concept of capital. To deal exclusively with physical forms of capital is a serious mistake. The formation of physical capital is only part of the investment story. A more important part consists of human capital. The formation of human capital is omitted in national income and capital accounting, which is misleading. It arises from the convention of treating investment in human capital as current consumption or as welfare expenditures. Additions to the stock of human capital that improve the acquired quality of the population – improvements in health, more and better schooling, the acquisition of skills, and training at work – are usually high-yielding investments over the long term in their contribution to economic growth including agricultural productivity.

Investment in agricultural research requires both facilities and competent agricultural scientists. The research in turn contributes to the stock of both physical and human capital. A new high yielding variety of rice, for example, is a form of physical capital. Information on better crop rotations that farmers derive from agricultural research becomes a part of their human capital. Advances in the sciences contribute importantly to knowledge which becomes a part of the stock of human capital.

Having adopted an all-inclusive concept of capital, the next step is to face up to the implications of the heterogeneity of capital since the various forms of capital are far from homogenous. I agree with Hicks[6] that the capital homogeneity assumption is the disaster of capital theory.

Capital is two-faced, and what these two faces tell us about economic growth, which is a dynamic process, are, as a rule, inconsistent stories. It must be so because the cost story is a tale of sunk investments, and the other story pertains to the discounted value of the expected stream of services that such capital may render, which changes with the shifting sands of growth.[7] The existing stock of capital at any given date consists of many different specific forms of capital. In terms of investment costs that were incurred, it is rare indeed that the present yields on each form of such capital would be the same. Even though all past investments were optimum with respect to expected yields, the realized yields are altered, as noted, by the dynamics of economic growth.

Current public and private investments are, of course, constrained by available resources. Here, too, various investment options entail capital heterogeneity. The expected rates of return to the specific forms of capital are constantly subject to changes because the dynamics of growth and inequalities in the realized rates of return occur. Inequalities in the rates of return to the various specific forms of capital are inevitable as a consequence of economic growth. Nor would a catalogue of all existing growth models prove that these inequalities are not pervasive. But why try to square the circle? If we were unable to observe these inequalities, we would have to invent them because they provide the compelling economic signals of growth.

4 Organization

Capital theory despite its limitations provides a useful economic rationale for investment, but there is much controversy about the principles of economic organization. The controversy persists in the realm of ideas and theory on centralized control versus markets. Meanwhile world wide experiences of recent decades indicates clearly that centralized control of agriculture is inefficient. No government that has imposed direct economic controls on agriculture with little or no reliance on markets has been successful because an efficient allocation of resources on each and every farm cannot be achieved from the top.

In modernizing agriculture, the institutions that are essential parts of economic organization include both particular government activities and viable free markets. It is not all one or the other. It is necessary at this point to distinguish between those economic activities in which governments have a comparative advantage and those in which they do not.[8]

5 Advantages of Government

Leaving qualifications aside, stable, well-managed governments have a comparative advantage in the following activities.

(1)   In collecting and reporting agricultural statistics governments have an advantage and these statistics are important sucres of information for producers and consumers. In this area of statistics the USDA has a good record.

(2)   Governments have an advantage in providing standards of measurement of things that are bought and sold along with the enforcement of such standards in trading. In both national and international markets these standards are exceedingly important in pricing agricultural commodities and agricultural inputs.

(3)   In determining the property rights of buyer and sellers the government is the primary authority.

(4)   In reducing the occurrence of or spread of plant and animal diseases and of pests governments have a comparative advantage. Closely related is health inspection of food products.

(5)   Maintaining a stable level of prices and thereby not having periodic

inflation or deflation, is an important function of governments. It is beyond the capability of consumers, farmers, laborers, or business men to maintain a stable general level of prices.

(6)   Agricultural research acquires special institutional organization in which governments are much involved.

Organized agricultural research is a recent development and we have learned a good deal during recent decades about the economics of agricultural research. This research contributes much to the increases in agricultural productivity. The rates of return on the expenditures are in general decidedly favorable. These rates of returns tell us that it is a worthwhile activity; they also give us the implicit price of this research. But rates of return, no matter how high, do not tell us who should pay for it and how it should be organized. Consider experiment stations, laboratories and other university research related to agriculture. They do not sell their product; they make their findings available to the public. Nor do they provide the funds that cover the costs of doing this research. Who benefits and who bears the costs require some elaboration. In Asia less than five percent – in the United States it is 25 percent – of all expenditures on agricultural research is accounted for by the industrial sector. Industrial firms, understandably, restrict their agricultural research to projects from which they expect to derive a profit. The economics of this part is both simple and straightforward.

It could be argued that the same economic logic shows that farmers should pay for the research from which they profit, just as industrial firms do. The first difficulty in applying this logic is that under competition the reductions in real costs of producing agricultural products that are realized as a consequence of the contributions of agricultural research are transferred in large measure to consumers. Farmers who first adopt a new high yielding variety do benefit. But when most farmers have adopted such a variety most of the benefits shift to consumers. Even where farmers are the beneficiaries, it is beyond the capacity of the individual farmer to do the required research on his own. Nor are farmers collectively up to organizing and financing national agricultural research.

Although over time most of the benefits from agricultural research accrue to consumers, it is not feasible for them to organize and finance national agricultural research enterprises. The only meaningful approach to modern organized agricultural research is to conceptualize most of its contributions as *public goods*. As such, they must be paid for on public account, which does not exclude private gifts used to produce public goods.

There is a serious unresolved organizational quandary (it is far from solved) in supporting the more basic research with public funds. Most of such research is done by universities. The allocation of research funds for this purpose and the regulations that follow in their wake, seriously impair the on-going research of scientists. The institutions serving agricultural research in high income countries have a longer history and are in better repair than are the institutions in low income countries. The major unsolved problem is the tendency to over-organize and over-control agricultural research from the top.[9]

6 Advantages of Markets

Markets, despite all the talk about market failures, are not obsolete. Although many regulations and government interventions distort market prices, markets continue to survive; they continue to perform essential price-making functions that the economy requires. That markets should continue to be as robust as they are under the burden of the constraints that are placed upon them should tell us a good deal about how essential markets are in production, trade and consumption. It is easy to list the adverse economic effects of the failure to rely on viable markets.

1 As already noted, no government that has "abolished" markets has been successful in modernizing agriculture. The inefficiency in the allocation of resources in agriculture in all centrally controlled economies is no longer in doubt. The Soviet Union with all of its farm machinery, fertilizer, and other large investments in agriculture, continues to be incapable of developing a modern efficient agricultural sector. I know from discussions that I have had with managers of collective farms while in the Soviet Union that they are intelligent and capable human beings. They are not to blame for the poor performance of Soviet agriculture. Orders from Moscow are poor substitutes for market prices.

2 In South Asia, where under colonial rule food grains were frequently obtained by force from farmers to cope with poor crops caused by bad monsoons, some governments continue to procure food grains at below market prices to provide cheap rice and wheat for fair food shops, mainly for the benefit of urban consumers.[10] The effect of such procurement is to distort the incentives of farmers and in doing so, reduce the economic possibility of farmers to modernize agriculture.

3 The government of India some years ago abolished wheat markets by assuming direct control of the distribution of wheat. The resulting

disorganization verged on chaos and the government abandoned its noble experiment.

4   Governments of the European Community are vastly over-pricing major agricultural products within these countries. This over-pricing is a costly and wasteful policy. There is a growing recognition in these countries that this is not a viable policy. Free trade at going international prices would be a boon for consumers in the European Community.

5   By contrast, many low income countries, despite their urgent requirements for more food, are under-pricing their agricultural products. In most of these countries free trade and internal prices at the prevailing international prices would be a boon for the modernization of their agriculture.

6   Some low income countries have in effect nationalized the pricing of fertilizer by controlling imports, production, and the distribution of fertilizer. The inefficiency and waste of these governmental endeavors are well documented.

I have recently edited a set of essays by competent, experienced international agricultural authorities on the *Distortions of Agricultural Incentives*.[11] These distortions take a large economic toll in both low and high income countries. The economic necessity of market prices bears repeating. Any price on which buyers and sellers freely agree, each having only a small influence on the price, is a price that approximates the real economic value of the thing that is exchanged.

7   Social and Cultural Values

Is it possible to reconcile social and cultural values with the economic values on which I have concentrated? Whether the objective is to expand the provision of social services or to improve equity, governments and markets perform essential roles. Economists are fond of saying, "there is no free lunch." What is noteworthy about this phrase is that it is true for any society (country) regardless of its culture, social structure and political organization. Free food, free housing (no rent) or free health care can conceal the economic value of these services, but they cannot eliminate the costs of producing them. The marginal cost and the marginal utility of anything that is not free must be brought into harmony or there will be waste and misuse of scarce resources.

Social and cultural values do matter. They must be properly included in the economic analyses as they are in most studies pertaining to human capital. Studies of investment in education do not debase the cultural part of education because future cultural satisfactions that students expect to derive from their investment in education are a part of their returns. This is true for any other investments in human capital, for instance, in undertaking investments to improve and maintain one's health. In principle, any cultural or social value that entails the use of scarce resources is not free. Under these conditions it becomes necessary to solve the problem of harmonizing (equating) the marginal cost and the marginal utility of the social value. The concept of externalities is not new in economics; it goes back to Pigou[12] and his analysis of the social costs of smoke that factories belch into the air. The regulatory approach in solving this class of pollution problems are inefficient compared to charging factories for their pollution, which would be an explicit price. There are also other externalities. There are also worthwhile public goods that the market cannot afford to produce. I have featured organized science and agricultural research that contribute to our stock of knowledge that enters the public domain as valuable public goods.

8   Concluding Remarks

I have dealt mainly with investment in people and knowledge and with the organization of economic activities. In the case of investment in knowledge, I have concentrated on agricultural research. Modern organized agricultural research is a decisive activity in improving the productivity of agriculture. Although it requires substantial funds (resources), it is usually a high yielding investment, one of the best that a country can make in achieving economic growth.

The issues that pertain to economic organization are high on my agenda. In many countries the major economic inefficiencies over any extended period of time are consequences of the pervasive bias against the role of markets. Since agricultural research is predominantly in the public sector, the organizational problems are specific to the performance of that sector. Instability of governments thwarts agricultural research. Where there is stability and a commitment to support agricultural research, there are three sets of research entrepreneurs: top government officials, research directors and agricultural scientists. Each set has information that is required in making research decisions. All too often there is a lack of arrangements for negotiations between and among them to bring the information that each possesses to bear in an orderly way in arriving at research decisions.

In the offices of national capitals, the farmer is the forgotten man. Yet it is he who produces our food. It is he who knows his parcel of land and the terraces that protect his soil. He knows that the rains, the winds and the sun are indifferent whether or not he and his family survive. Pests, insects and diseases are ever hostile to his crops. Nature is niggardly. This forgotten farmer is an indispensable economic agent in the modernization of agriculture. He calculates his marginal costs and returns to a fine degree. He is no less concerned about improving his lot and that of his children than we are. The dynamics of agriculture in no small measure depend on the incentives and opportunities that farmers have to increase their productions.

Notes and References

1 Alfred Marshall, *Principles of Economics* (Macmillan and Co., London, 1930).

2 This is the central theme of my Nobel Lecture, "The Economics of Being Poor," reproduced in Theodore W. Schultz, *The Economics of Being Poor* (Blackwell, 1993), Part I, No. 1.

3 The recent large contributions of agricultural research to the productivity of agriculture are presented in Theodore W. Schultz, "The Economics of Research and Agricultural Productivity." (IADS Occasional Paper, New York, 1979).

4 Theodore W. Schultz, "Investment in Population Quality Throughout Low-Income Countries," for United Nations Fund for Population Activities, published in Philip M. Hauser (ed.), *World Population and Development: Challenges and Prospects* (Syracuse University Press, 1979), 339–60; see also Theodore W. Schultz and Rati Ram, "Life Span, Health, Savings and Productivity," *Economic Development and Cultural Change*, 27, No. 3 (Apr. 1979), 399–421.

5 In Japan and the United States over half of the income of farm families is derived from off-farm sources, mainly from off-farm work.

6 John Hicks, *Capital and Growth* (Oxford University Press, Oxford, 1965), chapter 3, p. 35.

7 Schultz, "The Economics of Being Poor."

8 For a more extended analysis of this issue see Theodore W. Schultz, "Markets, Agriculture and Inflation," L.J. Norton Lecture, University of Illinois, Urbana-Champaign, June 11, 1980.

9 Schultz, "The Economics of Research and Agricultural Productivity;" see also Part III, No. 2 above, "The Politics and Economics of Research,", and Part III, No. 3, "Distortions of Economic Research."

10 Theodore W. Schultz, "Distortions of Information about Food," Agricultural Economics Paper No. 80(7) (lecture at Macalester College, Saint Paul, Minnesota, Mar. 20, 1980, published by University of Chicago).

11 Theodore W. Schultz (ed.), *Distortions of Agricultural* Incentives (Indiana University Press, Bloomington, Indiana, 1978).

12 A.C. Pigou, *The Economics of Welfare* (Macmillan and Co., New York, 1920).

5

The Changing Economy and the Family*

Although we have learned a great deal about the economics of the family, the ability of the family to cope with the disequilibria that occur as a consequence of changes in economic conditions has not been on our research agenda. Three issues are considered in this paper. First, the reasons why the family is not fading away as an economic entity are discussed. My argument is that, despite the declines in various economic functions of the family and the increases in divorces and in other failures, the survival capacity of the family is both strong and robust. Second, our economic approach should now be extended to deal with the effects of the life-span revolution; with the large secular shifts in relative prices in commodities, durables, and services; with the changes in the permanent and transitory income components; and with the entrepreneurial ability of the family on the economic behavior of the family. Third, viewed as a hypothesis, what families do over one or more generations in distributing their endowments has less effect on the personal distribution of endowments and rewards than have the general increases over time in real per capita incomes, the changes in the composition of that income, its permanent and transitory components, and the increases in the ratio of the income derived from human capital in terms of wages, salaries, and entrepreneurial rewards relative to that derived from property.

The economics of the family is not blissful. It seems doubtful that the family can survive the dismal propensities of economists. It is not that we belong to the Club of Rome. We stay true to our classical vows. Being true to our logic, our findings are not cheerful. We find the stability of the family being impaired by increases in human capital, by the secular rise in the value of human time, and by generous income transfers. The US

* First published in *Journal of Labor Economics*, 4, No. 3, part 2 (1986). © 1986 by The University of Chicago. I am indebted to Mary Jean Bowman, John Letiche, Margaret Reid, Vernon Ruttan, and T. Paul Schultz for their critical comments.

divorce rate has doubled since 1960, and the illegitimate birth rate also has doubled.[1] The better the performance of the economy and the larger the earning power of women, the greater the decline of the family. It would be premature, however, to infer from all this that the family is fading away.

For better or worse, the bearing and rearing of children will not fade away. The comparative advantage of producing one's own children is not in doubt. As yet there is no acceptable biological substitute for bearing them and no all-inclusive social substitute for rearing them. We have the theory and supporting evidence to explain fewer children per family. How few are enough is not revealed to us. Even China, with its centrally controlled society, is not capable of enforcing its "one-child family" policy.

The family is not an economic entity on a par with that of the firm, the household, or the market. The family is in essence a biological, cultural, legal, and economic institution. But we do not treat these characteristics of the family as an institution. Marriage, however, is much less troublesome whether it is sanctioned by church or by civil authorities, including common-law marriages. When it comes to data and empirical work, it is inconvenient to find that large numbers of couples who are living together are not married.[2] Marriage as an institution has not been a fruitful source of economic hypotheses, whereas the marriage market idea has opened an important new research area.

The family as a biological, cultural, and legal entity has a long history in dealing with political and economic changes. The short view of this process is heavy with pessimism and is stated succinctly by Becker at the outset in *A Treatise on the Family* (p. 1): "The family in the Western world has been radically altered, some claim almost destroyed, by events of the last three decades". In his last chapter, "The Evolution of the Family," the long view emerges on the basis of many historical accounts. It implies a strong survival capacity on the part of the family.

By no means are all aspects of the recent decline of the family bad, hard as it is to distinguish the bad from the good. Taking the long view, the survival ability of the family is more than Darwinism.

1 Family Entrepreneurship

It will not suffice to treat the family as a passive entity. Its actions are not routine and repetitive. The family is not a robot. It is a calculating entity; decisions are made and actions are taken. I find it useful to think of the family as dealing with changes in conditions that originate either from within the family or from outside the family. A placid society, serenely free of disturbing changes, has not been the lot of families during the past. In my view it is inevitable that future families will also be dealing with changes.

In reality there are few if any families that manage throughout their family life span to attain and maintain at all junctures an equilibrium as changes occur. What we should endeavor to determine are the incentives that induce the members of the family to bring it into equilibrium. The disequilibria are not restricted to the economic domain since they also occur in the biological, cultural, and legal domains of the family.

Since we specialize in the economic behavior of families, I find it hard to understand why the entrepreneurial function of families has been omitted in our family economic research. Milton Friedman's studies have not been in the mainstream of the family economics under consideration here, and yet he, in his classic "consumption function" book, features entrepreneurial families in both the theoretical and the empirical parts of that book.[3]

Our economic approach tends not to get at the interacting effects of the performance of the economy and the behavior of the family. It is not that we postulate a wholly self-sufficient family. What we tend to do, however, is to abstract from the changes in the economy by treating them as data that are given. Much, and perhaps most, of what we want to know about the economics of the family, in addition to what is now known, are the effects of the performance of the economy on the opportunities, on the composition, and on the functions of the family. A part of the supporting argument is that the options, roles, and economic importance of the family are strongly linked to the performance and achievements of the economy over time. The family is not spared from even short-run periodic changes, be they business cycles, fluctuations in employment, good and bad monsoons (India), or large shifts in the rates of economic growth. Studies of long periods of accumulative economic changes, with notable large increases in per capita income, would substantially increase our understanding of US families at this juncture.

When we take a long view of changes in the family, during which economic possibilities were being extended, we observe that the market specializes in and produces at a lower cost many services that families formerly produced for themselves. Specialization also alters the composition of families as prime adults, other than wife and husband, leave the family and establish separate households. Accumulative increases in family income make it financially possible for parents to support the marriages and the separate households of their children at an age before they are prepared to earn enough to do it on their own. The favorable personal income also makes it possible for retired couples and individuals to maintain a household that is separate from that of their adult children. Thus the composition of the family changes as the number of adults who are in it declines as a consequence of the increases in opportunities created by economic growth. The entrepreneurial function of families continues to be important as a consequence of the changing economic conditions that characterize economic growth.

2   Decline of the Family

The number of kinfolk attached to the wife-husband family core declines. The economic self-sufficiency of the family declines. The support that adult children provide their parents over the last years of their parents' lives – and also earlier when adversities strike – declines. Since research on these issues is still fragmented, these changes in the family may be viewed as a hypothesis. For reasons already presented, I see it as an acceptable proposition on a par with the widely observed worldwide decline of the economic importance of the agricultural sector and closely related on a par with declines in the share of national income derived from the Ricardian "original properties of the soil" in the form of land rent.

Research on the economics of the family has reached the point where it should be possible to give a provisional answer to the question, When will these particular declines pertaining to the family have completed their downward course? The increase in the fraction of married women who are in the labor force, part- or full-time, as yet has not peaked. There are no apparent reasons for believing that the value of the time of women will not continue to rise as a consequence of modern economic growth. As the demand for labor requiring brute strength declines and as that for skills requiring less physical effort increases, it is plausible that the value of the productivity of the time of women will rise relative to that of men and, in so doing, will narrow the gap in wages or salaries between them. As yet, a general economic equilibrium in the allocation of the time of women among bearing children, household activities (including the rearing of children), and work in the labor market is not at hand.

The utility implications of these various elements in the decline of the family as an economic entity await analysis. Meanwhile, the accumulative increases in personal family income, taking the long view, are likely to continue. With respect to the observable decline in family economic self-sufficiency over time, I have no doubt that a careful reckoning would show that families enhance the utility they derive from their increasing dependency on the performance of the market. Fewer kinfolk and less dependency on one's children during old age are also sources of some utility.

3   Interactions between the Economy and the Family

Applications of economics to the behavior of families have produced an impressive body of new knowledge. But our theory has not been extended to deal with the nature and significance of economic changes that originate not from within the family but from within the rest of the economy, and it has not been extended to deal with the infractions between them. Consider the following unsettled issues.

3.1   *The Life-Span Boom*

In most low-income countries since the late 1940s, the costs of acquiring a longer life have declined relative to the value that people place on their own additional life time. The resulting observable increases in life expectancy must be viewed as an extraordinary achievement. It took Western Europe and North America much longer than it has taken many low-income countries more recently. In India, as a case in point, the life expectancy at birth of males increased 43% and that of females 41% between the 1951 and 1971 censuses.[4] By 1981, life expectancy at birth of the Indian population was 52% as estimated by the World Bank,[5] an increase of 63% percent over that in 1951. India exemplifies this "life-span boom" of the last three decades. It has enhanced human well-being, unevenly to be sure. A large part of it has had its origin in advances in knowledge. Families benefited from collective efforts to suppress malaria and to reduce tuberculosis and various endemic diseases through the availability of modern drugs, the service of health centers, and improvements in nutrition from more and better food. It seems to me that we want to know (1) the economics of the observed decline in the price of an additional year of expected life; (2) the economics of the rate at which families respond to this lower price; and then (3) the economics of the resulting changes in family composition, in age profiles of its members, and in the functions of the family. My assumption is that an important part of the explanation of the life-span boom is in the economics of the decline of the price of the extensions in life expectancy.

I am always on my guard when I am with an economist who is reluctant to be associated with changes in relative prices. If he is beholden to a centrally managed economy, it is the better part of wisdom to discuss poetry. In reality, changes in relative prices are the mainspring that produce the necessary incentives for economic efficiency in the process of modernization.

We, too, in many of the applications of our approach to family behavior, have, for reasons of empirical convenience, concentrated on changes in earned income (wages and salaries). But the origins and the effects of changes in relative prices of commodities, changes in the relative rents paid for the use of property (houses, automobiles, household durables), and changes in relative prices of services are rarely being analyzed.

Changes in relative prices create the incentives that result in changes in composition and the size of the stock of capital and in the source of family income. The interactions between these changes and those of the family, as the following cases suggest, should be on our research agenda.

3.2   Wheat-Rice Price Ratios

Wheat and rice are the world's major food grains. Wheat has become very cheap, much more so than rice. At least half the family income of most rice eaters is spent on food; many, if not most, wheat eaters spend a small fraction of their income on food. In the United States, only 12% of personal incomes goes for food.

On the London "world market," during 1867–77, wheat prices exceeded those of rice by 30%, but by 1911–14 they were about the same. For some years now, world wheat prices have been half those of rice.[6] Since the nutritional value per ton of these two food grains is virtually the same, there is a dual puzzle: Why has the cost of producing wheat declined so much relative to that of rice? Why has wheat been a weak substitute for rice?

In reckoning the changes in the demand for labor, in the case of wheat it has become a man's job; in rice, however, in the parts of Asia where people are poor, much of the work in planting and harvesting rice is a woman's job. What are the male and female labor demands and earnings implications for family behavior?

3.3   Labor in Corn and Milk Production

In the United States between 1929 and 1979, the hours of labor required to produce 100 bushels of corn dropped from 115 to 3 hours, and those required to produce 100 pounds of milk fell from 3.3 to .3 hours. The deflated corn price declined 30% while that of milk rose 13%. Real farm wages rose more than threefold ($0.49–$1.59; nominal $0.25–$3.41 per hour). There is only a small demand for the labor of women in corn production; in milk production (dairy farming), however, the demand for the labor of farm women is sufficient to reduce their off-farm employment compared to that of women on farms that specialize in producing field crops. Sumner's[7] study of off-farm labor supply and earnings of farm family members from a sample of Illinois farms shows "that wives of dairy farmers are less likely to work off the farm" than are wives on other types of farms.

3.4   Changes in Relative Prices

Evidence to test the role that changes in relative prices play in the behavior of families is hard to come by. A recent study by T. Paul Schultz[8] based on evidence for Sweden from 1860 to 1914 shows that the decline in the price of rye relative to butter led to increases in the wages of women relative to those of men and to the fertility transition. The conclusion is that "County level data for this fifty year period in Sweden suggests that the appreciating value of women's time relative to men's, played an important role in the Swedish fertility transition, holding constant for real wages of men, children mortality, and urbanization" (p. 22).

4   Family Entrepreneurship and Transitory Income

Explain, if you can, why the theory and empirical work on the permanent and transitory components of family income have been so grossly neglected in our research on the economics of the family. I have in mind the neglect of the family income studies of Dorothy S. Brady et al.[9] based on US 1935–36 data covering small cities, villages, and farms and the neglect of the analyses of the large differences in the transitory component in the income of families in various data sets by Margaret G. Reid.[10] Even more serious has been the neglect of the advance in theory and of the applications of that theory by Milton Friedman.[11]

Dorothy Brady's transitory income clue is in the changes in assets and liabilities of urban, village, and farm families during 1935–36. Margaret Reid extended the search by examining various forms of capital formation by families and by analyzing the behavior of other families at other dates and locations. Milton Friedman drew, in part, on Brady's and Reid's findings and proceeded to establish a strong linkage between entrepreneurship and transitory income, namely, that the ratio of permanent consumption to permanent income has been decidedly higher for families of wage earners than for entrepreneurial families and that the difference between entrepreneurial and nonentrepreneurial families in the ratio of permanent consumption to permanent income "seems larger and better established than any other we have examined."[12]

Having given thought to the possible reasons for this neglect, I rule out intellectual hostility on our part to the concepts of permanent and transitory income. I also rule out that family income studies using these concepts were not known by us. The reason is that Brady, Reid, and Friedman were analyzing the economic behavior of families under a wide array of changes in economic conditions. In their approach they did not exclude events that required entrepreneurship to reestablish an economic equilibrium. On this important issue, the analytical domain of a nonstandard approach to the economic behavior of families is decidedly more restrictive.

5   On Distribution of Economic Rewards

In closing, I acknowledge the theme assigned to this conference. It is not my cup of hemlock. I shall explain why I am so shy.

For me, the observable changes in the distribution of economic rewards as income or as wealth are, in part, a consequence of what is done by families during a generation and in distributing their endowments over two and even more generations. Both in theory and in regard to its application, our knowledge pertaining to this part is substantial and useful.

Another part of this distribution of economic rewards is a consequence of changes in economic conditions over time. Clearly, it is this part that is central in my thinking on the issue at hand. A decline in the price of food improves the economic lot of poor people more than that of people who are not so poor. In Ricardo's day, the families of laborers were giving up half and more of their wages for food. In North America and most of Western Europe, as modernization has proceeded, the fraction of family income spent on food has dropped to less than one-fifth of personal family income. Gains in the productivity and economic efficiency of agriculture, for reasons stated, reduce the inequality in the personal distribution of income. The share of national income going to landlords declines as Ricardian land rents become smaller relative to other sources of income. Here, too, income inequality is reduced. Kuznets[13] takes a fairly long view of the decline in the share of national income derived from property from about 45 percent–25 percent, while labor's part rose from 55 percent to 75 percent.[14]

My hypothesis is that the fivefold increase in real wages per hour of work in the United States since 1900 has swamped the within-family and the intergenerational personal distributions of income. Thus what matters most are the increases in the value of human time over time.

6   Conclusion

What I have done is to leave family reforms to others. Producing one's own children is a family matter. The family is not about to fade away. The family, in its economic behavior, is a flexible and robust entity. By no means have all the recent changes in the family been bad; quite the contrary, most of them are not inconsistent with optimal economic behavior.

While we have learned a great deal from our economic approach to family behavior, it is my contention that our analytical work should be extended to relate the economic changes in the rest of the economy to those in the family exemplified by the "life span revolution" and by large shifts in relative prices in commodities, durables, and services. There is the hard-to-explain neglect of the highly competent family income studies based on the permanent and transitory income concepts. Then, too, the entrepreneurial behavior of families as economic conditions change is being neglected in our analytical work.

What families do to the distribution of their economic endowments is far less important than are the distributional effects of the general increases over time in real per capita incomes, the changes in the composition of that income, its permanent and transitory components, and the increases in the ratio of that income derived from human capital, namely, from wages, salaries, and entrepreneurial rewards relative to that derived from property.

Notes and References

1   See Gary S. Becker, *A Treatise on the Family* (Harvard University Press, Cambridge, Mass., 1981), figs. 11.1, 11.5, pp. 237–56.
2   Ibid., fig. 11.6, p. 248. The number of such couples is now about 2 million.
3   Milton Friedman, *A Theory of the Consumption Function* (Princeton Uni-

versity Press, Princeton, NJ, 1957).

4 Rati Ram and Theodore W. Schultz, "Life Span, Health, Savings and Productivity," *Economic Development and Cultural Change* 27 (Apr. 1979), 399–421.

5 *World Development Report 1983* (World Bank, Washington DC, July 1983).

6 See Theodore W. Schultz, "On Economics and Politics of Agriculture," in Theodore W. Schultz (ed.), *Distortions of Agricultural Incentives* (Indiana University Press, Bloomington, Indiana, 1978), updated on the basis of US Department of Agriculture statistics. See also A.J.H. Latham and Larry Neal, "The International Market in Rice and Wheat, 1968–74," *Economic History Review*, 2nd ser., 36 (May 1983), 260–80, app. 2, cols. B, G. The text shows the market linkages between rice and wheat in India and in London.

7 Daniel Sumner, "Off-Farm Labor Supply and Earnings of Farm Family Members," unpublished PhD dissertation (University of Chicago, 1977).

8 T. Paul Schultz, "Changing World Prices, the Wages of Women and Men, and the Fertility Transition: Sweden 1860–1910," *Journal of Political Economy* 93: 6 (Dec 1985), 1126–1154.

9 Dorothy S. Brady et al., *Changes in Assets and Liabilities of Families, Five Regions* (US Department of Agriculture, Miscellaneous Publication No. 464, Consumer Purchases Study: Urban, Village and Farm, US Government Printing Office, Washington DC, 1941). See also their *Family Income and Expenditures, Five Regions, Farm Series* (USDA, Miscellaneous Publication No. 465, US Government Printing Office, Washington DC, 1941).

10 Margaret G. Reid, "Effect of Income Concept upon Expenditure Curves of Farm Families," in *Studies in Income and Wealth*, 15 (National Bureau of Economic Research, New York, 1952).

11 Friedman, *A Theory of Consumption Function*.

12 Ibid., p. 227.

13 Simon Kuznets, *Modern Economic Growth* (Yale University Press, New Haven, Conn., 1966).

14 See also my elaboration of Kuznets' analysis in Theodore W. Schultz, "The Economics of the Value of Human Time," in Theodore W. Schultz (ed.), *Investing in People* (University of California Press, Berkeley and Los Angeles, 1980).

Part V

Government, Economics, and Politics

Part V

Government, Economics, and Politics

1

Role of Government in Promoting Increases in Income*

As a people we value highly both prosperity and progress. The civic capacity to achieve these goods matters greatly. But as yet we do not know the organizational requirements and the skills that are needed to achieve the optimum increases in income.

My remarks are restricted, in the main, to poor countries,[1] and my thesis is that in most poor countries there is not much economic growth to be had by merely taking up whatever slack may exist in the way the available resources are being utilized. To achieve economic growth of major importance in such countries, it is necessary to allocate effort and capital to do three things: increase the *quantity* of reproducible goods; improve the *quality* of people as productive agents; and raise the *level* of the productive arts. The first of these represents additions to the stock of particular tangible resources and the second and third as adding to the stock of particular intangible resources. Some economic growth, also, may be had from enlarging the scope of the market. In the opposite direction, a part of the gain from these several sources, varying from country to country, is canceled by diminishing returns against such non-reproducible factors as exist.

What, then, is the role of government in promoting economic growth? It depends not only upon how one envisages the process of economic growth but also upon one's conception of what are the best ways of acquiring and allocating the effort and capital to increase the stock of these resources and of achieving a larger market. All too much attention is being directed to taking up the existing slack in countries that now have a poor collection of resources on the assumption that there are

* First published in Leonard D. White (ed.), *The State of the Social Sciences* (University of Chicago Press, Chicago, Ill., 1956), pp. 372–83. © 1956 by the University of Chicago.

many underemployed resources readily available for economic growth. Moreover, there has been all too much emphasis on particular tangible resources relative to the stock of intangible resources required to achieve an optimum rate of economic growth from some given expenditure of effort and capital. The redirection of both private and public efforts here implied will be considered later in this paper.

One needs to take cognizance of the great differences in beliefs that are now held about the role of government in promoting economic growth. The issues are most unsettled. Nor is it any wonder, given the state of affairs in the world, that there should have arisen such widespread differences about the relevant facts and the standards or values by which they should be rated. Economic development has become a major objective in many countries where our concept of a good society is suspect. Received Western values are on the defensive, as are its forms of social and political organization. For one, a new vigorous nationalism has taken root in soil just freed from colonialism. It is striving for internal unification and control, and it views with fear the entry of foreign capital, economic aid, and assistance. Some of the basic ideas of mercantilism come closer to explaining the economic policies of this new nationalism than do the prevailing notions among us about economic development. The vast struggle for political power among nations that is now under way cannot help but leave its scars. At the level of propaganda it is obvious that the respective economic systems are pitted one against the other. But what is not so obvious is the relevance of the economic experiences of Russia and China, on the one hand, and of the recent upsurge in production and income, especially in western Europe, on the other, to the role of government in bringing about economic growth. One needs to recognize, however, that the climate of opinion has become charged by ideological conflicts, and as a consequence it is increasingly difficult to discuss and communicate and not be misunderstood. Moreover, politics and economics are being fused once again under the white heat of the international struggle for power. It is hard to believe that these issues have not and will not seriously impair our perspective on the role of government.

One notes, also, that governments are not entirely neutral in selecting advice as they bestir themselves. Most of them preside over poor countries. At best, they want to undertake measures which will increase the production, income, and wealth of their countries. The compulsion is to do it rapidly; the operating horizons are almost always exceedingly short. As governments, they turn for advice to those few countries that have become rich or to those that are now making impressive progress although still quite poor. Nor should one be surprised to find that the advice they want and usually receive is mostly governmental advice featuring the role of government. This note is sounded here not to condemn the process or the advice but to characterize it.

A comment on the meaning of economic growth will be necessary. It is here taken to mean a rising stream of income where the rate of increase in output exceeds that of the population. Economic growth, as I shall use the term, accordingly means a rise in per capita income. There are several reasons for taking this as my definition. A rate of increase in income which is somewhat greater than that of population is the goal of most countries now entering upon programs to promote their economic development. Then, too, the data on which I want to draw are cast in these terms. Nor do I want to become enmeshed in the age-old problem, still present in all too many countries, of population growth absorbing all the additional output, so that no rise in per capita incomes occurs. The many conceptual and measurement difficulties that arise in determining income are acknowledged, but I shall not enter into them here. Nor shall I consider the personal distribution of income except as it is affected by measures to improve the quality of people as productive agents.[2]

I shall now elaborate somewhat on the proposition that most countries cannot achieve economic growth simply by putting so-called underemployed resources to more productive work. A contrary belief about the facts is widely held. A large literature has appeared in recent years based on the belief that countries, however poor the collection of resources at their disposal, can do wonders by recombining the resources already at hand. The mainspring of this view has been the notion that in agriculture one finds many workers whose marginal productivity is not only far below that in other sectors but that it is zero,[3] and, of course, the agricultural sector bulks large in nearly all poor countries. One suspects that this view of an abundance of underemployed resources is a piece of the aftermath of the mass unemployment of the 1930s.

I know of no evidence for any poor country anywhere that would even suggest that a transfer of some small fraction, say, 5 percent, of the existing labor force out of agriculture, with other things equal, could be made without reducing its production. I am, of course, ruling out putting new and additional non-labor resources into farming, the substitution of capital for the labor withdrawn, or the introduction of a better technology. Given the wide range for substitution among factors so characteristic of agriculture, it is all but impossible to construct even a theoretical model which would permit the possibility of a zero marginal product for any appreciable part of the labor supply.

In Peru a modest road was recently built down the east slopes of the Andes to Tingo Maria, using some labor from farms along the way mostly within walking distances; agricultural production in the area dropped promptly because of the withdrawal of this labor from agriculture. In Belo Horizonte, Brazil, an upsurge in construction in the city drew workers to it from the nearby countryside, and this curtailed agricultural production.

The marginal productivity of labor in agriculture in poor countries is very low because of the poor collection of resources, but it is not zero. Moreover, in such a country it is very low for labor generally. And in situations, and there are many, where for many years, often for decades, agriculture has approximated a kind of stationary state, one is likely to find the average and the marginal values of labor more nearly the same than would be the case in a rapidly developing economy like that of the United States. The more sophisticated presentation of this under-employment notion by Eckaus,[4] based on a "technological restraints hypothesis," falls not on its logic as a bit of theory but on its relevance.

The record, as I see it, is as follows: A poor country which has been virtually stationary for a long period is not likely to reveal any appreciable malallocation of factors, say, as between agriculture and the rest of the economy or within agriculture, whereas a country undergoing rapid economic growth, more likely than not, will have in it areas that have been bypassed and others that have become depressed as a consequence of its economic development. There is more malallocation of resources of this kind in western Europe, the United Kingdom, Canada, and the United States, for example, than in poor countries that have as yet achieved little or no economic growth.[5]

There are, however, a few countries where exceptional circumstances exist which led me at the outset to qualify this part of my thesis. These exceptional countries can achieve considerable increases in output by taking up the existing slack. I would place the Argentine and Chile and, perhaps, also Paraguay in this exceptional class. The case of the Argentine, which is not so poor, is clear enough. A study[6] of the earlier growth and recent decline of the agricultural sector of that country indicates that agricultural production currently is fully one-third less than one would have predicted from the characteristic of these agricultural resources, and the progress that was under way up to the early 1940s, and from the growth of agriculture in other countries with comparable resources. The Argentine, however, has been engaged in a very special kind of economic folly for which it has paid a high price. And the Argentine could, if it would, produce much more than it has by simply utilizing more efficiently the fine set of resources at its disposal.

Chile, also far from poor, is operating a long way below its optimum, given the collection of resources that it has at hand, mainly because of what it has done in living with its inflation. I would venture the guess from observations and such data as are available that Chile is foregoing between a fifth to a fourth of its normal output in order to indulge itself in a vast, chronic imbalance in governmental receipts and payments. Inflation itself need not give rise to serious resource malallocations. With flexible product and factor prices, flexible foreign-exchange rates and interest rates attuned to the declining value of money, what would remain may be represented as a special tax on money and near-money. The rub, however, is that where there is inflation the government, as a rule, feels compelled to act and by all manner of devices impairs the flexibility of prices and places restrictions on foreign exchange and trade. Moreover, many administrative and even entrepreneurial talents, always scarce especially in poor countries, are employed to administer these controls. As controlled prices and rates diverge increasingly from the underlying structure of "real" values, the incentives for corruption mount, and, although such corruption acts as a partial corrective of some extreme distortions, it is a high price to pay in terms of public and private integrity.[7]

Suffice it then to say, on the first part of my thesis, that not much economic growth is to be had from efforts to put existing underemployed resources to work because they are relatively unimportant, except in a few countries like the Argentine and Chile. The widely held notion that a substantial fraction of the labor in agriculture in poor countries has a marginal productivity of zero is an illusion. On the contrary, it is very doubtful that any appreciable part of the labor in agriculture in such poor countries is far below the average in its productivity. In general, it appears to be true that such factor disproportionality as does exist does not provide a firm foundation from which to launch a government program of economic growth. Therefore, to place a government into this position and role is a mistake.

Let me now take an affirmative tack and explore that part of my thesis which says that economic growth of major importance is dependent upon increasing the stock of particular intangible resources represented by the *level* of the productive arts and by the *quality* of human agents, and by adding to the stock of conventional reproducible goods. Both sets require effort and capital; both need to be augmented at the same time; and it is a mistake to concentrate solely on the tangible set as is the case where industrialization is viewed as the way of achieving the optimum rate of economic growth.

In my remaining remarks I can give only the bare bones of an approach. Most theorizing about economic growth is based on the belief (assumption) that capital narrowly conceived, namely, where it is restricted to the stock of reproducible goods, is the fundamental variable. To the best of my knowledge, no evidence has been produced to support this particular belief on the all-important role that additional reproducible capital goods play in economic growth as herein defined.

The economic history of the United States as interpreted by Fabricant, drawing upon the research riches of the National Bureau of Economic Research, certainly does not support this belief on the contribution and role of capital when it is restricted to reproducible goods.[8] During the last eight decades (1869–73 to 1949–53) the per capita output of the United States rose at a rate of 1.9 percent per year (compounded). In exploring where this remarkable economic growth (i.e., output per capita) came from, Fabricant ascribed only about one-tenth of it to the rise in the stock of tangible capital consisting of structures, including housing, equipment, inventories, and net foreign assets (but excluding consumers' equipment, military assets, and land and subsoil assets).[9]

Fabricant puts it thus, "With a given 'dose' of labor and tangible capital we have learned to produce a larger and larger volume of goods for consumption and investment: output per unit of input has risen somewhat under fourfold, or about 1.7 percent a year on the average . . . [This] Improvement in national efficiency has been a remarkable persistent process." He also points out that this upward trend in *national efficiency* occurred in each of the several major parts of the eight decades and in all corners of the economy. Thus, according to Fabricant, about nine-tenths of the remarkable economic growth of the United States (the rise in output per capita) since about the Civil War has come from sources other than increases in labor and in the stock of tangible capital. One need not endorse these precise results, nor would Fabricant, I am sure, contend that they will not have to be revised substantially as the underlying researches proceed. But the direction and the magnitudes of these estimates, even allowing for the many conceptual and measurement difficulties to be resolved, are so decisive that they cannot be put aside in theorizing about economic growth.

One, of course, would prefer to have comparable estimates for one or more poor countries in process of achieving economic growth, for instance, for Mexico and Brazil and for Japan with its development of longer standing. But, unfortunately, no such estimates are at hand; nor can they be had without undertaking years of difficult and often very tedious research. We must build, therefore, with the straw and clay we have.[10]

How, then, is economic growth to be represented? The economic experiences of the United States since the Civil War – and these are not inconsistent with one's observations of the process of economic development in poor countries – do not support the view that economic growth (rising per capita output) is wholly or even primarily dependent upon increases in the stock of reproducible goods. The major key to this rise in output per capita Fabricant has called the "improvement in national efficiency," namely, the observed increases in the ratio of output to inputs of labor and of reproducible goods. This means that economic growth is determined in part by adding to the stock of reproducible goods and in part, and probably much the larger part, by factors which give rise to the improvements in national efficiency.

Economic growth, therefore, is here represented as some function of three basic variables, each determined (presumably in large part) by the amount of effort and capital allocated to its development, that is, to increasing its magnitude; these variables are, as stated at the outset of this paper: (1) the quantity of reproducible goods; (2) the quality of people as productive agents; and (3) the level of the productive arts. In addition, a larger market improves the national efficiency and becomes a special factor in this process. These variables must then be cast into a framework which takes account of whatever diminishing returns occur as a consequence of the nonreproducible factors and the drag that these place on economic growth.

In advancing this formulation, I take it to be meaningful to approach the quality of human agents and, also, the level of the productive arts as economic variables, that is, as variables which are at least in substantial part determined by resource allocations, namely, largely determined by the effort and other inputs that are committed to their development. It might be argued that this approach is simply an extension of the theorizing about economic growth which is based on increasing the existing stock of capital. I would not disagree with such an interpretation; however, if viewed as an extension, it drastically redefines the role of capital and related effort on which economic growth is dependent.

My closing remarks will be addressed to some of the implications of this approach to the role of government. I enter upon these with some misgivings for reasons already touched upon.

Let me first restate two major inferences which emerged from the first part of this paper.

1 Quite aside from whether it is a proper role of government, it is a mistake for governments of poor countries to undertake programs of economic development based on so-called underemployed resources.
2 It is also a mistake for governments in poor countries to key all programs of economic development to industrialization. To do so creates "factor disproportionality" where none had existed before.

I consider the rest of these observations as tentative and exploratory.

1   The growth in output to be had in most poor countries from additional effort and capital allocated to improving the quality of its people as productive agents is, so it would appear, substantially higher than that from equivalent inputs to increase the stock of many forms of reproducible goods, although these goods usually are given top priority in programs of economic development. This statement implies that relatively more resources should be allocated, for example, for health services, for extending knowledge about nutrition, and for education. Of the resources devoted to measures which improve the quality of people as productive agents, the health services appear to fare relatively better than does education.

What is the role of government in this exceedingly important area? Surely it cannot be rated as minor. I would cite Puerto Rico as outstanding example of what can and should be done in improving the quality of its people preparatory to entering upon rapid economic development. Mexico, also, has been doing unusually well in broadening its educational base and in acquiring depth in terms of trained personnel. Puerto Rico and Mexico may well be exceptions to the rule that most poor countries allocate all too few of the resources at their disposal to these services. In both of these countries the respective governments have performed a distinctly positive role in this area.

2   Efforts and capital expended to raise the level of the productive arts – scientific work, technological research, development of new techniques of production and their dissemination – by universities, research institutes, agricultural experiment stations, and extension services and in other ways, indicate a rate of return, measured in economic growth, that is undoubtedly very high. Poor countries presumably may draw upon the technology of rich countries where the level of the productive arts is much higher. The possibilities of doing so, however, are more restricted than is commonly believed. Rich countries have evolved a technology that is appropriate to an economy where labor is dear relative to capital. Basic scientific and technological knowledge can be drawn upon, but the gap between this knowledge and useful techniques of production applicable to a poor country is usually very considerable.

The excellent joint work on corn of the Rockefeller Foundation and of the government of Mexico demonstrates that it is no easy matter to take the scientific knowledge on corn hybrids and on corn-breeding already established in the United States and develop useful corn varieties for Mexico. Experiment stations that do well are hard to come by. In the United States there are still all too many states that have not established satisfactory conditions for such agricultural research. Extension services organized to disseminate useful knowledge to farmers are a fairly recent innovation and as yet not well understood.

The role of government in this area is most complex. It is all too easy for governments to underrate the contributions of business, foreign and domestic, as effective carriers of new technology. It appears that more useful techniques are being transferred from the United States to Latin America by business firms than through any other single channel, although very important contributions are being made by foundations, universities, Point Four, and by United States – supported religious activities in agriculture, education, and health. Governments, nevertheless, can and, virtually of necessity, must play an important role not only in creating conditions that facilitate the functioning of business as a carrier of technology but also in institutionalizing scientific work, technological research, experiment stations, and extension services.

3   In the area where effort and capital is allocated to increase the stock of reproducible goods there is, as I have already stressed, in many poor countries, all too much emphasis on industrialization relative to that placed on improving the quality of people as productive agents and on raising the level of the productive arts. Also, other sectors, that is, agriculture, mining, transportation and communication, financial institutions, distribution, and the service industries, usually receive too little attention in programs of economic development. Here, again, let me call attention to the achievements of Puerto Rico and Mexico with the inference that they have come closer than have most countries in finding the optimum combinations of effort and capital in promoting economic growth in this complex area.

4   Let me also restate a truth, long accepted as a truism, namely, that the instability of government which is all too characteristic of many poor countries hangs like the sword of Damocles over all effort and capital devoted to economic growth.

We shall continue, as a people, to value prosperity and progress highly. We want these for ourselves, and we are prepared to help many other countries achieve them. But our understanding of economic growth is far from satisfactory, and we do quite badly in our endeavors to help poor countries and their governments in achieving this important national objective. It has been the burden of this paper that we could and should do much better in this particular civic art.

Notes and References

1 This paper is being restricted to "poor" countries and, in the main, to countries that have as yet achieved little or no economic growth, although most of the second and positive part of my thesis is equally applicable to "rich" countries.

2 The definition of economic growth which I have offered is closely parallel to that employed by Professor W. Arthur Lewis in *The Theory of Economic Growth* (George Allen & Unwin, London, 1955), chapter I.

3 See P.N. Rosenstein-Rodan, "Problems of Industrialization of Eastern and South-Eastern Europe," *Economic Journal*, 53 (June–Sept. 1943), 202.

4 R.S. Eckaus, "Factor Proportions in Underdeveloped Areas," *American Economic Review*, 45 (Sept. 1955), 539.

5 But even in these Western countries these depressed pockets and by-passed communities do not provide enough resource slack on which to base an appreciable economic growth.

6 I refer here to a study made by Marto Ballasteros at the University of Chicago.

7 Paraguay is a special case where an exceedingly rough-and-ready policy of reaching for public revenue by "taxing" foreign-trade transactions has greatly impaired the output of its principal industry, the raising of cattle.

8 Solomon Fabricant, *Economic Progress and Economic Change*, in the 34th Annual Report of the National Bureau of Economic Research (New York, May 1954).

9 Of course, it took a large amount of additional capital of this type simply to stay abreast of the growth in population. This particular achievement in output and the contribution that such capital has made to it we are leaving aside, for we are here concentrating on the rise in output which is in excess of the growth in population.

10 There are some sector data: for example, those growing out of the work of Clarence Moore, while at the University of Chicago, to determine the changes in outputs and inputs on agriculture in Mexico and Brazil.

2

*Tensions between Economic and Politics**

In the invitation to write this essay on my part in economic development, I was asked: "Did your professional efforts make a difference?" The answer was "No" whenever I testified before congressional committees. The more I lectured throughout Latin America the greater became the economic distortions. In India the Fabian drums prevailed over my impeccable economics. Nigerian officials and I agreed that the high export tax on palm fruit was killing the goose that produced the revenue. It did. The officials and I were right. My first venture into the USSR was in 1929. In 1960 the Soviet Academy of Sciences made the mistake of asking me to lecture and since then crop failures have become a part of the natural order. My lecture at Peking University and a series at Fudan University in 1980 also made a real difference. Agricultural economic policy was promptly put on the right track and Chinese graduate students opted for Chicago to master the hard core of economics.

While it is obvious that both political activities and economic activities entail human actions, it is not obvious that there is a division of labor between them. We accept Allyn Young's assessment that the most fruitful and illuminating generalization in all of economics is that "the division of labor depends on the extent of the market."[1] The new analytical idea that there is a political market is in its infancy. What are the properties of this political market? Are they comparable to those of the economic market when it comes to the division of labor, specialization, and the gains to be had from extensions of political activities?

As yet we do not know the optimal combination of these two markets. At issue is the extent to which people belonging to a particular nation

*First published in Gerald M. Meier and Dudley Seers (eds), *Pioneers in Development*, © 1984 by The International Bank for Reconstruction and Development/World Bank. Reprinted by Permission of Oxford University Press, Inc. I am indebted to J.J. MacGregor and Gerald M. Meier and to three anonymous readers at the World Bank for their critical comments.

would be served better by substituting part of the activities of one of these markets for the other. Meanwhile, there is no lack of tension.

Tensions between economics and politics, like those in marriages, are part of the human condition. Appeals to the idea of the political market have not reduced these tensions, nor has development economics. The dominating effect of development economics has been to overburden the political sector with economic functions that governments are not capable of performing efficiently. As a policy legacy it is a liability. Gerald M. Meier closes his essay, "The Formative Period," with an excellent summary of this new branch of economics: "Some may . . . summarize the mainstream development economics of the 1950s as being structural, shaped by trade pessimism, emphasizing planned investment in new physical capital, utilizing reserves of surplus labor, adopting import-substituting industrialization policies, embracing central planning of change, and relying on foreign aid."[2] Would that we had a critique on why this variety of development economics had such a bad start.

When it comes to the economics of agricultural production, some governments are about as sophisticated as farmers who allegedly planted crops in accordance with the phase of the moon. Famines provide still another perspective. Most of those occurring in parts of Africa are in considerable measure consequences of internal African governmental policies. It is always convenient to attribute food catastrophes to droughts.

Most people throughout the world, whether they are rich or poor, have both economic and political expectations. Economists are rarely privy to these expectations. People search for useful information, but they seem to place a low value on the information that economists produce. Politicians are wary of academic economists who specialize in the long view that is of little value to politicians. When considering the question, "What will be the future costs of agriculture products?" I once wrote:

> Seeing the pure economic opportunities the prospects for lower costs are good, but in view of what is being done politically the prospects for lower costs are less favorable. Meanwhile, international food conferences produce a lot of weak reports and social thought produces strong ideologies. But reports and ideologies do not produce food. Fortunately, plants and animals do not read reports nor do they discriminate against the ideology of any government.[3]

On his own turf the lowly traditional farmer has an advantage over the expert from a rich country who comes knowing only economics. The farmer knows a great deal about his parcel of land, the local weather, and what he can expect for his efforts that is unknown to the so-called expert. The farmer also knows that the rain, wind, and sun are indifferent whether or not he and his family will survive. Pests, insects, and diseases are ever hostile to his crops. Nature is always niggardly. This unknown farmer is an indispensable economic agent in the modernization of agriculture. He calculates his marginal costs and returns in pennies, not in dollars. He is no less concerned than we are with improving his lot and that of his children.

Wholly self-sufficient farm families are few and far between. Increasing specialization has long been the order of the day. The supply of food has not been divorced from the economic productivity of agriculture, nor is agriculture a unique economic entity. Nevertheless, what a farmer does in traditional agriculture seems too simple to qualify as an economic activity at all. It looks like unskilled labor of zero value. Illusions abound from what we think we see.

Theory and evidence are critical in assessing our knowledge, whether of economics or of politics. I shall begin my assessment by calling attention to various misleading ideas, false concepts, and invalid theoretical fragments that have burdened economics in its treatment of agriculture. Whatever the reasons, agriculture has been the victim of more than its share of bad economics. It seems to me that I have devoted all too much of my career to exposing this particular class of economics.

Close at hand, in the United States, parity prices for farm products based on 1910–14 relative prices is a vulgar economic concept. While at Iowa State College, I did my best to expose the false economic logic inherent in this concept. I buried it but it would not die! Parity farm income is worse, but it has done less economic harm. Agricultural supply management, production control by means of acreage allotments, and the economics of dumping farm products abroad to the tune of Food for Peace are bad economics. I also had a little bout on the value of sub-stituting margarine for butter. These are a few of the fragments of pseudo-economics on which some agricultural policies of the United States have been, and to some extent continue to be, based. Some high-income countries are not altogether immune to this type of bad economics.

During the 1950s I concentrated on human capital to solve the mystery of the part of economic growth that could not be explained by increases in the traditional factors of production. I then turned to the productivity of agriculture in low-income countries, mainly to find out why the agricultural sectors in these countries were doing badly compared with the United States.

I turned for guidance to development economics, that new branch of economics designed to chart the optimal rates of economic growth of low-income economies. In my innocence I overlooked the fact that this branch was created by economists living in high-income countries – economists whose thinking was not encumbered by any knowledge of agriculture and whose theories were produced for export. Given my agricultural bias, I was appalled by their treatment of the role of agriculture in the economic growth of low-income countries. The thrust of their argument was as follows: Agricultural opportunities are the least attractive source of economic growth; investment in agriculture is not warranted; first and foremost is industrialization. Agriculture can provide a substantial part of the capital that is required to mount industrialization; it can provide an unlimited supply of labor for industry; it can even provide much labor at zero opportunity costs because a considerable part of the labor force in agriculture is redundant in the sense that its marginal productivity is zero. Policies and administrative means are required to keep farm food prices down in favor of urban consumers and thereby to promote industrialization. Farmers in developing countries are not responsive to normal economic incentives but instead often respond perversely, with the implication that the supply curve of farm products is backward sloping; and the indivisibilities of modern agricultural inputs are such that large farms are required to produce farm products at minimum costs.

My critique of this line of thinking and its policy implications is set forth in my *Transforming Traditional Agriculture*.[4] I argued (p. 10) that this approach to development economics "is rooted in the economic thinking associated with the mass unemployment of the Great Depression. . . . the concept of "disguised unemployment". . . was extended to countries that have little or no industry, and in the transition it gave birth to the doctrine that a considerable fraction of the labor in agriculture in these countries has a marginal productivity of zero value."

An important first step in my analysis was to establish the critical attributes of traditional agriculture. The next step was "to determine whether it is profitable to transform this type of agriculture by means of investment" (p. 24).

When farmers are limited to traditional factors of production they . . . can make little or no contribution to economic growth because there are few significant inefficiencies in the allocation of factors . . . and because investment made to increase the stock of traditional factors would be a costly source of economic growth. These two propositions, i.e., efficient allocations of factors and a low rate of return to investment at the margin will be formulated as hypotheses that can be tested empirically. There is then another presumption to the effect that there are laternative factors which would be relatively cheap sources of economic growth (pp. 24–25).

On the allocative efficiency of traditional agriculture, my task was to test the hypothesis that "there are comparatively few significant inefficiencies in the allocations of factors of production in traditional agriculture" (p. 37). For data I turned to field studies of anthropologists Sol Tax, with his yen for economics, and W. David Hopper, who after his field work and PhD dissertation opted for economics.

> For Panajachel, Guatemala, the data in the study by Sol Tax in *Penny Capitalism* show that although people were *very poor they were efficient*. This study opens with the words, it is "a society which is "capitalist" on a microscopic scale" (pp. 41–44).
>
> For Senapur, India, the analysis is based on a study by W. David Hopper, "The Economic Organization of a Village in North Central India" (PhD dissertation at Cornell University, 1957). People in Senapur *were poor but efficient* (pp. 44–48).

I was not surprised that my critique of the doctrine of agricultural labor of zero value touched a sensitive nerve. My conclusion stands:

> that a part of the labor working in agriculture in poor countries has a marginal productivity of zero is a false doctrine. It has roots that make it suspect. It rests on shaky theoretical presumptions. It fails to win any support when put to a critical test in analyzing effects upon agricultural production of the deaths in the agricultural labor force caused by the influenza epidemic of 1918–19 in India (p. 70).

When I wrote *Transforming Traditional Agriculture*, the political market was seriously impairing the economic market. Strong ideological differences weakened the consensus among economists. But, in retrospect, older economists who were spared our particular ideological tensions had different sets of misleading doctrines. According to the Physiocrats only agriculture produces an economic surplus – their third rent. A few agrarian fundamentalists still believe this doctrine. And lest we forget, Smith, Ricardo, and Hume viewed agriculture as an unprogressive sector.

Hume accused farm people of having a predisposition to indolence. His defamation of them is terse: "A habit of indolence naturally prevails. The greater part of the land lies uncultivated. What is cultivated, yields not its utmost for want of skill and assiduity in the farmers."[5] Smith and Ricardo saw manufacturing and commerce as progressive, whereas agriculture was the sinecure of an unprogressive landed aristocracy. Although the libel of indolence has lost its sting, in the view of some development economists farmers in parts of Africa would do better if subjected to greater pressures, whether from higher rents or lower farm product prices. I strongly disagree.[6]

The belief that there is a historical law of diminishing returns – which in the case of agriculture is made of steel – is widely held not only by the Club of Rome but by some distinguished economists. Alfred Marshall did not free himself wholly from the static dictates of Ricardo's diminishing returns to agricultural land.[7]

No less an economist than Colin Clark, no longer ago than 1941, came to the conclusion that the world was in for a dramatic rise in the prices of primary products. He predicted that by 1960 "the terms of trade of primary produce will improve by as much as 90 percent from the average of 1925–34."[8] (To speak of such a violent increase in these prices as an "improvement" is a neat twist.) His projection went off in the wrong direction. What went wrong? It was not the population variable that did it. The upsurge in population that occurred was larger than he had assumed. So, too, was the rate of increase in industrialization. Clark simply assumed a lot of secular diminishing returns against land which turned out not to be valid.[9] Could it be the less agricultural land the better, as in Hong Kong and Singapore? Mark Twain would have enjoyed this aspect of economics.

Over fifty years ago in my first professional paper,[10] I presented evidence that secular "increasing returns" had occurred in agriculture, and I argued that the concept of diminishing returns based on stationary equilibrium conditions does not suffice in analyzing the returns when economic conditions change. In that paper, I opted for the phrase "in view of progress," which I would not use now knowing that I might be liable to a class action suit! The "changing state of the economy" is a safer phrase. I know of no economy in which all economic activities are routine, repetitive, and blissful. Economic changes are evident worldwide. These changes entail risk and uncertainty, successes and failures beset with tensions, and conflicts of interest. For Adam Smith, "the progressive state is in reality the cheerful and hearty state" while "the stationary state is dull." John Stuart Mill disagreed. He wrote, "I am inclined to believe that it [the stationary state] would be, on the whole, a considerable improvement on our present condition." I consider it fortunate that the choice between hectic progress and a serene repetitive economic life is not determined by scientists, economists, or the World Bank.

A major mistake of much new development economics has been the presumption that standard economic theory is inadequate for analyzing the economic behavior of people in low-income countries and therefore a different economic theory is required.[11] Models developed for this purpose were widely acclaimed, until it became evident that they were at best intellectual curiosities. Gunnar Myrdal reacted by turning to cultural and social explanations for the poor economic performance of India. Some scholars in these fields are uneasy about this use of their studies. When I have used the data of anthropologists, they have been generous in helping me. Increasing numbers of economists have now come to realize that standard economic theory is as applicable to the scarcity problems that confront low-income countries as to the corresponding problems of high-income countries.

Another mistake has been the neglect of economic history. Classical economics was developed when most people in Western Europe were barely scratching out subsistence from the poor soils they tilled and they were condemned to a short life span. As a result, early economists dealt with conditions similar to those prevailing in low-income countries today. In Ricardo's day, about half of the family income of laborers in England went for food. So it is today in many low-income countries. Marshall tells us that "English labourers' weekly wages were often less than the price of a half bushel of good wheat"[12] when Ricardo published his *Principles of Political Economy and Taxation* in 1817. The weekly wage of a plowman in India is now approximately the price of two bushels of wheat.[13] Knowledge of the experience and achievements of poor people in Europe a century and more ago can contribute much to an understanding of the problems and possibilities of low-income countries today. Such understanding is more important for my purposes than more detailed facts about the surface of the earth, its ecology, or tomorrow's computers.

Standard economic theory has its limitations. I shall presently consider some of them. These limitations, however, are not specific to low-income economies.

1   The Fine Art of Shedding Blame

It is all too convenient to conceal economic policy mistakes that impair the performance of agriculture by blaming it on bad weather, or on farmer's perversity, or on man's fecundity. Shift the blame to bad monsoons or to a spell of droughts. Reared in the Dakotas, I know that the reoccurring good and bad effects of weather are an integral part of the normal expectations of farmers. So it has been for ages in Ethiopia. The food tragedy in Ethiopia at present is in no small measure a consequence of the economic policy of that government. Keith Griffin, president of Magdalen College, Oxford University, reports:

> In 1982 I was asked by the Government of Ethiopia to head a large team of Western economists and to prepare a comprehensive study of economic policy. In our report of September of that year we emphasized the deteriorating condition in the countryside and stated quite frankly that the major weakness in the economy has been agriculture. In the agricultural sector as a whole production increased only 1.7 percent a year (from 1974–75 to 1979–80). That is, agricultural output per head declined on average about 0.8 percent a year. A continuation of this trend would have dire consequences as it would result in the rapid impoverishment of the sector which contains 85 percent of the nation's population. Clearly, this cannot be allowed to continue.
>
> Alas, it was allowed to continue. Our warning was ignored, our policy suggestions were rejected and the report itself was suppressed by the Government with the acquiescence of the sponsoring United Nations agency.[14]

The poor performance of agriculture in the USSR, Poland, and a fairly long list of other countries is not the fault of *nature*.

In terms of their true economic interest, farmers in low-income countries are not bound by tradition. On this issue there is now strong evidence that when opportunities to improve their economic lot are to be had, they take advantage of them. That farmers in China did not respond to the command to make a great leap forward was a clear case in which the economic incentives were wholly wrong for them to do so.

It has become fashionable to jump on the fecundity of the population. I do not wish to imply that high rates of population growth do not give rise to some serious problems, for surely the additional costs of health facilities and of schools must be reckoned. But population increases should not be used as a cover-up of economic policy mistakes.

In the case of poor performance of agriculture, the real culprit is the lack of economic opportunities that are rewarding to farmers.

2   Analytical Apparatus

Not all of the useful parts of economics were at hand when economists began to study the economic behavior of people in low-income countries. We now have a comprehensive concept of capital that does not exclude human capital; a concept of knowledge, the economic value of which can be identified and measured; a concept of the economic disequilibria that occur during modernization; a concept of human agents with ability to deal with disequilibria; and a concept of the nature and significance of the distortions of economic incentives. I shall comment briefly on each of these in turn.

2.1   *Irving Fisher's All-Inclusive Concept of Capital*

Although Marshall acknowledged Fisher's masterly argument in favor of a comprehensive concept of capital, he argued that Fisher takes "too little account of the necessity for keeping realistic discussion in touch with the language of the marketplace."[15] Fisher's concept, however, did not spawn the specialization in human capital research. It emerged out of the endeavor to account for the increases in national income that could not be explained by the increases of conventional factors of production.

In the opening paragraph of my American Economic Association presidential address, I stated:

> Although it is obvious that people acquire useful skills and knowledge, it is not obvious that these skills and knowledge are a form of capital, that this capital is in substantial part a product of deliberate investment, that it has grown in Western societies at a much faster rate than conventional (nonhuman) capital, and that its growth may well be the most distinctive feature of the economic system. It has been widely observed that increases in national output have been large compared with the increases of land, man-hours, and physical reproducible capital. Investment in human capital is, propably, the major explanation for this difference.[16]

My initial concept of human capital led me to investment in human beings, that is, in their schooling, health, work, and entrepreneurial experience. I soon learned that the capital homogeneity assumption in capital theory is a disaster. After more than a decade of applications of the concept of human capital with special attention to the schooling of farm people in the United States and then in various low-income countries, I made a survey of the policy issues and the research opportunities in human capital.[17]

The advances in thought and in research, as of 1971, were of two basic parts: "The 'capital' part rests on the proposition that certain types of expenditure (sacrifices) create productive stocks embodied in man that provide services over future periods. The other part rests on the allocation of 'time,' which has led to the economic treatment of a wide array of nonmarket activities." The linkage between these two parts is close and strong:

> The discovery of human capital in the growth context revealed the importance of earnings forgone in the formation of human capital. The development of micro theory extending the concept of earnings forgone led to the formulation of the theory of the allocation of time. This extension with

special reference to micro theory of the household opened a new frontier in analyzing nonmarket activities.

A strong case can be made for using a rigorous definition of human capital. But it will be subject to some of the same ambiguities that plague capital theory in general and the capital concept in economic growth models in particular:

> Capital is two-faced, and what these two faces tell us about economic growth, which is a dynamic process, are, as a rule, inconsistent stories. It must be so because the cost story is a tale about sunk investments, and the other story pertains to the discounted value of the stream of services that such capital renders, which changes with the shifting sands of growth. But worse still is the capital homogeneity assumption underlying capital theory and the aggregation of capital in growth models ... This assumption is demonstrably inappropriate in analyzing the dynamics of economic growth that is afloat on capital inequalities because of the differences in the rates of return, whether the capital aggregation is in terms of factor costs or in terms of the discounted value of the lifetime services of its many parts. Nor would a catalogue of all existing growth models prove that these inequalities are equals. But why try to square the circle? If we were unable to observe these inequalities, we would have to invent them because they are the mainspring of economic growth. They are the mainspring because they are the compelling economic force of growth. Thus, one of the essential parts of economic growth is concealed by such capital aggregation.

There is little room for doubt that investment that enhances people's abilities really makes a difference in economic growth and in the satisfactions derived from consumption.[18] We now know that the omission of human capital biases the analysis of economic growth. Land gets overrated. The declining economic importance of agricultural land as modernization proceeds is not perceived.[19] We are beginning to see that specialization and increases in human capital go hand in hand. I shall return to the interaction between specialization and human capital. Some serious investment policy mistakes by international suppliers of funds, including the international donor community, are mainly consequences of underrating the value of human capital.

2.2　Marshall's Dictum: "Knowledge Is the Most Powerful Engine of Production"

We now have considerable information about the costs and returns from agricultural research. Both for analytical work and for investment policy, the achievements in this area over the past several decades have been impressive. The contributions of agricultural research to economic growth are being identified and measured. Organized research is being treated as a subsector of the economy that specializes in the production of knowledge.

Studies of the economic value of agricultural research began to flourish following the classic work of Zvi Griliches on "Research Costs and Social Returns: Hybrid Corn and Related Innovations" at the University of Chicago. He set the research stage for a series of PhD dissertations in this area, and others elsewhere have added much to this part of the analytical work.[20] For discovering and establishing the international dimensions of agricultural research, we are greatly indebted to many highly competent agricultural research entrepreneurs: George Harrar, F.F. Hill; the three venturesome scientists – Richard Bradfield, Paul Mangelsdorf, and E.C. Stakman; also Frank Parker, Ralph Cummings, Norman Borlaug, David Bell, Nyle Brady, and others belong on this list.[21]

The success of International Agricultural Research Centers is not in doubt. There are now thirteen centers supported by thirty-five donors, and their annual budgets total more than $190 million.[22] They have an international dimension that owes much to the Rockefeller Foundation and to the pioneering entrepreneurship of the late George Harrar, to F.F. Hill while he was vice president of the Ford Foundation, and to other key research entrepreneurs.

Successful as these centers are, I see four limitations: (1) they are not substitutes for ongoing national experiment stations and laboratories in low-income countries; (2) the relationship between them and the major research-oriented universities and experiment stations in high-income countries is too tenuous; (3) the central management, which allocates funds to each of the centers, is becoming overorganized in the sense that the research personnel spend too much time on paper work "justifying" research; and (4) several centers, such as the one in Nigeria, concentrate on local food production and neglect the important export commodities. More generally, research restricted to food production, especially throughout Sub-Saharan Africa, is inconsistent with the economic comparative advantage: larger gains in real income are to be had from the growth in exports, primarily of tree and fiber crops. A recent *World Development Report* is clear and cogent on this point.[23] Because of the economic importance of comparative advantage in production and trade, agricultural research to promote only food crops in parts of Africa is not optimal.

The annual agricultural research expenditures worldwide (in constant 1980 US dollars) rose from about $2 billion in 1959 to more than $7 billion in 1980.[24] The world food supply, ten to fifteen years from now, will be decidedly larger than it could have been had these investments in agricultural research not been made. Real costs of producing farm food products will continue to decline. Agriculture as a sector of the economy will also continue to decline.

No country in which the government distorts agricultural incentives benefits fully from the contributions of agricultural research. The rates of increase in agricultural production derived from new high-yielding varieties and from other discoveries are highest in open market economies in which incentives are not distorted. Such distortions are clearly evident in centrally planned and controlled economies, notably so in the USSR. They are also evident in Egypt, throughout much of central Africa, in parts of Central America, and elsewhere.[25]

2.3   *Economic Growth with No Economic Disequilibria Is Not Possible*

For the purpose at hand, this proposition has two implications. The first is that even under the most favorable circumstances, when changes in production and distribution give rise to increases in real income, economic disequilibria are inevitable. They cannot be prevented by law, by public policy, and surely not by rhetoric. The second implication pertains to the incentives to human agents and the actions that are taken to bring the economy into equilibrium.

If agriculture were to arrive at a long-run equilibrium, the economic activities of farm people would be those of traditional agriculture. Farming would be essentially routine. There would be no new technology, no alterations in the land being farmed, in the equipment used, or in the labor employed. The productivity of each of the various agricultural resources would remain constant, and the demand could be such that there would be no changes in relative prices. Under these conditions, long-run costs, risks, and returns would be known almost with certainty. Accordingly, there would be virtually no entrepreneurial function; routine management would suffice.

But agriculture is not in such an equilibrium state. On the contrary, the transformation of agriculture into an increasingly more productive activity, a process that is commonly referred to as "modernization," entails changes in what farmers do as new and better opportunities become available. The value of the ability to deal with disequilibria is high in a modernizing economy.[26]

The number of models that assume steady, smooth, and blissful economic modernization is large; whereas the actual process of modernization is beset by various classes of uninsurable risk, by some true uncertainties that give rise to unanticipated gains and losses, and by political tensions that are consequences of changes in economic conditions. Although a market-oriented economy has a comparative advantage over a centrally managed economy, market economies are nevertheless subject to inflations and deflations, booms and depressions, and various types of economic irregularities.

The implications of equilibrium theory and the economic behavior of farmers in traditional agriculture appear to be virtually identical. But the implications of equilibrium theory and the behavior of economic agents, including farmers, as they deal with changes in economic conditions appear to have little in common. Can research-based equilibrium theory be extended to deal with changes in economic conditions? One approach is to establish the linkage between disequilibria and entrepreneurial actions. In support of this approach there is compelling evidence, often referred to by economists, that when any part of an open market economy experiences a disequilibrium there are incentives for economic agents to take actions that have the effect of reestablishing an economic equilibrium. In Lyle Owen's language, like the earth's gravity, which pulls in rocks and metal fragments that come near enough from outer space, economic equilibrium tends to absorb disequilibria when there are incentives to reallocate resources.[27]

The nature of these incentives and their economic significance in the actions of economic agents are unfinished parts of economic theory.

2.4 *Economics Without Entrepreneurs*

Economic theory that omits the role that entrepreneurs play in modernization is on a par with omitting the Prince of Denmark in presenting *Hamlet*.[28]

Farmers the world over, when dealing with costs, returns, and risks, are calculating economic agents. Within their small, individual, allocative domain they are fine-tuning entrepreneurs, tuning so subtly that economists from high-income countries fail to see how efficient they are. Although farmers differ for reasons of schooling, health, and experience in their ability to perceive, interpret, and respond to new events pertaining to their farm enterprises, they provide an essential human resource which is entrepreneurship. On most farms there is a second enterprise, the household. Housewives perform economic activities and are entrepreneurs in allocating their own time and in using farm products and purchased goods in household production. This talent of entrepreneurship is supplied by millions of men and women on small-scale producing units, and it makes agriculture a highly decentralized sector of the economy. Where governments have taken over these entrepreneurial functions, they have been far from efficient in modernizing agriculture. Where governments have not nationalized agriculture, the entrepreneurial roles of farmers and of farm housewives are important and the economic opportunities open to them make a difference.

No matter what part of a modernizing economy is being investigated, we observe that many people are deliberately reallocating their resources in response to changes in economic conditions.

> The ability to reallocate is not stricted to entrepreneurs who are engaged in business. People who supply labor services for hire or who are self-employed are reallocating their services in response to changes in the value of the work they do. So are housewives in devoting their time in combination with purchased goods and services in household production. Students likewise are reallocating their own time along with the educational services they purchase as they respond to changes in expected earnings and changes in the value of the personal satisfactions they expect to derive from their education. Consumption opportunities are also changing, and inasmuch as pure consumption entails time, here too people are reallocating their own time in response to changing opportunities.[29]

In agriculture it is clearly evident that

> millions of farmers in low-income countries have substantial ability to alter the use that they make of their land, labor and their opportunities . . . The necessity of dealing with disequilibria is a good teacher. Although any farmers in low-income countries have little or no schooling, their recent performance reveals considerable ability to learn; it wit, in their success in the adoptions of new highyielding varieties of food grains. In view of the contributions of agricultural research oriented to the requirements of low-income countries and the large amounts of additional capital being committed to agricultural development in these countries, the observed ability of this new breed of farmers to transform these research contributions and the additional capital into increases in food production is clear and substantial.[30]

Meanwhile, theory is silent on the economic value of the function that entrepreneurs perform, and empirical studies using standard production function theory provide no estimates of the value of the contributions that entrepreneurs make to production.

2.5   Distortions of Economic Incentives

Nations have governments; the actions of governments pertaining to the economic domain are in effect responses to the "political market." The political market in many high-income economies overvalues agricultural products, whereas in most low-income economies it is the other way around.

The new development economics, as I noted at the outset, advocated economic policies that seriously distorted agricultural incentives in low-income countries. I protested then and I continue to do so. What appears not to be understood by governments and by some economists is the critical allocative role that producer incentives play in attaining optimal increases in productivity. Because of wrong incentives the real economic potential of agriculture is not being realized. This unrealized economic potential is a measure of a pervasive economic disequilibrium in world agriculture.[31]

Correct governmental actions do occur. A notable case in point occurred in the mid-1960s. David Hopper's account of this case is telling.[32] Despite arguments in New Delhi early in 1966 calling for government prohibition of imports of high-yielding seeds, the minister of agriculture decided to import the new Mexican dwarf wheat seed. Some 18,000 tons of this wheat arrived from Mexico in late spring. The new seed was suited to the agriculture of the Punjab and to adjacent areas. The farm price of wheat in India was somewhat below the price of imported wheat. Even so, the increase in the yield of the new seed enhanced the profitability of producing wheat. The farm entrepreneurs of the Punjab quickly adopted the new variety because the incentives to do so were favorable. Wheat production in India rose from 11 million tons in 1966 to 46 million in 1984. Landowners profited; real wages of farm labor rose. We called it a Green Revolution. But before they had evidence, many critics in India and abroad turned to making predictions about the unfavorable social side effects of this type of economic "progress" instead of searching for ways of duplicating the Punjab success in other parts of agriculture. Ways could be found, but they are at present suppressed by the lack of adequate incentives. The state of incentives is such that in many countries it is unprofitable for farmers to undertake modernizing investments that would increase the productivity of agriculture.

3 Improving the Quality of Inputs

The process of improving the quality of the inputs raises three questions: (1) What are the properties of quality? (2) What do these properties cost? (3) When the returns from quality exceed cost, what determines the process and the time that is required to attain a new equilibrium? The properties of quality can be identified and measured; the cost of these properties can also be ascertained, and so can the equilibrating process.[33]

We owe much to Griliches' pioneering studies of inputs, starting with his PhD research on hybrid corn. Three of his papers rank high in presenting his approach and findings. They are "Measuring Inputs in Agriculture: A Critical Survey"; "The Sources of Measured Productivity Growth: United States Agriculture, 1940–60"; and "Research Expenditures, Education, and the Aggregate Agricultural Production Function."[34] Griliches" studies along with those by others that followed tell us more about the economics of the inputs in agriculture than is known at present about this issue for most other sectors of the economy.

In view of the improvements in official agricultural output and input statistics, it might be said that academic research has not been in vain.[35] These statistics, however, do not treat adequately the heterogeneity of physical capital; they exclude the investments in human capital and the economic value of the services rendered by the acquired abilities of farm people. The costs and value of the contributions of agricultural research are omitted. Under normal conditions, ideal statistics would show that the value of the realized output is equal to the services of the inputs plus profits or minus losses. What they show instead for the United States is that the increase in output exceeded that of inputs 3.5 to 1 during the 1970s. We may, of course, take comfort in this productivity at a time when there is so much ado about declining productivity.

The acquired quality of people as economic agents is revealed in the work effects and allocative effects of their health, education, and training.[36] These sources of quality entail investment in human capital. The returns from such investments are not to be had on short notice, and their value extends over the life span from youth through adulthood.

The core of the economics of these improvements in quality consists of: (1) the inputs that farmers purchase (an important source of quality, as increases in purchased inputs over time have a strong effect on agricultural modernization); (2) the nonfarm sectors which are the primary sources of this set of quality inputs; the incentive to buy them depends on how profitable they are; (3) the current costs as well as the private and public costs of research; and (4) improvements in the quality of farm people achieved by investment in their human capital.

4   Specialization and the Human Capital Approach to Economic Growth

"Truly, the most distinctive feature of our economic system is the growth in human capital. Without it there would be only hard manual work and poverty except for those who have income from property. In William Faulkner's *Intruder in the Dust*, there is an early morning scene of a poor, solitary cultivator at work in a field. The man without skills and knowledge leaning terrifically against nothing.[37]

Division of labor, specialization, and increasing returns to human capital go hand in hand in the process of economic modernization. Our dear self-sufficient Robinson Crusoe, or a self-sufficient family living somewhere in splendid economic isolation, or a small population on a small Caribbean island with little or no international trade are micro entities with a minimum of division of labor, with traditional forms of specialization, and with small returns to human capital.

Nations differ greatly in natural endowments, in producible physical capital, and in human capital including knowledge. I venture to generalize. The performance of a small set of not so rich economies in East Asia is significantly better than that of most countries. Consider Hong Kong, the Republic of Korea, Singapore, and Taiwan: no oil, no iron ore; two of them are city-states with no agriculture. The cultivated area per capita in Korea and in Taiwan is far less than that in China. Harry T. Oshima has compared the rapid productivity growth, the marked rise in employment and education, and the sharp decline in birth rates in Hong Kong, Korea, Singapore, and Taiwan (he also includes Japan) with the less successful performances of Indonesia, Malaysia, the Philippines, and Thailand.[38]

My assessment of the economic performance of three selected sets of countries is as follows: (1) the aggressive, successful four East Asian entities are at the top in growth rates; (2) another four, Indonesia, Malaysia, the Philippines, and Thailand may be next by this test (Malaysia comes close to qualifying for membership in my first "gang of four"); and (3) throughout most of tropical Africa and parts of the Caribbean and Latin America, there are economies that are performing poorly.

Why the large differences in economic performances? Are they the consequences of having or not having coal, oil, iron ore, and other minerals? Are they the result of differences in the acreage and productivity of cropland? My interpretation of the evidence is that the answers are No. Where trade extends the market there are incentives for specialization based on the increases in productivity from divisions of labor, and there are increasing returns to human capital as economic modernization is achieved.

The tale of Singapore and Jamaica, as told in table 1, contains the secret of the connections between specialization and development. The key to the secret is in the division of labor, which depends on the extent of the market. The market is large for Singapore, small for Jamaica. Allyn

Table V.1 A Tale of Two Small Nations: Singapore and Jamaica

Item	Singapore	Jamaica	Unit
In common			
Population mid-1982	2.5	2.2	Millions
Life expectancy of females,			
1982	75	75	Years
External debt, 1982	1.4	1.5	Billions of dollars
Differences			
Area	224	4,232	Square miles
Population density	11,160	520	Per square mile
Economic (GDP) growth rate,			
1970–82	8.5	−1.1	Percent
Exports, 1982	20,800	730	Millions of dollars
Imports, 1982	28,200	1,370	Millions of dollars
Per capita GNP	5,910	1,330	1982 dollars

Source: World Bank, *World Development Report 1984*: Oxford University Press, New Yorik, 1984).

Young's classic paper, "Increasing Returns and Economic Progress" reveals the secret. Securing increasing returns depends on a progressive division of labor that gives rise to increases in outputs without increasing their costs proportionately. In Young's language, "Economic changes become progressive and propagate themselves in a moving equilibrium."[39]

A notable advance on this issue is made by Sherwin Rosen in his "Specialization and Human Capital."[40] His argument is:

> Incentives for specialization, trade, and the production of comparative advantage through investment are shown to arise from increasing returns to utilization of human capital. Indivisibilities imply fixed-cost elements of investment that are independent of subsequent utilization. Hence the rate of return is increasing in utilization and is maximized by utilizing specialized skills as intensively as possible. Identically endowed individuals have incentives to specialize their investments in skills and trade with each other for this reason, even if production technology exhibits constant returns to scale. . . . The enormous productivity and complexity of modern economies are in good measure attributable to specialization.

In the long run, the critical component in economic modernization and development consists of human capital – that is, in the abilities and knowledge embodied in people rather than in the properties of land, other natural resources, or other forms of physical capital. First and foremost over the decades are investments in population quality.

5   Self-Appraisal

Self-appraisal was requested; against my better judgment I indulge in it. I had given much weight during the 1930s and 1940s to the importance of reducing international trade barriers in bringing about the economic recovery of US agriculture. But when I then turned to world agriculture, I gave too little weight to the economic function of trade in my *Transforming Traditional Agriculture*, 1964. I also neglected it in my *Investment in Human Capital: The Role of Education and Research*, 1971. When it comes to getting rid of the vast array of price distortions within countries, the elimination of the barriers to trade is an important means of achieving economic efficiency and gains in welfare.

It took me decades to learn that time spent on preparing and presenting congressional testimony, however valid my analysis, had no discernible effect on the actions of Congress. I also have been slow in learning that serving on international economic committees and doing assignments for governments or international agencies is to place a low value on my time. I have become stubborn in my belief that my comparative advantage is in thinking about the long pull.

I derive professional pleasure when someone makes a point for or against me citing a passage from what I have published. I want to be read, especially by concerned people. I value translations of my books more than royalties. I bask in the fact that my *Investing in People* is available in nine languages.

6   The Bottom Lines

1   Do international agencies, the donor community, governments in low-income countries, and private people invest enough in human capital? Taking the long view, the answer is No!

2   Is enough being invested in the knowledge-producing sector? The record is fairly good in the area of agricultural research. The prospects are that in the long run the rates of return on investment in knowledge are likely to continue to be higher than the normal return on other investments.

3   Is the economic contribution of agricultural land overrated by governments and international agencies? The answer is Yes, in part

because of the prevailing Ricardian Rent bias, and the failure to see that most of the productivity of agricultural land is man-made and that substitutes for agricultural land are being produced by agricultural research. The declining economic importance of agricultural land is clearly evident.

4 Does the organization of the economy provide optimal economic incentives? In the case of agriculture, they are at their worst in a centrally planned economy. In many high-income economies the incentives established by governments overvalue agricultural products, and in most low-income countries, despite food shortages, the opposite occurs.

5 Is the economic value of the ability of entrepreneurs to deal with the economic disequilibria that occur as a consequence of modernization being fully realized? The answer is No. Unfortunately, standard economic theory tends to omit the entrepreneur. In economic policy he is also forgotten as an economic agent which explains many of the mistakes that are made in economics.

6 The economic gains from specialization and human capital go hand in hand.

How could I know whether or not my professional efforts have made a difference? What I do know, however, is that there is much about economic development that remains unknown to me.

Notes and References

1 Allyn Young, "Increasing Returns and Economic Progress," *Economic Journal*, 38 (Dec. 1928), 527–42.
2 Gerald M. Meier and Dudley Seers (eds), *Pioneers in Development* (Oxford University Press, 1984), p. 22.
3 See above, Part IV, No. 2.
4 Theodore W. Schultz, *Transforming Traditional Agriculture* (Yale University Press, New Haven, Conn., 1964).
5 David Hume, *Writing on Economics*, ed. Eugene Rotwein (University of Wisconsin Press, Madison, 1955), p. 10. I am indebted to Nathan Rosenberg on this point.
6 A long shelf of empirical evidence shows that, in Africa, when the export price of cocoa, cotton, coffee, peanuts, or palm fruit becomes profitable, the supply response of farmers is highly elastic. It is wrong thus to malign African farmers, and it is a serious error to reach for that all too handy colonial stick.
7 Alfred Marshall, *Principles of Economics* (Macmillan, London, 1930); see

the preface, p. xv, which is from the 8th edition and dated October 1920.

8 Colin Clark, *The Economics of 1960* (Macmillan, London, 1943), p. 52. The introduction is dated May 15, 1941.

9 Discussed in Theodore W. Schultz, "Connections between Natural Resources and Economic Growth," reproduced above as Part II, No. 2, "Connections between Nautral Resources and Increases in Income."

10 Theodore W. Schultz, "Diminishing Returns in View of Progress in Agriculture," *Journal of Farm Economics*, 14, No. 4 (Oct. 1932), 640–49.

11 This paragraph and the next two are from my Nobel Lecture, reproduced in Theodore W. Schultz, *The Economics of Being Poor* (Blackwell, 1993), Part I, No. 1.

12 Marshall, *Principles of Economics*, p. xv.

13 Theodore W. Schultz, "On the Economics of the Increases in the Value of Human Time over Time," in R.C.O. Matthews (ed.), *Economic Growth and Resources*,vol. 2 (Macmillan Press Ltd., London, 1980), reproduced in *The Economics of Being Poor*, Part III, No. 7, as "A Long View of Increases in the Value of Human Time."

14 Letter to the Editor, *The Times* (London, Nov. 10, 1984). J.J. MacGregor called my attention to this letter.

15 Marshall, *Principles of Economics*, app. E, "Definitions of Capital," pp. 785–90.

16 Theodore W. Schultz, "Investment in Human Capital," *American Economic Review*, 51, No. 1 (Mar. 1961), 1–17, reproduced in *The Economics of Being Poor*, Part II, No. 1.

17 Theodore W. Schultz, "Human Capital: Policy Issues and Research Opportunities," in *Human Resources*, 50th Anniversary Colloquium VI (National Bureau of Economic Research, New York, 1972), pp. 1–84. The quotations that follow are from pp. 2–3 of this work.

18 See Theodore W. Schultz, *Investing in People: The Economics of Population Quality* (University of California Press, Berkeley, Ca., 1981). Various studies sponsored by the World Bank deserve a high mark in this connection. Notable is the book by Dean T. Jamison and Lawrence J. Lau, *Farmer Education and Farm Efficiency* (Johns Hopkins University Press, Baltimore, Md, 1982); and George Psacharopoulos, "Returns to Education: An Updated International Comparison," in Timothy King (ed.), *Education and Income*, World Bank Staff Working Paper No. 402 (Washington DC, 1980), 73–109.

19 See above, Part II, No. 1, "Declining Importance of Agricultural Land."

20 Relevant here is Theodore W. Schultz, *Investment in Human Capital: The Role of Education and of Research* (Free Press, New York, 1972), chapter 12.

21 See the index of Elvin Charles Stakman, Richard Bradfield, and Paul C. Mangelsdorf, *Campaigns against Hunger* (Harvard University Press, Cambridge, Mass., 1967).

22 For an extended analysis of these centers see Vernon W. Ruttan, *Agricultural*

Research Policy (University of Minnesota Press, Minneapolis, Minn., 1982), chapter 5.

23 World Bank, *World Development Report 1982* (Oxford University Press, New York, 1982), 40–77.

24 J.K. Boyce and R.E. Evenson, *National and International Agricultural Research and Extension Programs* (Agricultural Development Council, New York, 1975); and M. Ann Judd, J.K. Boyce, and R.E. Evenson, "Investing in Agricultural Supply," Yale University Economic Growth Center Discussion Paper No. 442 (New Haven, Conn., 1983).

25 A large part of the uneven gains from research discoveries is a consequence of price and trade distortions. This issue is examined in Theodore W. Schultz, "Uneven Prospects for Gains from Agricultural Research Related to Economic Policy," in T.M. Arndt, D.G. Dalrymple, and V.M. Ruttan (eds), *Resource Allocation and Productivity in National and International Agricultural Research* (University of Minnesota Press, Minneapolis, Minn., 1977), 578–89; and also in Theodore W. Schultz, "The Economics of Research and Agricultural Productivity," (IADS Occasional Paper, New York, 1979).

26 See above, Part I, No. 3, "The Value of the Ability to Deal with Disequilibria."

27 Lyle Owen, "The Mincy Meteorite," *The Ozarks Mountaineer*, 31 (Dec. 1983), 40–43.

28 From William Baumol, "The theoretical firm is entrepreneurless . . . the Prince of Denmark has been expunged from the discussion of Hamlet," in "Entrepreneurship and Economic Theory," *American Economic Review*, 68 (May 1968), 68–71. In the common display of macro theory, the entrepreneur is unknown.

29 See above.

30 Theodore W. Schultz, "Investment in Entrepreneurial Ability," *Scandinavian Journal of Economics* (1980), 437–48, reproduced in *The Economics of Being Poor*, Part III, No. 6.

31 D. Gale Johnson, "Food Production Potentials in Developing Countries: Will They be Realized?", Macalester College Bureau of Economic Research Occasional Paper No. 1 (St. Paul, Minn., 1977); and D. Gale Johnson, "International Prices and Trade in Reducing the Distortions of Incentives," in Theodore W. Schultz (ed.), *Distortions of Agricultural Incentives* (Indiana University Press, Bloomington, Indiana, 1978), 195–215.

32 David Hopper, "Distortions of Agricultural Development Resulting from Governmental Prohibitions," in Schultz (ed.), *Distortions of Agricultural Incentives*, 69–78.

33 See Theodore W. Schultz, "On the Economics of Agricultural Production over Time," *Economics Enquiry*, 20 (Jan. 1982), 10–20.

34 Zvi Griliches, in *Journal of Farm Economics*, 42 (Dec. 1960), 14; *Journal of Political Economy*, 71 (Aug. 1963), 331–446; and *American Economic Review*, 54 (Dec. 1964), 961–74.

35 See *Economic Indicators of the Farm Sector: Production and Efficiency*

Statistics, 1979, US Department of Agriculture Statistical Bulletin No. 65 (Feb. 1981), 90.

36 Finis Welch, "Education and Production," *Journal of Political Economy*, 78 (Jan.–Feb. 1970), 35–59; and also "The Role of Investment in Human Capital in Agriculture," in Schultz (ed.), *Distortions of Agricultural Incentives*, 259–81.

37 Schultz, "Investment in Human Capital." (The Free Press, New York, 1971) p. 47.

38 Harry T. Oshima, "The Industrial and Demographic Transition in East Asia," *Population and Development Review*, 9 (Dec. 1983), 583–607.

39 Young, "Increasing Returns and Economic Progress," 533.

40 Sherwin Rosen, "Specialization and Human Capital," *Journal of Labor Economics*, 1 (1983), 43–9.

Index